UP THE CREEK

*Parachute Creek's Pioneer Families
and Energy Development
1875-2015*

Ivo E. Lindauer

Copyright © 2016 Double F Inc. Press
269 Lodgepole Cricle
Parachute, CO 81635

All rights reserved, including the right to reproduce this book or portions thereof in any form, store in a retrieval system, or transmit in any form or by any means, electronic, mechanical, photocopy, recording, or otherwise without permission in writing from the publisher, except by a reviewer who may quote brief passages in a review.

Up the Creek: Parachute Creek's Pioneer Familes and Energy Development 1875-2015

ISBN: 978-0-692-58587-0
Library of Congress Control Number: 2016917562

Ivo E. Lindauer

Editor: Elizabeth A. Green

Layout: Lisa Snider

Photos are reproduced with permission from their owners

This book is dedicated to the community of Parachute
and all the pioneers who have lived there.

◇

Paul Lindauer's first North Water cabin, ca. 1930s.

A LITTLE CABIN AWAY FROM TOWN

A Little Cabin Away from Town
Mid nature's varied smile and frown,
An easy chair when day is done,
We watch at eve the setting sun.
To watch the cattle on the hill
The evening chant of the killdeer

A horse will whinny from around the corral
A coyote howl from the north water creek,
The quakers stir its leafy fronds
To rhythm to a wind mill song
Evening breezes blow softly o'er
To stir the columbines around my door.

The moon will rise, the stars come out
The cares of life will be put to route
As there I will find at the close of day,
The vagrant heart content to stay, in a
Little Cabin Away from Town, when
night begins to settle down.

– **Paul R. Lindauer**
ca. 1940s

Photo contributed by Carl Lindauer

Brothers Karl and Louis Lindauer harvested this record deer on the East Fork cattle range in 1932. It scored 255.25 in Boone-Crocket and was ranked as 19th non-typical head when taken, but ranks 49th today. Louis Lindauer's son Carl is the keeper of the head today.

Parachute Creek Drainage

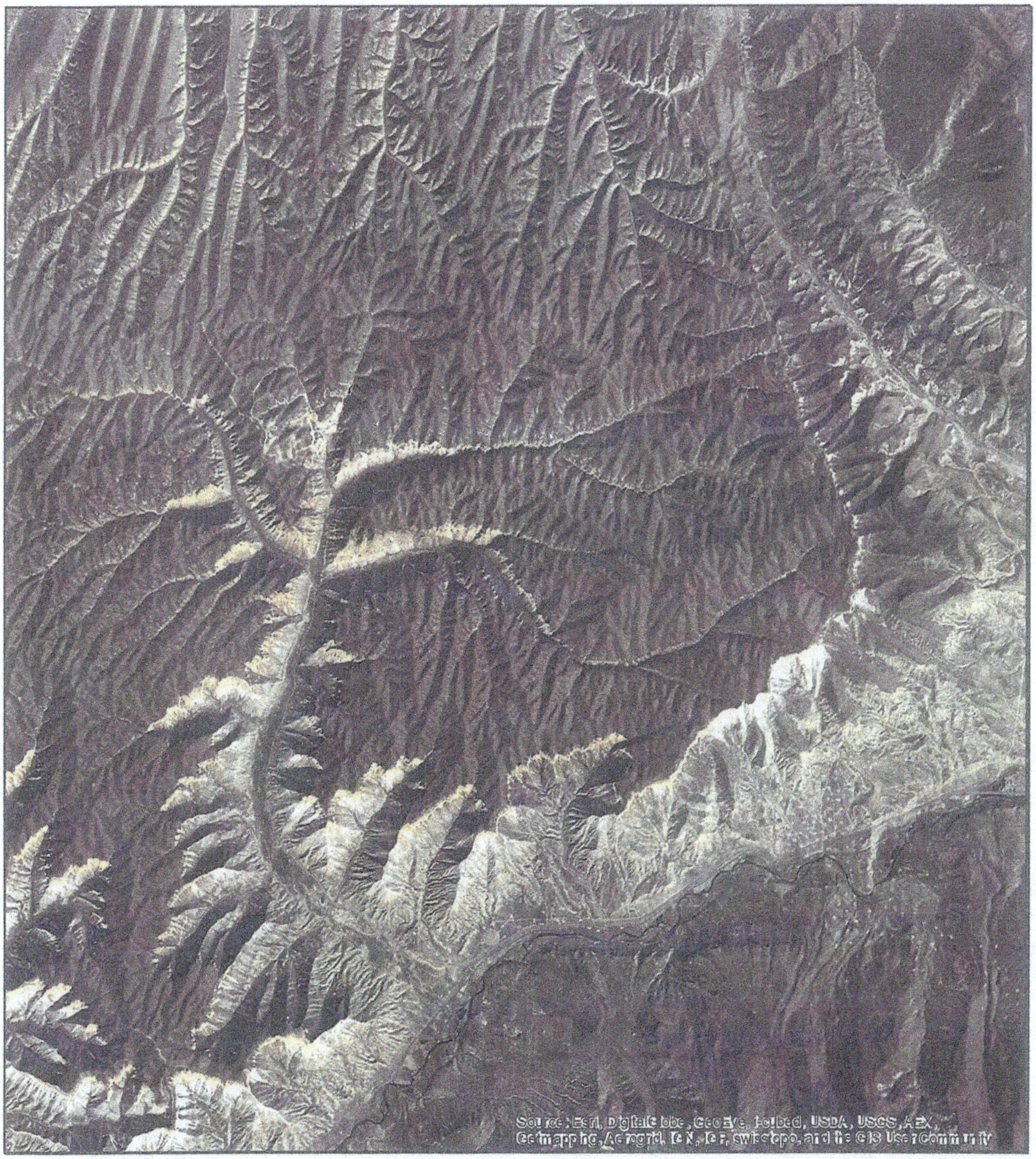

Provided by Colorado River Valley Field Office
Isaac Pittman Rangeland Management Specialist
September 4, 2013

No Warranty is made by the Bureau of Land Management as to the accuracy, reliability, or completeness of these data for individual use or aggregate use with other data.

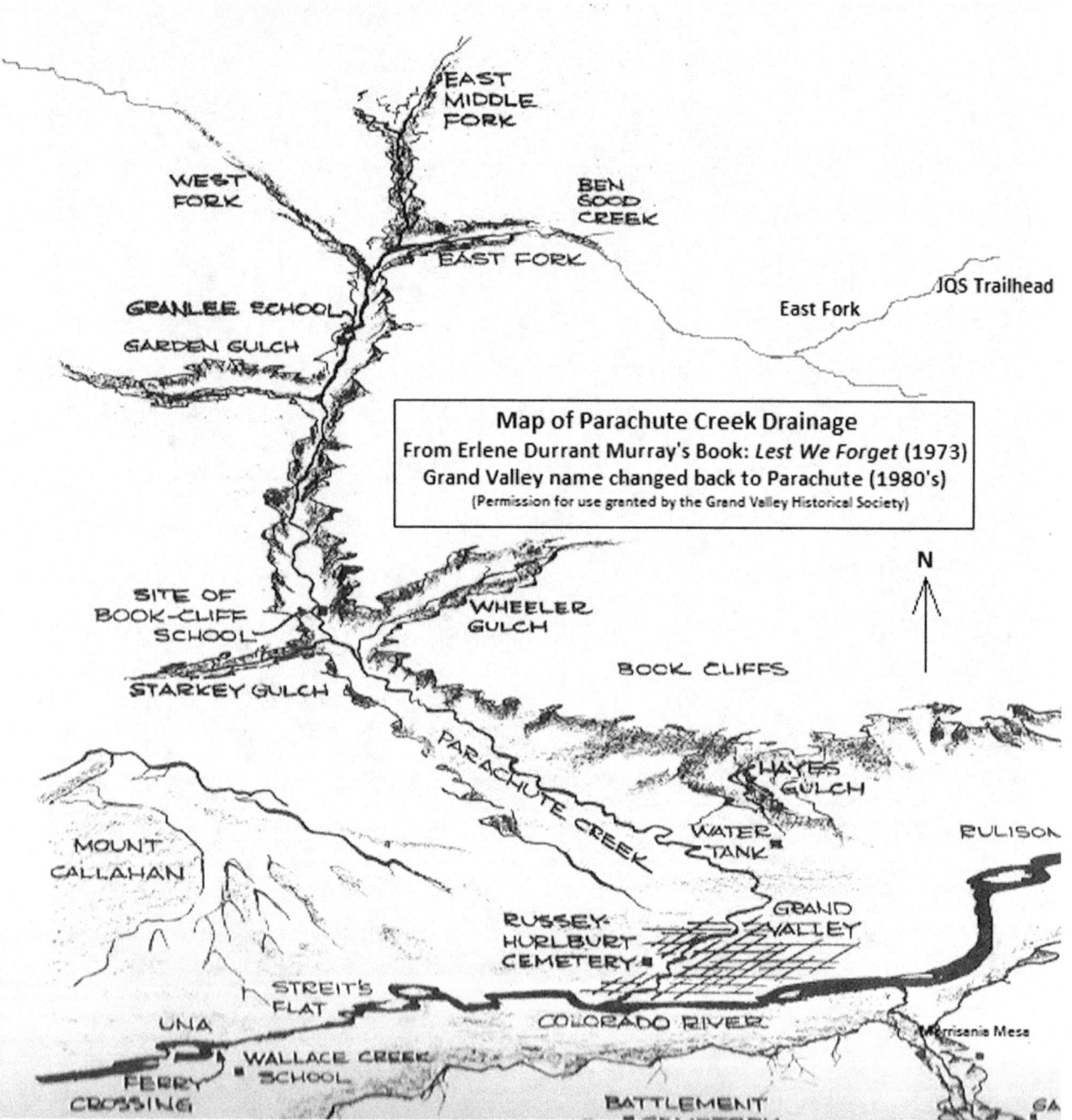

TABLE OF CONTENTS

Foreword by Andrew Gulliford xi

Preface and Acknowledgments xiii

Chapter 1   Geographical and Geological Description of Parachute Creek 1

Chapter 2   The Name Parachute – A Misnomer from Ute "Pahchouc" 3

Chapter 3   Ute Indians: The First Inhabitants of Parachute Creek 5
                   New Tribes are Formed 7
                   Problems with the Meeker Indian Agent 7

Chapter 4   The Formative Years of Parachute Creek History: 1868-1882 13
                   Sheep and Cattle Wars 13
                   Grazing on Public Lands 15

Chapter 5   Pioneer Families of Parachute Creek: 1882-1945 17

Chapter 6   Early Pioneers on the Upper Half of Parachute Creek 21

Chapter 7   Early Pioneers of the Lower Half of Parachute Creek 67
                   Other Stockmen on the Parachute Creek Drainage 126

Chapter 8   Life along the Creek 129
                   Recollections of Early Pioneers of Parachute Creek and Grand Valley ... 129
                   Early Life of a Cowboy in the Parachute Creek Area 130
                   Tragedies of the Area 131
                   Last Train Robbery 132
                   Local Newspapers 134
                   Early Day Blacksmiths 134
                   Wolves on Parachute Creek 135

Chapter 9   Parachute Creek Ranching and Farming Community Becomes an Industrial Site 137
                   Parachute Mining District (PMD) 137
                   Oil Shale Mining on Parachute Creek 137
                   Soda Ash and Sodium Bicarbonate on Parachute Creek 141
                   Natural Gas Industry on Parachute Creek 142
                   Encana Energy Enters the Gas Industry on Parachute Creek 144

Chapter 10   Changes in the Parachute Creek Valley in the Last 80 Years 147
                   The Exodus of Pioneers and their Families from Parachute Creek 147
                   Impact of Closing Public Access to West, Middle,
                   and East forks of Parachute Creek 148

Appendices 151
                   I maps showing well pads along Parachute Creek 151
                   II Water Flow and Flooding of Parachute Creek 153

Bibliography 155

Index 159

FOREWORD

Thanks to the 1862 Homestead Act, by the 1930s fifty-eight families lived up Parachute Creek north of the Colorado River. Now it is an industrialized landscape of pipes, well pads, bulldozed gravel roads and locked gates with only one family still owning ranch property along the creek. That family is the Lindauers, pioneers themselves. The patriarch of the family, Ivo Lindauer, has fulfilled an important goal and dream. He has written about Parachute Creek history and a vanished world of small ranches, orchards, one-room schools, dangerous accidents, babies born and buried, and successful Grand Valley High School graduates who left the area never to return.

Ivo Lindauer has an impressive resume: cowboy, rancher, teacher, scientist, biologist, consultant for the National Science Foundation, and now author of this book. He has squeezed several lifetimes and careers into his eighty-five years including almost four decades of teaching and research at the University of Northern Colorado and sixteen Grand Canyon float and field trips teaching ecology and geology.

Working with the editing and design team of Beth Green and Lisa Snider, Lindauer has researched and written about each member of the fifty-eight families that once homesteaded and lived up the three drainages that comprise Parachute Creek flowing into the Colorado River at Parachute, Colorado. Though Erlene Durrant Murray described the region in 1973 in her book *Lest We Forget*, Lindauer has dug much deeper into archival, genealogical, and census sources to provide important verbal snapshots and valuable photos of families and their descendants who have moved away. This is an in-depth history of pioneer life along a Colorado creek.

It's all here. Geology. Ute Indian history. The hardships of the early settlers and how they traveled by covered wagon to arrive at Parachute Creek always seeking better opportunities, good land, and government grass for cattle and sheep.

The book is peppered with phrases unknown to a younger generation. In the parlance of the Western Slope to "take up" or "to locate" a homestead was to begin to grub sagebrush and pinon juniper trees out of local hillsides to design gently sloping hayfields where it took years to dig ditches and properly drain the fields. To keep financially afloat, men often "worked out" as carpenters, teamsters, trappers, or cowboys to bring a little cash back home.

Pioneers "filed on the land" as farmers, but some of them also became intrigued with "the rock that burns" or oil shale and started the Parachute Mining District in 1890. The fledgling industry began in the 1910s with a sensational report by the US Geological Survey and a 1919 article in *National Geographic* predicting a "gasoline famine" and describing millions of barrels of oil locked in the kerogen layer of mahogany shale. The industry sputtered and never succeeded, but hopes for it revived during the 1950s and resulted in offers for families to sell out to Sinclair Oil & Gas Co. or Union Oil Company of California.

Readers will learn about cow camps, sheep camps, home canning, the occasional poached deer, and a baby carried off by a mountain lion. Pioneers arrived when "there were still teepee poles on their land" from recently departed Ute Indians. Ivo Lindauer has captured the flavor of pioneer lives and tells tales of hard labor but also of friendships, shared values, and working together during hay season and cattle roundups. Lindauer writes about saddle makers, house builders, rodeo cowboys, and one errant husband who liked to gamble. He left the house with his wife's horse and buggy and when he returned on foot from gambling in town she met him on the porch with a shotgun.

Lindauer explains the importance of federal grazing and how families created hayfields to feed their stock from December to May but in the summer ran their herds up a variety of trails to graze the high country on top of the Book Cliffs. By 2012 only one family was left up the creek—the Lindauers.

Murray's book came out in 1973. A few years later I traveled up Parachute Creek researching my Ph.D. thesis on the history of oil shale, which was published as *Boomtown Blues: Colorado Oil Shale*. I remember a fine autumn day and a red log homestead set back among huge old cottonwood trees. Amidst a swirl of golden leaves, I stepped to the door to interview a pioneer woman who I'd been told had a serious reputation for running off oil industry representatives, especially anyone come to try and buy her ranch and water rights. They brought suitcases full of cash. She didn't care.

Gingerly, I knocked. She came to the screen door and asked my business. When I told her what I was trying to do she smiled and let me in. We had a wonderful afternoon at her kitchen table and she made clear that her ranch and home were not for sale. Her husband had built the log house we sat in so why would she ever sell it?

That woman was Bessie Lindauer and her property is still in the family today. Her son is Ivo and this book is his gift to a vanished community.

It's not often we get to pay back old debts and obligations incurred over a lifetime of living in the same place. During the Great Depression in the 1930s families "got by" because they helped each other. Sure, there were squabbles, but there were also generosity and an intimacy unknown today. Once families were "beholding" to each other—pronounced beholdin' on the Western Slope—and they owed each other debts that could never be paid in cash. They helped each other out and knew where the coffee cups were in their neighbors' kitchen cupboards. Those days are gone now, but Ivo Lindauer brings them back.

Enjoy this book. It is a valuable pioneer and genealogical history with important updates on the energy industry in Parachute that now includes oil shale, soda ash, and natural gas. The world the settlers made is gone. But it lives again within these pages.

– Andrew Gulliford
Durango, Colorado

Andrew Gulliford is a professor of history and environmental studies at Fort Lewis College, in Durango, Colorado. Dr. Gulliford has won both the Colorado Book Award and the New Mexico-Arizona Book Award—twice. He can be reached at gulliford_a@fortlewis.edu

PREFACE AND ACKNOWLEDGMENTS

The story that follows was initiated when a fifteen-page document was found that had been audio-recorded and typed, single-spaced, by Dr. Betty Jo Lindauer from conversations of her father-in-law, Paul Robert Lindauer, and a neighbor, Harry Hansen, who stopped by the ranch frequently for coffee and discussions of the "old days" on Parachute Creek. As I read this copy, the history and the first settlers on Parachute Creek Valley began to come alive.

The first historical information found in the Betty Lindauer document had been recorded on several occasions between 1972 and 1974, but was set aside and not found again until some thirty-eight years later. Little of this information had been published and is not generally available to the public. Consequently, the efforts of this writer were to gather as much information as possible and put it into some form that is accessible for the general public.

Additional historical information was obtained from living original property owners, and then from their children and grandchildren who have remained in the general area. Other information has been obtained from Garfield County Courthouse records,[1] Google and the Internet, Ancestry.com,[2] local libraries, interviews, and obituaries. Valuable data and stories were gathered from published documents which can be found in the Biography section, the Internet and, of course, Erlene Murray's publication, *Lest We Forget*, which has been a valuable and primary resource for this project along with several others that were helpful in gathering the necessary information to complete this historical venture.

Several maps of Parachute Creek and its major tributaries are shown on preceding pages. On page xvi, you will find a map with numbers associated with the Parachute Creek Families identifying most landowners' homesites along the drainage.

To tell the story of the original settlers of Parachute Creek in a logical manner, a geographic approach has been used, tracing the settlements from the headwaters of the stream down to the Colorado River. By taking this approach, there is some jumping back and forth with families and timeline. However, it is the writer's desire to take the readers on a journey downstream and introduce them to the settlers along the way. Several small maps have been included within the text to help readers locate a site where the settler under discussion established his or her ranch and home. Some photos have been included where specific individuals lived or were located.

As the author and several friends were discussing the early history of Parachute Creek and the surrounding areas, it became apparent that little history of this area and its original settlers had been recorded. Erlene Durrant Murray's general historical document on the local history of the Grand Valley area, including Parachute Creek, Battlement Mesa, Wallace Creek, Rulison, and Holmes Mesa devoted several pages to Parachute Creek.[3] However, most of the text that she and others members of the Home Culture Club of Grand Valley were able to gather was devoted to residents of the town called Grand Valley, whose name had been changed from Parachute in 1908 but changed back in the 1980s. Murray's text has been invaluable as a resource for many of the early historical events of the area and of individuals and their earlier experiences in the settlement of the valley. The information gathered for this document has been generally restricted to the years between 1875 and 2015.

One of the first settlers in the Parachute Creek Valley who supplied much of the early history was

---

[1] Garfield County Clerk & Recorder's Office.
[2] Ancestry.com.
[3] Murray, *Lest We Forget,* 1973, Pp. 7-18.

Mark Hurlburt who turned ninety-three years of age in 1970. It is impossible to verify the exact dates, events, or the early pioneers who settled the valley beyond those which Hurlburt and Murray's text reported, since little was recorded during that time and only a few of the sons, daughters, and grandchildren of the early pioneers are living today. An effort was made to contact as many remaining longtime residents as possible to gather the information for this story, but undoubtedly, some have been missed. After several years of searching and gathering information, much is still missing. Hopefully, this will be a first effort in completing the history of this unique drainage of western Colorado that, today, has suffered with oil shale development and now is nearly covered with natural gas pads and production facilities.

For more than 100 years, the potential development of an oil shale industry in the Parachute Creek Valley and adjacent areas has persisted. The oil products from the Green River Shale are of high quality but difficult to extract. Several booms followed by busts occurred during the early, mid-, and late 1900s. Dr. Andrew Gulliford, a professor of history and environmental studies describes in great detail in his award-winning book *Boomtown Blues: Colorado Oil Shale 1885-1985*, the problems and outcomes of a dreamed-about energy industry that has never materialized but remains on the horizon. His book includes details on the impact to residents of Parachute Creek and the surrounding area during and after the 1982 boom ended. Professor Gulliford has been a mentor to this project and has guided and encouraged the author in completing this manuscript.

Carol Crawford McManus wrote of early historical settlements in the area in her widely read text, *Ida*[4], and then followed up with a second text, *Bess*[5], which described the experiences and hardships of early ranchers and those who came first to the mesa and valley of Wallace Creek that is located a few miles south of the town of Parachute. If something was not done soon, the few remaining longtime residents and their children of Parachute Creek would be gone and much of the original history would be lost. Thus, Carol encouraged Charline (Benson) Allen and the author to develop a map along the drainage of Parachute Creek and identify the location of some fifty-eight ranches that existed there between the years of 1882 when the first white resident arrived and the end of WWII in 1945. Such a map was produced with Carol doing most of the work and is included in the front of this text.

A major source of information for this text came from Paul R. and Bessie E. (Shults) Lindauer, the author's father and mother, who detailed stories of the ranchers and their earlier experiences up and down Parachute Creek. Their stories and history are included later in this text. The recall of historical events from these early Parachute Creek individuals was impressive. Some of the information in this text has been edited for clarity and changed as documented details were found. Efforts were made to document dates and times individuals came into the valley, but it is impossible to verify all the information. Almost none of the earliest individuals, except their sons, daughters, and grandchildren, are living today and few records from individuals or documents remain except those found in the Garfield County Courthouse, libraries, newspapers, and obituaries.

Without considerable encouragement and help from noted author Carol Crawford McManus and Charline Allen's secretarial experience, this history could not have been compiled and prepared in a format that could become available to the public. They both lived on or near Parachute Creek for much of their lives and knew the early residents. They helped to identify individuals and resources,

---

[4] McManus, *Ida: Her Labor of Love,* 1999.

[5] McManus, *Bess: A Woman's Life in the Early 1900s,* 2004.

and to gather photographs for the text. Their efforts in editing and correcting names, places, and early events have been extraordinary. Also, special thanks are extended to the various editors that helped to bring this text into a readable format. These include citation editors Joel Kirkpatric and Nathan Humphreys, a computer specialist. Also, my granddaughter Delcia Orona and grandson Dylan Ivo Lindauer provided the expertise for bringing all the photographs to the text, reading, and correcting the draft. Among those who spent many long hours on the text was editor Beth Green. She has done an outstanding job of bringing a very rough manuscript to a readable document. Thanks also to Lisa Snider, design and layout specialist, for the work and effort she and Beth have done in preparing this document for publication. I also wish to extend thanks to my wife Betty JoAnn and my family for their support these last five years.

Photographs of the early residents of Parachute Creek were sought from all sources that could be identified. Consequently, some families have none and others several. Those submitting photographs have given permission for their use in this text. Those who submitted photographs and information are as follows: Stanford Dere, Gloria (Kramer) Jasinowski, Charlene (Kramer) Semsack, Roberta (Benson) Wambolt, Margie (Benson) Lange, Bill Ogden Jr., Howard and Marshall Wilson, Gerald and Zoe Lindauer, Larry and brother Carl Lindauer, David Crawford, Eileen Bumgardner, Ella (Lewis) Hendrick and brother Charles Lewis Jr., Eyer Bruckner, Sherrill (Davidson) La Donne, Ted McQuiston Jr., Betty (Allen) McQuiston, Dena (Nelson) Thompson, Pauline (Walters) Threlkeld, Marlene (Hansen) Trent, Vera (Stanton) Madden, Ruth (Bailey) Roberts, Wayne and Alberta Payton, Fred Alber, Christy (Hayward) Koeneke, Judith Hayward, Gary Miller, Norman and Diane Lindauer, Evalee McKay, Lois (Power) Hurla, Robert Eugene Green, Charline (Benson) Allen, Carol (Crawford) McManus, Colorado State Historical Society, and the Grand Valley Historical Society.

Thanks to my good friend Dr. Lee Shropshire for providing me a well-written description of Parachute area geology.

A serious effort was made to identify correct dates and names. However, a number of individuals and their history could not be found and a number of early pioneers are missing from this text. The author of this document must assume responsibility for any errors and omissions that occur or may be found in this document.

– Ivo Lindauer
Parachute, Colorado
Summer 2016

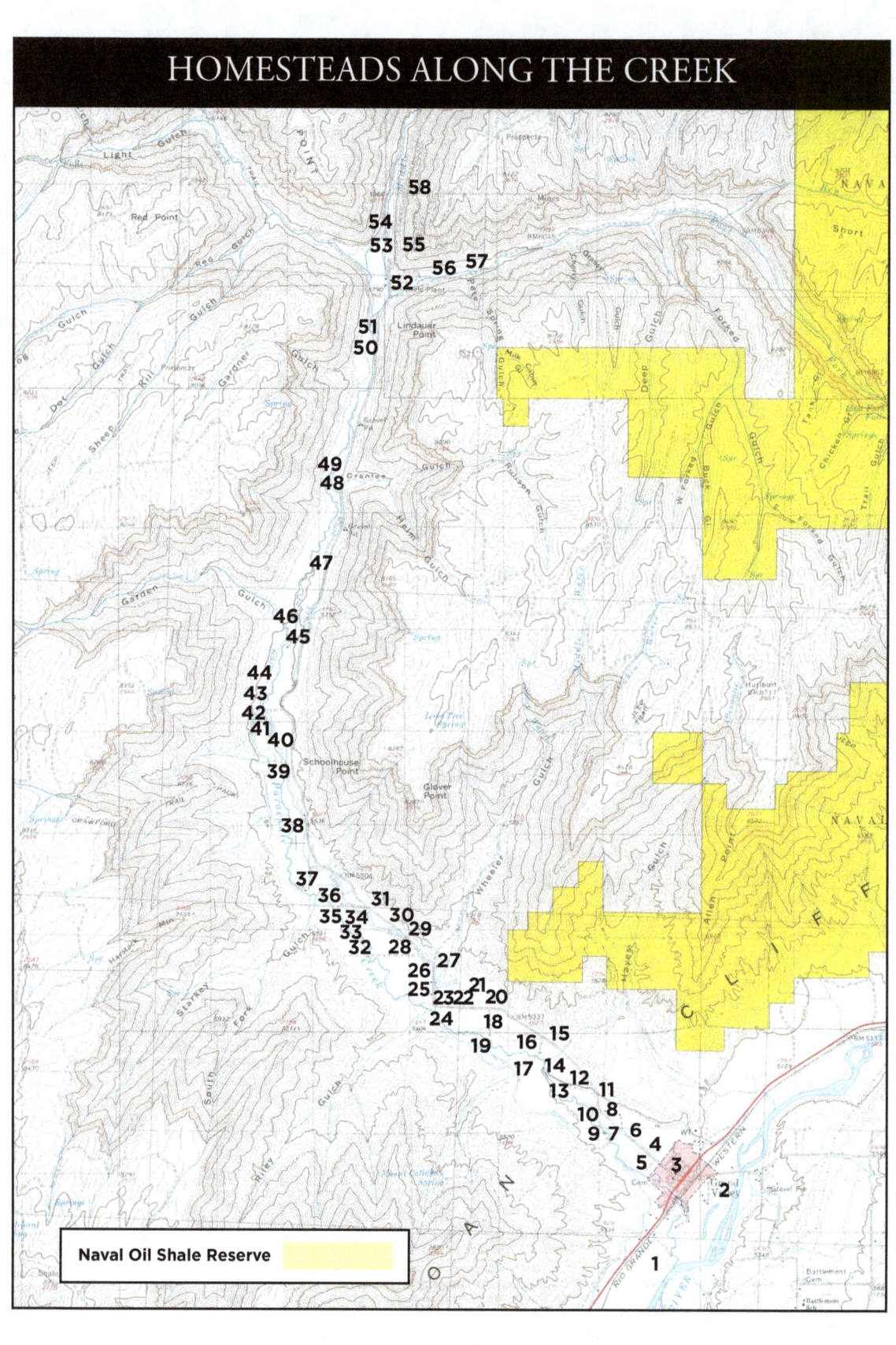

Parachute Creek Families

1. Van Horn/Paul Lindauer
2. JB Hurlburt/Mark Hurlburt
3. Parachute/Grand Valley
4. Garris Mahaffey
5. Albert & Gladys/John & Lola Allen
6. Yellow Barn – Havelmeyer/Albert Allen
7. FJ Lenhart/Elmer Wheatley
8. Lloyd Power/Williams/Eyer Bruckner
9. Lloyd Blue/Paul & Bessie Lindauer
10. Al & Mildred Mabee/Sid & Ruth Lindauer
11. Stanley & Evelyn McKay, Family etc.
12. Yone & Jessie Baughman
13. Ray & Iris Huber/Carl Jr. & Leona Alber
14. Darrell Seaman/Carl Alber
15. Charles & Mabel Patterson/Lou Tuck's sons
16. George & Fay Bendetti/Julius & Betty Lindauer
17. Tom & Maud Cline/Chester & Mabel Payton/John Cline
18. Otto & Sadie Letson/Fred Brasher, Sr.
19. Lavern & Frances Bailey
20. David Hoffman/William Zediker/Tucker
21. Lavern, Joy & Frances Bailey/new home
22. Bruce "Red" & Viola Walters
23. Francis & Emma Stanton
24. Robert & Anna /Reuben & Leila Nelson
25. Mile High Ranch-Gibbons/Ogden/ Rookstool
26. Harry Hansen/Ted McQuiston/ Gene Bumgardner/Riley Gulch
27. Martel & Mae Sherwood
28. Floyd & Maude Bruckner
29. Ernest & Blanche Sandstrom/Andy & Olive Davidson
30. John & Jennie Wheeler
31. Book Cliff School
32. Charles Lewis/Benton/Shults/Hayes
33. Tom Glover Family/Birdie DeWitt
34. DeWitt Family/Roy Jenson/etc.
35. Marcus Dee Freeland/Doc Wilson
36. Doc Wilson/Christenson/Fender/Enos Yeoman/G. Power/ Orland Lindauer
37. Jack & Vesta Crawford
38. Gabriel/Jack Crawford & George Sherman
39. John Crawford/Bob & Cora Bumgardner
40. Sig Cox & son Clifford
41. George & Ollie Kerlee
42. George & Doris Kerlee
43. Bainter Family/George Kerlee
44. Mae Kerlee & Hack Ferris/Charles Lewis, Jr./ Sig & Mae Cox
45. Families: Killian/Allen/Ogden/Zediker
46. Arcadious & Bertha Benson/Charlie & Ruth Benson
47. Bill Hughes/Power/Paul & Bessie Lindauer
48. Milton & Clara Granlee/Orland & Alice Lindauer
49. Granlee School
50. George & Mary Gardner
51. Community Oil Shale Building/ Louis & Midge Lindauer
52. Felix & Edith Lindauer
53. Families: Davenport/Rowley/Trimmer/ Peter & Margaretha Lindauer
54. Karl & Iva Lindauer
55. Julius & Betty (Baughman) Lindauer
56. Hallie & Madeline Parkhurst/Paul & Bessie Lindauer
57. Robert & Mabel Wheeler
58. Philip & Chris Dere/Charles & Flora Dere

CHAPTER 1

Geographical and Geological Description of Parachute Creek

Parachute Creek is a major drainage of the Roan Plateau found between the towns of Rifle and De Beque in west-central Colorado. The Parachute Creek Valley entrance lies between two majestic escarpments: Mt. Callahan on the south side at 8,606 feet in elevation and Allen Point at a similar elevation on the north side. The two peaks are separated by a distance of about two miles and rise over 3,000 feet above the valley floor.

Parachute Creek extends westward from the town of Parachute and the Colorado River for some five miles and then turns northward another five miles until it reaches the confluence of three smaller drainages: West Fork, Middle Fork, and East Fork. The mountains and high plateaus on the opposite side of these narrow drainages rise some 2,000 feet above the valley floor and prominent peaks are formed on either side of the drainage. These three forks come together from their respective directions to supply the water that makes up Parachute Creek.

Each valley extends in its cardinal direction some seven to fifteen miles with the East Fork branch being the longest and Middle Fork the shortest. East Fork extends eastward some six miles to a major waterfall and then on east for nearly eight more miles, reaching its headwaters near the top of the JQS trail at an elevation of almost 9,000 feet (shown on map, page viii). Parachute Creek empties into the Colorado River just south of the town of Parachute at an elevation of 5,075 feet.

The town of Parachute is found at an elevation of 5,095 feet and is bordered on the east by the Grand River, or Colorado River, as it is now known. The name of this river was changed to the Colorado River by the state legislature in 1907 and finally approved by the US Congress in 1921.

Above the Colorado River on the east side is the unincorporated community of Battlement Mesa with a population of 4,471 according to the 2010 Census.[6] West of the Colorado River, across from Battlement Mesa, is the town of Parachute, which had a population in 2013 of 1,085, according to the town clerk.

Geologically, only two relatively young rock formations are present within the Parachute-Roan Plateau area. The lower one is the Wasatch Formation, named for its type locality in southwestern Wyoming. It consists of interbedded layers of brightly colored (red, green, brown, etc.) sandstone and shale, and was deposited during the Paleocene Epoch about 50 million years ago (just a young teenager in geological time). It was deposited by streams and in ponds on a relatively flat landscape that was much lower in elevation than today's. The Wasatch is about 1,000 feet thick in the Parachute area, and can be seen in the valley of Parachute Creek for a short distance upstream from the town. The salinity and alkalinity of the soils of the valley originate from this formation as it eroded. Many soluble salts make the soil alkaline, often with a pH of 7.5 or greater. This condition ties up the transfer of nutrients so that plants cannot get such elements as nitrogen and phosphate, which are strongly needed for growth.

Above the Wasatch Formation, separated by a conspicuous but conformable boundary, is the Green River Formation, named for its type locality near Green River, Wyoming. This formation, which is about 3,000 feet thick in the Parachute area, underlies most of the Roan Plateau and is very prominently exposed in the cliffs above Parachute and the Colorado River. It is mostly various shades of gray in color and consists of shales, fine-grained sandstones, and thin beds of limestone. The Green

---

[6] City of Parachute administrative office, accessed 2012.

River Formation occurs only in northwestern Colorado, southwestern Wyoming, and northeastern Utah. It was deposited during the Eocene Epoch more than 40 million years ago in and along the shores of ancient Lake Uinta, which existed for a few million years. The water of Lake Uinta had an unusual assemblage of dissolved elements, and from it were deposited several minerals found nowhere else on earth. Near the top of the Green River Formation is a brown layer known as the Mahogany Ledge. It weathers brown because it contains kerogen, a semisolid hydrocarbon substance which causes that part of the formation to be called "oil shale." Please see pgs. 137-140 for information on the development of this oil shale resource.

On the south-facing slopes of these high mountains that directly face the sun, little vegetation exists, with the exception of herbaceous species that may be present if moisture is available. On the north and some west-facing slopes a greater diversity of plant species exists. These include a variety of shrubs including sagebrush, rabbit brush, mountain-mahogany, and some grasses, including cheat grass and Indian rice grass. More woody species occur in this foothills zone (5,500 - 7,500 feet) that are typical of the foothills ecosystem of Colorado. At higher elevations where more moisture is available, several juniper species, gambel oak, and Douglas-fir are common. Typically, above 7,500 feet elevation and in the montane life zone (7,500 – 8,500 feet elevation), aspen, gambel oak, and Douglas fir, and subalpine fir occur. At the highest elevations (above 8,500 feet) on the plateau, spruce and fir are common. On the less fertile valley floors greasewood, rabbit bush, sagebrush, cacti, cheat grass, kochia, mustards, and a large variety of other herbaceous species occur.

In this valley of Northwest Colorado, the annual precipitation ranges from below ten inches to eighteen inches and above on the upper plateaus. The precipitation in the valley classifies it as a cold desert ecosystem. Consequently, all ranches in the valley must have sufficient farmland and irrigation water necessary to raise the feed for their livestock to survive during the winter months when little pasture is available.

On the south side of the Colorado River, the rich volcanic soils attracted settlers who had great plans for the development of orchards and berry patches. This mode of farming existed well into the 20th century, but today most are replaced with small ranches or ranchettes. Soils on the west side of the river contained much calcareous material and were not as attractive, but the grass growing on the high mesas and in the valley suggested good grazing and ranching would be very profitable. To the north, the cliffs below Mamm Peak are remnants of the Green River Formation that contains the oil shale. West, south, and to the north from Parachute, the rich mahogany shale veins may be found at the base of the cliff northwest of the Colorado River. These veins are found near an elevation of 7,150 feet at the forks of Parachute Creek.

CHAPTER 2

The Name Parachute – a Misnomer from Ute "Pahchouc"

The name Parachute is assumed to be a misnomer since a June 30, 1910, issue of the *Grand Valley News,* located in the Colorado Historic Newspaper Collection in Denver, presents a different story by a government employee:[7]

> PARACHUTE, a Misnomer According to Government Employee—is a Ute Word.
>
> The writer for many years has often wondered how the creek in this valley ever got the name of Parachute. So far as the contour of the valley and the mountains were concerned, it seemed far-fetched to call it Parachute for, after all, to the closest observer, there cannot be seen any resemblance to a parachute. We have often asked the question. "How did it get the name?" Some time since while the writer was coming in from Denver he met a gentleman who some 30 odd years ago was in the employ of the government among the Ute Indians and was all over this section. He said at that time this creek was known as Pahchouc, meaning twins or the same and that the two mountains one on each side of the mouth of the creek were known at that time among the Indians as the Pahchouc because of their similarity and that in his reports to the government and mentioning this section he always referred to it by the above name. Then later, it was corrupted from Pahchouc to Parachute, which should follow very naturally. His version of the change is very probable. It should also be remembered, as he called the writer's attention to it, that the creek was called by the name of Pahchouc by the Indians before the day of the parachute. The parachute is not so very old. The *News* would like to submit that the name Pahchouc is far more appropriate than that of Parachute. Parachute signifies nothing unless it is to let a fellow down easy. Pahchouc keeps one of the old landmarks in the early Indian language and is both unique and romantic. Why not call it that today? It sounds better; it has a distinctiveness about it that in the other name has not. What do you say? Let's call the creek Pahchouc!

There has been much controversy concerning the name of the town of Parachute over the years; however, no evidence has been presented, other than the above article concerning where the name originated and why the name was given to the town. Some have suggested that F. V. Hayden named the town when he was conducting his geological and geographical surveys of western Colorado in the mid-1879s. However, the location of Parachute Creek and the town of Parachute were Ute Indian territories. The US government had signed the Treaty of 1868 and the Brunot Treaty of 1873 reaffirming the position never to permit other persons to pass over or settle within this reservation.[8] Consequently, Hayden's surveyors would not have surveyed the Parachute Creek Valley. No evidence could be found that F. V. Hayden had named Parachute Creek or the town of Parachute in any of his surveys or progress reports.[9]

The unincorporated town of Parachute was founded in 1885. It wasn't but a few years following

---

[7] *Grand Valley News*, "Parachute a Misnomer According to Government Employee—Is a Ute Word." June 30, 1910, pg. 1.

[8] Fritz. *Colorado, the Centennial State*. 1941.

[9] Hayden et al, *Ninth Annual Report of the United States Geological and Geographical Survey, 1875.*

the Meeker Massacre in 1879 that the US government opened this area for settlement. Following the movement that forced the Ute tribes out of the area in 1881, some went to the Four Corners states of Colorado, New Mexico, and Arizona, but most to northwest Utah. The Western Slope of Colorado was now ready to receive applications for settlement. They came from all directions: north, south, east, and west, since the land appeared good for farming and the large high mesas covered with grass would be ideal for grazing livestock. Hungry Mike, a recluse from Hungary, was the first to purchase land on Parachute Creek. Prior to 1882, he purchased land from the government and built a cabin at the mouth of Parachute Creek where it enters the Colorado River.

The first newspaper, called the *Parachute Index*, a four-page weekly publication, was published on October 15, 1895, with a notation that it was "Devoted to the Advancement of the Grand Valley, and Published in the Interest of Parachute and Vicinity." The town kept this name until 1908, when it officially incorporated with the new name of Grand Valley. The name was retained by the town for some seventy years, after which it was changed back to Parachute in the 1980s. The town has the name Parachute since that date. Of the fifty-eight families that homesteaded or bought claims and ranched along the Parachute Creek drainage, most are now gone. They have been replaced by gas drilling pads, associated facilities needed to prepare the gas for sale, and miles of pipelines.

CHAPTER 3

Ute Indians: The First Inhabitants of Parachute Creek

The Ute Indians were the original inhabitants of the Parachute Creek drainage. Thus, any story of this historical region must begin with them. It is important that one understands the difficulties that the Ute Indians were subjected to during their struggle to survive in the last 1,000 years or so. They have continued to remain a viable tribe that has maintained their culture, traits, and customs.

The early Indian inhabitants valued the valley of the Grand (Colorado) River that extended upstream from Grand Junction to Rifle, including Parachute Creek, as a special place where there was an abundance of game and plant material needed for their survival, especially during the winter months. They often camped along the floodplains of this river. During the summer months, hunting parties roamed the high mountain plateaus to find the migrating game needed to meet their needs. Ute Indian families often lived alone or in small groups in brush *wickiups* and *ramadas* in the western and southern areas of Colorado. They hid tepees in the eastern and southern reaches of their territory and believed that staying in one place meant certain starvation. The remains of their campsites are found throughout the valley, documented by the many wickiup remains and sites found by archeologists in the region. They were true stewards of western Colorado and adapted well to the varied mountainous and valley environments where they lived.

In the Ute Reservation Treaty of 1868, the first definite boundaries were set for Ute lands in Colorado. The area included all of the Colorado Territory west of the 107th meridian and south of a line fifteen miles north of the fortieth parallel (the northern boundary of Rio Blanco County). This area was reserved for the Ute Indians and no one, except necessary government officers, was to be permitted to pass over, settle upon, or reside in this reservation, along with several other benefits. Hunters, trappers, and some prospectors passed over the lands; however, no settlement in the Parachute Creek drainage occurred until the Utes were forced out in 1882.

It is not known when the Ute Indians arrived in Colorado but scholars believe that they were descendants of the desert cultures. Their true origin is not known at this time. Records of early cultures such as the Basketmakers and Fremont people date back nearly 10,000 years in Colorado, but had no direct ties to the Ute Indians. The Anasazis—"The Ancient Ones"—were present in western Colorado nearly 1,000 years ago, but left before the Ute bands roamed the mountains.[10] The Ute Indians occupied an area of some 225,000 square miles, extending from the Front Range west 500 miles, encompassing a good portion of Utah and some of northern New Mexico. The Ute language is Shoshonean, belonging to the Numic group of Uto-Aztecan. This language is shared by most of the Great Basin Tribes. Donald J. Hughes, in his text *American Indians in Colorado,* identified seven different bands of Ute Indians occurring in this area. These tribes were described as follows:

> The Uintah band occupied the Uintah Basin of Utah; the Yampa band, later known together with the Parianuc Utes as the White River band living in the Yampa River area in northwestern Colorado; the Parianuc, or Grand River band resided along the Colorado River; the Tabeguache, later known as Uncompahgre band, inhabited the valleys of the Gunnison and Uncompaghre Rivers in western Colorado; the Weeminuche band roamed

---

[10] Crow Canyon Archaeological Center, "Peoples of the Mesa Verde Regions."

throughout the San Juan River drainage in the Four Corners area; the Capotae band occupied the San Luis valley and the surrounding San Juan and Sangre de Cristo ranges; and the Mouache band ranged across southern Colorado and northern New Mexico from the Sangre de Cristo Mountains east out onto the plains.[11]

The Ute Indians did not have one major chief nor were they known as a unified tribe. Those of western Colorado traveled over much of the northern Colorado Plateau. The Parianuc, better known as the Grand (Colorado) River band, traveled across the continental divide over Trail Ridge in Rocky Mountain National Park, west to the Colorado Plateau. On numerous field trips to the Rocky Mountain National Park alpine region, the author of this document observed evidence of the old Ute Trail that crossed through the park above timberline. They arranged their travels from high mountains to the desert areas as their hunting and gathering required. Most anthropologists agree that by AD 1500 the Ute Indians were well established in this region. They adapted to their environment by wandering widely and taking advantage of food and material sources in the different ecological zones. Men hunted deer, antelope, buffalo, mountain sheep, rabbits, reptiles, amphibians, and other small animals such as birds, and insects. Women gathered seeds, especially of the Indian rice grass, that they could grind and make into flour. Using woven baskets, they also gathered piñon nuts, chokecherries, berries, roots, and green vegetables. They dried fruits whenever possible, crushed the piñon nuts and chokecherries, then added meat and fat for the preparation of a dried transportable food called *pemmican*. Hides were used for making teepees, clothing, and utensils. Fishing was also a primary source of food whenever they were near streams or lakes, of which there were many in the mountains. The Sevier Lake Ute Indians called themselves Pah Vant and were the only Ute band that cultivated plants prior to the horse. When horses were introduced to the Ute population, they became a major part of the Ute culture.[12]

Mormons entered into Ute Indian Territory in 1847 as the first settlers to establish communities in east-central Utah and western Colorado. They were friendly with the natives for a few years; however, as the Mormon population became stronger in numbers, their treatment changed, resulting in abuses, loss of hunting grounds, and destruction of the graves of native ancestors. As Mormons appropriated more and more of the Ute lands, the Indians retaliated with a series of raids against isolated Mormon settlements. A powerful and legendary leader in the Ute Tribe, Chief Walkara (also known as Wilson), became disenchanted and upset by the way his people were being treated. He spoke Ute, English, and Spanish and served his people as a leader in trading furs, horses, slaves, and commercial products. When a Ute warrior, a relative of Chief Walkara, was killed in a minor trade disagreement, Walkara's group demanded the death of a white settler in retribution. When their demand was not met, the Walkara (Walker) War of 1853-1854 was on. This was the beginning of the "open hand, mailed fist" Indian policy of Mormon Leader Brigham Young—feeding when possible, fighting when necessary.[13]

As part of this "non" war, the Walker War and other attacks on Mormon settlement, Captain John W. Gunnison was killed and massacred along with seven members of his survey party. Gunnison's party was seeking a railroad route through the Rocky Mountains to the Pacific Coast.[14] Their bodies were mutilated and some, (both Caucasian and Indian) said Mormons were to blame since they

---

[11] Hughes, *American Indians in Colorado*, 1977.

[12] Conetah, Fred A. *A History of the Northern Ute People*, 1982, Pp.1-26.

[13] Davis, "Ute Indians" Blog. September 20, 2010.

[14] Alexander. "The Walker War." Utah History to Go website.

feared the encroachment of their population within the Utah Territory. The Mormons, also, encouraged Indians to protect their own hunting areas. Governor Brigham Young believed that the Indians should not be unduly censured for their conduct and he took no action to punish the guilty parties. Three of eight Indians were charged in the event, and given three-year sentences; however, all escaped and no additional charges or prison time was served. A peace was eventually reached.[15]

As Mormon and other settlers entered the Utes' territories, conflicts continued, which eventually resulted in the Northern Ute Indians being forcibly removed in 1869 to the Uintah Valley Reservation. In 1881, the White River Ute Indians from Colorado joined them. The Uncompahgre Ute Indians moved to the adjoining Ouray Reservation the following year. In the latter part of the nineteenth century a division in these Ute Tribes occurred. Details of this division are discussed in the following paragraphs.

NEW TRIBES ARE FORMED

This division resulted in the creation of the Northern Ute band for those Indians that resided in Uintah-Ouray Reservation near Fort Duchesne in northeastern Utah. A separate group was created for those residing at the Ignacio Reservation called the Southern Ute Indians. However, after a few years, the Ignacio group separated and a new band moved west and became known as the Ute Mountain Ute group. This group settled west of Cortez forming the town of Towaoc, Colorado. President Lincoln initiated this division when he established the Northern Uintah-Ouray Reservation in 1861.

Restricting the Utes did not satisfy the white population who wanted to prospect in the area. In 1871 and 1872, valuable mineral deposits were discovered in the San Juan Mountains and demands were made for opening this area for prospecting; however, the Indians refused to negotiate. With continued pressure from the white population, the Brunot Treaty was signed by the Ute Indians on September 13, 1873, and ratified by Congress, ceding an additional part of their reservation in the San Juan Mountains, (recognized as a rectangular strip sixty-five miles wide and ninety miles long) to the United States. This treaty required the United States to pay the Ute Indians $25,000 annually and reaffirmed the promise of 1868 never to permit other persons to pass over or settle within this reservation.[16]

Chief Ouray obtained 304 signatures of Indians for the Brunot Treaty, but in spite of it, Indian troubles continued and ended in the Ute conflict (Meeker Massacre) of 1879 near the town of Meeker, Colorado. By that time, the amount the Ute Indians were to be paid had risen to over $65,000 and they had not received any reimbursement in the form of cash or annuities.[17] The treaty had been violated in several ways and tension rose between the settlers and the Indians.

When the Indians had not received the annuities promised to them for several years, bands of Indians continued to peacefully hunt and fish in the ceded grounds. The whites could not understand why the Indians needed so much hunting area and why the government troops did not keep them within the established boundaries.

PROBLEMS WITH THE MEEKER INDIAN AGENT

Nathan C. Meeker had been highly recommended by Horace Greeley for the position as agent of the White River Indian Agency. He was considered honest, was opposed to the use of liquor, and had been involved with the success of establishing an agricultural colony at Greeley, Colorado. Thus, he

---

[15] Hughes, *American Indians in Colorado*, 1977.

[16] Fritz, *Colorado, the Centennial State*, 1941, p. 286.

[17] Ibid.

was sent to the area to "civilize" the Indians. However, the White River Indians did not want to become farmers and live as the white population around them. Much of the wealth of the Ute Indians was tied to their horses. It was estimated that the Indians had some 3,000 head of horses in 1879. Meeker believed the large numbers of horses were eating all the grass needed by other livestock. The Indians often held races and competed in other events to show their superiority in horsemanship. In defiance of these activities, Meeker plowed up their main racetrack and threatened those who did not follow his recommendations with starvation. He wanted the Indians to stay on the reservation and work, which was totally against their culture. Meeker requested troops to curtail the Indian activities. Major Tipton Thornburg, with some 150 soldiers, was sent to his aid.

Captain Jack (Nickaagut), a leader of the Yampa White River Ute Indians who was raised in his early years with Mormons, could communicate with the whites. He went to see Governor Pitkin and asked that Meeker be removed as the agent. He intercepted Major Thornburg and urged him not to advance, rather try to settle the conflicts peacefully. Major Thornburg gave this serious consideration, but decided he should fulfill his orders and advance toward Meeker. Thornburg and his troops were ambushed at Milk Creek, some twenty miles northeast of the present town of Meeker on September 28, 1879. He and twelve of his soldiers were killed and forty-three wounded. Reinforcements were requested and Colonel Wesley Merritt arrived a week later with 530 men.

The day after the ambush at Milk Creek, a band of Indians attacked the White River Agency, killing all the white men and taking three women captive. The women were Arvilla Meeker (age sixty-four), her daughter Josephine Meeker (age twenty-one), Mrs. Flora Ellen Price (age not available) and two of her small children. According to Percy Fritz, the women were treated as "captured squaws" until Chief Ouray and Charles (General) Adams secured their release.[18] Details of the Meeker Massacre, can be found in several references, including the accounts by Robert Silbernagel, and Percy Fritz.[19]

The hostages were taken immediately to an Indian camp south of the Meeker Agency and later camped at various sites on their way to Mesa, Colorado. The first night they traveled some fifteen miles south of the White River toward Rio Blanco Hill and camped at the east headwaters of Piceance Creek, at a site called the Squaw Camp. They remained there for several days while women and others went back to the destroyed Ute Camp on the White River to obtain supplies. They were continually watching for the soldiers to come after them. On Thursday, October 2, they decided to move on. The direction they traveled from this camp is disputed.

There were several routes they could have taken on their next fifteen- to thirty-mile journey. One was over Rio Blanco Hill to the Grand River, with a camp just east of the present town of Rifle. From their camp on the river, they would travel downstream to the mouth of Roan Creek for the third camp near De Beque. They could then travel south over the Blue Stone region or up Plateau Creek to the present townsite of Mesa, Colorado. Another route, also described by Silbernagel, may have been up Cow Creek headed south toward the top of the Roan Cliffs and the JQS trailhead.[20] Here, scouts would have a wide and long-distance view in most directions overlooking the Grand River. From this point, the scouts could look back to Powell Park and the White River area where the massacre had occurred and the most likely location from which the military troops could be seen.

The Ute Indians were always on the alert for the troops they expected would be coming after

---

[18] Robert J. Silbernagel, *Troubled Trails: The Meeker Affair and the Expulsion of the Utes from Colorado*, 2011.
[19] Percy Stanley Fritz, *Colorado, the Centennial State*, 1941.
[20] Silbernagel. *Troubled Trails: The Meeker Affair and the Expulsion of the Utes from Colorado*, 2011.

them. They could have sent the major part of the large group of escaping Indians down the East Fork of the Parachute Creek, whose headwaters were nearby. From this point they would drop down into the valley and then on down to Camp 2 on the Grand River near the present day town of Parachute. Calvin Jennings, in his archeological report on Parachute Creek, identified the area as follows:

> Stories circulated by 20th century residents of the valley claimed that the historic Ute Indians used Parachute Creek and its tributaries as a trail from the Colorado River (originally called the Grand River) over to Meeker and the White River region. There were oral reports by early settlers of Parachute Creek about some 700 Ute Indians traveling down Parachute Creek in the fall of 1879. It may have been necessary to camp an extra night before reaching the Grand River. Some reported another route where the Indians came across the Piceance Creek Divide and down the ridge between Davis and Schutte Gulches to enter Parachute Creek.[21]

Assuming they selected this route, they most likely would have camped at a site near the present day town of Parachute. From this point downriver, they could have forded the Colorado River at Streit's Flat, three or four miles west of the present town of Parachute or farther down the river near De Beque. From here they would have headed southeast following Wallace Creek over the top of the Battlement mountain and down to where the town of Mesa is now located.

They remained at the Mesa campsite until the captives were released to Charles Adams and Chief Ouray on October 21, 1879, twenty-three days after being captured at the White River Indian Agency. Several warriors were charged with the killings at Meeker, but only three served time in confinement and then less than two years

During the summer of 1880, much discussion was directed toward moving the Ute Indians out of Colorado. Chief Ouray had finally agreed that if the tribe was to survive they had to abide by the rules and recommendations of the United States and its cavalry. Some of the Ute Indians refused to sign the agreement to move but were bribed by the payment of two dollars per person by Otto Mears and finally enough signatures were obtained.

During that summer, another blow struck the tribe when Chief Ouray died on August 24, 1880, as a result of Bright's disease. This was a tremendous loss to the Ute Tribe for Chief Ouray was the prime negotiator between the whites and the Indians. He was fluent in Spanish, Ute, and English and could easily communicate with all he encountered. He was a friend of President Lincoln and Kit Carson and had met with them on numerous occasions. However, it was obvious that the small population of Ute Indians could not compete with the large white population anxious to move into western Colorado.[22]

In the summer of 1881, the White River Ute bands were moved from western Colorado to reservations in northeastern Utah near the confluence of the White and Green rivers. The Uncompahgre Ute Indians were moved to the Four Corners area of Colorado, Utah, New Mexico, and Arizona where reservations had been established. Although some white officials reported that the move was cheerful and happy, others decried the move as sorrowful and downgrading since Ute Indians had occupied their western Colorado home for many centuries. Many were sullen and depressed but not hostile.

---

[21] Calvin Jennings, *A Cultural Resource Inventory of the Union Oil Company Property*, 1975.
[22] Smith, 1986

Some abandoned their blankets, personal possessions, and some livestock. Women and children wailed loudly as they were forcibly marched from their homeland. They were leaving their buried ancestors and their homes behind, not as warriors but as defeated and oppressed Indians. During the following two years, the Ute Indians were moved and forced from their promised land.

Within three days following the removal of Ute Indians from their ancestral homes, settlers were erecting houses, taking up land formerly occupied by Indians, and laying out lots and towns in the rich lands of the Uncompahgre. Thus, began the movement of individuals into western Colorado from all walks of life and professions. Since the mining industry was in a decline in the Leadville area, large numbers of miners from Denver, Leadville, central Colorado, and outside the state of Colorado came to establish homesteads. They brought livestock with them to take advantage of the large amount of free grazing and open range.

Many warriors and Indian hunters that had utilized the land for years refused to give up their hunting practices. They continued to hunt in the mountains and valleys of western Colorado into the late 19th century. Newly settled ranchers reported them stopping by their cabins and seeking food or other handouts. Some Indians returned but could not re-establish residence in the areas occupied by white populations.

The Ute Indians in the Uintah basin found their environment would not support their way of life and they continued to hunt and fish in the surrounding areas. During this time, agents did the farming for them and attempted to convert the Indians to an agrarian culture. Adding the White River Ute Indians to the reservation created additional problems with suspicion, jealousy of land, and money. In 1905 the US government allotted new reservations and opened the remainder for white entry. Each Ute received an 80- to 160-acre plot for farming and access to a communal grazing district. Allotment reduced Ute land holdings by over 85 percent and limited the potential for a successful livestock industry. Construction of expensive irrigation projects did little to improve Ute farming and led to extensive leasing and alienation of yet more land. During the years of 1906 to 1908 some 400 Ute Indians fled to South Dakota in an effort to maintain their Indian identity.

During the early 1900s, the Northern Ute Tribe was formed. Those living on the reservation survived on wages earned from whites and meager per capita distributions received from the tribe. Since that time, the Northern Ute Indians have benefited from successful federal claim cases and the development of oil and gas reserves on their reservation.

In 1879 the Southern Ute Indian tribe was formed from the remaining members of the Weeminuche, Capote, and Muache Bands that were living in Colorado. This tribe was placed on a temporary reservation in Southwest Colorado along the border of Colorado and New Mexico near Ignacio, Colorado. As this reservation (a strip of land fifteen miles wide and 110 miles long) became permanent, it was given to the Southern Ute Indians. Later, this reservation was then divided based upon options of allotments in severalty into an eastern portion for the Southern Ute Reservation and a western portion for the Ute Mountain Ute Reservation. The area was originally thought to be mostly grazing land with some farming, but the federal government failed to uphold native water rights, which restricted their farming and resource development until 1986. The Indian Reorganization Act of 1934 gave the Indians tribal sovereignty and they developed their own tribal government and constitution in 1936. Since the D&RG Railroad had purchased every other section for their railroad that ran through the reservation, it made the ownership checkerboard in nature as the unallotted land was sold to non-natives. The ownership by Hispanos, Ute Indians, and Anglo settlers made the competition for available land more severe. With the development of the gas reserves on the Southern Ute reservation, the Southern Ute Indians were no longer dependent upon outside sources for financial aid and have become major political and economic contributors within their communities and beyond.

The Weeminuche band of the Ute Mountain Ute Indians was formed into a tribe in 1897. This tribe was led by Chief Ignacio, and he opposed the allotments selected for the Southern Ute Indians. They moved and settled on arid land in the western part of the Southern Ute Reservation near the Four Corners area in 1896. This reservation is located near Towaoc and includes small sections of Utah and New Mexico. The tribe has a very successful casino on their land that provides employment for many of their own people. Ranching and farming provide a living for many. They developed their own tribal government and adopted a constitution in 1940. Following the preparation of their constitution, water was diverted from the Dolores River into McPhee Reservoir, providing for development of the large coal reserves on their reservation. In 1990, domestic water was piped to the reservation from Cortez. The tribe now controls its oil and gas development, has a successful farm and ranch enterprise, and a Weeminuche Construction Authority.[23]

---

[23] Davis, "Ute Indians" blog, 2010.

CHAPTER 4

The Formative Years of Parachute Creek History: 1882-1982

In early summer of 1882, two men, Abram W. Maxfield and Charles Marshall, traveled west from Battle Mountain in Eagle County downstream to the valley of the Grand (Colorado) River beyond Glenwood Springs, Colorado. They were leaving the mining fields of Battle Mountain looking for new land that they had heard was available farther west for settlement. These men brought with them, on two packhorses, cooking supplies, camping gear, and other items needed for an extended trip. They traveled fifteen to twenty miles a day and stayed at George Ferguson's ranch near the present-day town of Silt. The next day they went a few more miles west to a point where a mountain stream (Rifle Creek) entered the Colorado River. Abram Maxfield liked what he saw at this site and decided to stake out land for a ranch and home at a site now known as Rifle, Colorado.[24] The supply route to the ranch was nearly 100 miles east of Maxfield's ranch; however, a stage route of some forty-five miles was established two years later between the White River country and Rifle. A road through the rugged Glenwood Canyon was not built until 1906. Individuals traveling in western Colorado prior to 1880 became aware of the potential for grazing livestock on the high mountain plateaus and valleys where the winters were not so severe.

In 1882, John (JB) Hurlburt and Martin Billiter brought 2,000 head of sheep over the mountains from Meeker to a site where Parachute Creek joins the Colorado River. They had traveled from California to Meeker to establish a ranch and raise their sheep, but were convinced to travel to lower elevations where the winters were not so severe and the grazing was good. At this river site, Hurlburt and Billiter spent their first winter on Parachute Creek.

John "JB" Hurlburt
Oct. 4, 1839 - April 14, 1924

It was not long until the valley saw many new visitors. A railroad had been surveyed from Glenwood Springs to Rifle in the late 1880s and by 1892 a line had been completed from Glenwood Springs through Parachute and on to Grand Junction, Colorado, that brought many individuals to the area. They staked claims and established homes up and down Parachute Creek and some even on the high mountain plateaus. These individuals were hungry for a new start and recognized the potential economic value from growing fruit, ranching, and farming in the valley. There was a ready source of irrigation water from Parachute Creek to be used as needed for raising feed for livestock during the winter months.

CATTLE AND SHEEP WARS

The lush grazing potential in the west captured the attention of cattle barons and sheepmen who were looking for new grazing lands, and there was plenty of it on the mountaintops and valleys of Parachute Creek. Some ranchers in the 1880s and 1890s had created large herds and were looking to the west for new grazing opportunities. It wasn't long before conflicts occurred between cattlemen and sheepmen throughout the west. Cattlemen, who often were the first using the grazing land, saw sheep as invaders. These men noted that the habit of sheep eating grasses to their roots and their sharp hoofs trampling the grasses destroyed the land upon which they grazed. Also, the odor they left and the pollution of streams that occurred where sheep herds were bedded down altered the site and made it non-useable by cattle.

---

[24] Reading Club of Rifle, *Rifle Shots, Story of Rifle, Colorado,* 1973.

Sheep on their cattle range was a great fear of western Colorado cattlemen. Those in the northern part of Colorado considered themselves lucky that sheep had not moved onto their range. However, the inevitable was coming. The *Meeker Herald,* on January 14, 1888, warned that sheep were going to be brought in from Utah to use the White River grazing areas. A similar situation was occurring in other states.

In Texas, cattle-ranching was well established by 1870 and dominated the livestock industry, while sheep ranching was dominant in the southeastern states. By 1875, one of the first conflicts occurred on the Charles Goodnight Range on the border between New Mexico and Texas. Laws had been passed in Texas that required sheepmen to have their herds inspected for diseases, and if scabies (a mangy disease in sheep) occurred, they would be quarantined. This drove many sheepherders undercover.

In Arizona, some 4,000 head of sheep were driven into the Little Colorado River. Many died in the quicksand. For several years, conflicts and killings occurred between the war-prone Grahams/Blevins and Tewksbury families. This war resulted in revenge killings and had little to do with sheep after the initial encounter. Twenty-five people had been killed in a variety of conflicts by the end of 1892. Sheepmen with their large herds began moving west and north into Montana, Wyoming, and Colorado.

Shortly after JB Hurlburt and Billiter brought their sheep into the valley at Parachute, bad feelings developed between the cattlemen and sheepmen. Several cattlemen running large herds on the summer ranges were concerned that the sheep would destroy the grasses. With many settlers arriving and laying claim to any land available and with the competition for grazing increasing, the cattlemen were fighting for their existence. After several warnings to the sheepmen that they were not welcome, the Parachute cattle-sheep war was on.

In 1894, at a site some ten miles up Parachute Creek, 3,800 head of sheep were killed. Some were driven off the plateau over a several-hundred-foot-high cliff while others were clubbed to death. These sheep belonged to different local sheepmen. The sheepherder, Carl Brown, was shot in the hip as he came running out of his tent with a rifle. The cattlemen had brought a doctor with them, and Carl Brown was treated, placed on a horse, and sent to the valley to notify the owners of what had occurred. About 1,500 more sheep were destroyed that same year in the same county. The earlier event was reported in the *Craig Courier* newspaper on September 14, 1894, as follows:

> The owners (of the sheep) are residents of Parachute with rights to adjacent range and the posse made a futile race to apprehend the raiders. John Miller owned 1,700 sheep and Charles Brown, uncle of the wounded man, 2,100.

From various reports, JB Hurlburt owned many of the sheep killed in this conflict. He attempted to obtain retribution for the loss of a major part of his herd. However, no settlement was ever reached in his efforts with the state and he decided he could not fight the whole country, so he sold his remaining sheep. Sheep ranching did not resume in the valley until the early 1900s. The sheep and cattle wars lasted for fifty years, eventually ending in the 1920s. During this time, the Battle of Yellow Jacket Pass, located northeast of Meeker ended the last major conflict between sheep and cattle interests. The Colorado militia had to be called in to restore order.

GRAZING ON PUBLIC LANDS

The ranchers grazed large herds in the valley during the summer, and most of their cattle were trailed up to the high plateaus where there was extensive grass. With the increasingly large herds, overgrazing occurred. After sheep were introduced in the same area, the grasses were eaten close to the ground and trampled down. This created a habitat for weeds that began to replace the lush grass that had once been so common. Poison weeds infested the area as sheep and cattle conflicts continued.

The US government passed the Taylor Grazing Act of 1934, ending all conflicts. The act allotted grazing rights for sheep, cattle, and other livestock according to the base property of the owner and only to those ranchers that had sufficient feed/hay land to feed their herd over the winter months. The era of free grazing was over, and those permitted were assessed a fee per head for the livestock that ran on the range. The government assigned the responsibility of managing these grazing lands to the Department of Interior's Grazing Service, which later became the Bureau of Land Management. The US Forest Service has its own rules and management, but no national forest existed in the Parachute Creek grazing area.

The lush grazing did not last long. By the turn of the century, ranchers began to feel the impact. Many sold their operations or lost their property with high mortgages and bank loans called in during the depressions of the early 1920s and 1930s. These permits were restricted to ranchers, and when the allotment numbers were passed out, they were related to base property owned, prior use, and length of time. Most permits were effective during the summer from June 15 until October 15. The ranchers on Parachute Creek ran their livestock on the East Fork grazing allotment with a yearly updated management plan. Some had special permits on Forest Service property south and east of the Parachute Creek grazing area or grazed their livestock on private property.

As most of the available land became occupied, the ranches became smaller and changed from self-supporting to ranch/farms forcing the owners to take on second jobs to take care of their families and keep their operations running. Many of the landowners had orchards, raised large gardens, chickens, and pigs, milked their own cows, and sold the cream and eggs to neighbors and town folks. These served as a guaranteed food source for the families and provided much needed extra income.

Most of the ranchers grazing livestock on Parachute Creek were in a valley classified as part of the west cold desert ecosystem. Here, elevations range from a desert/shrub-land ecosystem at 3,500-5,500 feet to summer ranges in the montane ecosystem of 7,500-8,500 feet. The annual precipitation ranges in these zones from below ten inches in the desert to sixteen to eighteen inches in the montane. Grazing is not allowed during the off-season. Also, many ranch acreages are not large enough to raise the necessary hay to feed their livestock over winter and must supplement their winter supply by purchases. Consequently, most operations that once existed with self-sustaining properties have been sold and a few leased to larger operators.

In 1876, the US president was authorized by the General Land Office to withdraw forestland and create federal forest reserves to be managed by the Department of Interior and later the Department of Agriculture/Forest Service. At that time, permits did not regulate grazing rights, and first use had the priority. Other public lands would continue to be managed by the US General Land Office until a new agency was formed. It wasn't until 1946 that the Bureau of Land Management was created by the Department of Interior to manage most of the remaining public lands. The US Park Service was created earlier, but does not allow grazing on most of their managed parks. However, grazing does occur on thirty-two of their managed units.[25]

---

[25] Kerr, "Livestock Grazing on the National Park and Wilderness Preservation System," 2000.

CHAPTER 5

Pioneer Families of Parachute Creek: 1882 – 1945

Alice Boulton, in her text on early homesteads in Silt, Colorado, and surrounding areas, describes how advertisements encouraged people to come to the mesa and valley region of Garfield County, including the area adjacent to and east of Parachute Creek and Battlement Mesa/Parachute. As the railroad reached Parachute in 1892, potential settlers came from all directions, for they had heard of the free land to homestead and free grazing on the meadows and mountaintops. Homesteaders came from the eastern states, from Ireland, Eastern Europe, the eastern half of Colorado, and from the Leadville mines. All were in search of land that they could farm and ranch in their own way. Dugouts and log cabins provided housing for the early settlers, and an abundance of wild game provided a food source.[26]

The first settlers that arrived sought out land that had the greatest potential for farming and contained an appreciable portion of flat surfaces. JB Hurlburt and Morton Billiter found such land at the mouth of Parachute Creek and as others arrived, they found similar land partway up the creek. Fertile ground in and around Parachute and along streams provided sites for growing fruit to be sold to the miners upstream. Some found after a few years that the winters could bring much snow and the fields had to be irrigated from nearby streams or springs. Many settled on land where the soils were not fertile. Those that survived had to be tough, inventive, creative, and courageous—and many were just that.

As an introduction to those that first arrived, we will start with the location where East, West, and Middle forks converge to make up the major stream of Parachute Creek and list the settlers as one would travel down the creek. Maps throughout the text identify the location of each of the families by number. The numbers start with 58 and move downward to the town of Parachute and the post office as number 3 and on to number 1, Nolte property.

CW "DOC" WILSON | #36

In 1884, Charles William "Doc" Wilson, traveling from Piceance Creek, was the first white man to come down Parachute Creek. It was late in the fall and dark was overtaking him. He lay out overnight by an old corral west of Davis Point and lit a campfire for heat, light, and to keep the wolves away. He only had one bullet for a cap and ball pistol. According to his story, the wolves attempted to get to him, but would not come inside the light from the campfire. As the campfire burned down, they drew closer. He burned numerous logs from the old Indian corral that night to keep them back. The wolves left a little before daylight.[27]

Charles William "Doc" Wilson
1867 - 1953

Wilson was the first to explore the mountains east of Parachute Creek. Working his way through the cliffs on the point west of Granlee Gulch, he saw several elk around Mud Springs, but no other animals. After returning from his trip, he journeyed on to Rifle, where he took up management of the JQS Cattle Company. The JQS brand is one of the oldest in Western Colorado. He operated that

---

[26] Boulton, *Silt, Colorado, Homesteads, 1890-1940,* 2009.

[27] Murray. *Lest We Forget.* 1973.

ranch for about ten years, running some 7,000 head of cattle on the Book Cliffs (also known as the Roan Cliffs) west of the town of Rifle.

Doc Wilson was born in September 1867 in Kansas. His father, FB Wilson, was born in Kentucky in 1826 and moved to Missouri before settling in Kansas. His mother, LB Wilson, was born in Minnesota in 1827. The senior Wilsons had five children and Doc was the middle child. A younger brother, Frank, who had been living in Hesperus, Colorado, for some time, came north to join Doc. He later settled in Rifle and became the justice of the peace and a notary. (More details on Doc may be found later in this text under CW Doc Wilson and Family Section.)

HOMES & RANCHES 33-58

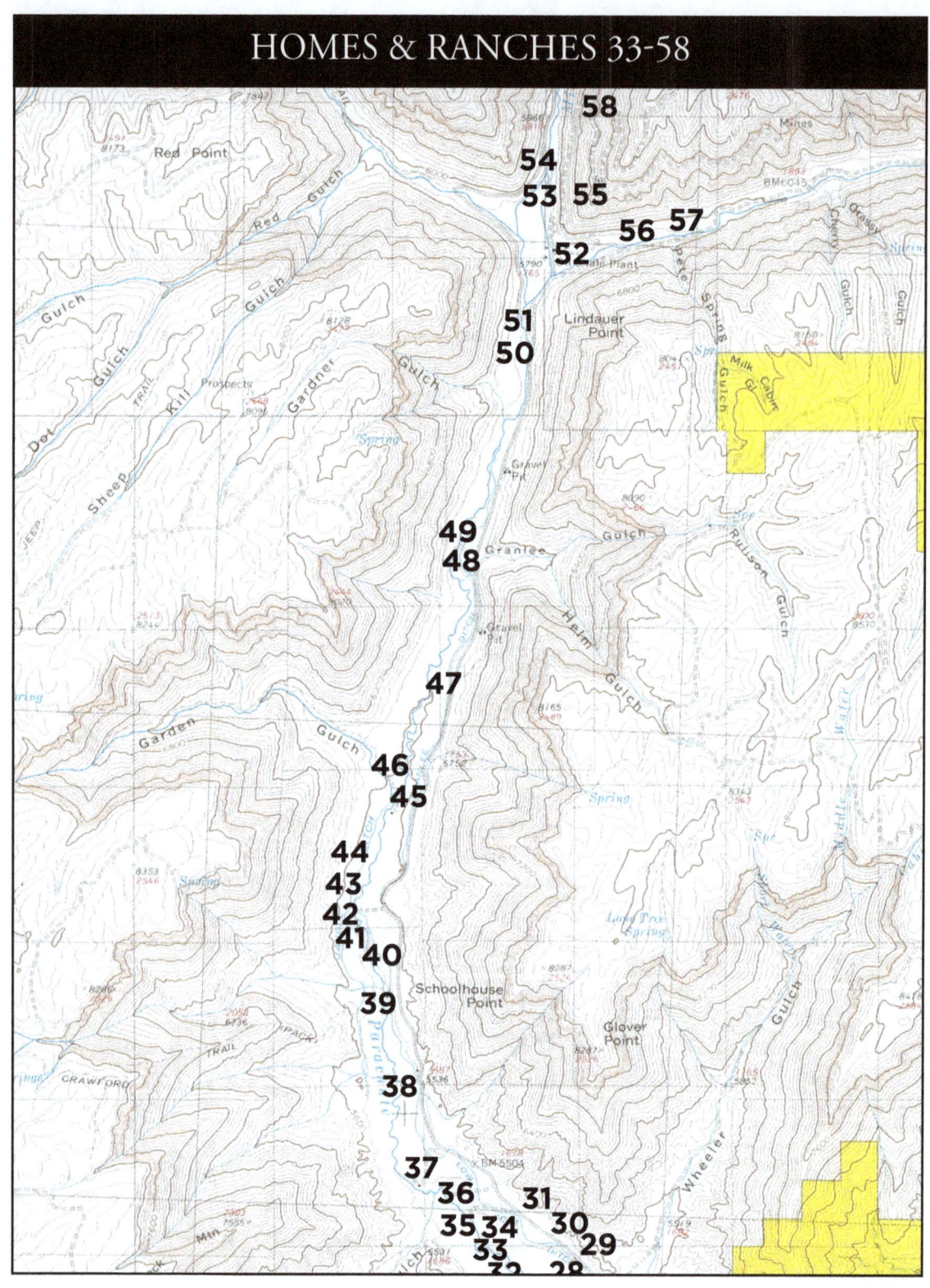

CHAPTER 6

Early Pioneers on the Upper Half of Parachute Creek

At one time, there were at least fifty-eight homes/ranches along Parachute Creek and its forks. Over the years, oil and gas companies have purchased almost all of the properties on the creek. Although some properties have been leased back to tenant farmers and ranchers, by 2012 only one of the original families still owned their ranch and farmed their property.

PHILIP GEORGE DERE FAMILY | #58

One of the earlier settlers on Parachute Creek was Philip George Dere. Sometimes referred to as George Philip, he was born in Frankfurt, Germany, on April 7, 1853. He immigrated to the United States in 1879. Philip married Anna Stoffer on November 4, 1879. She had immigrated to New York in 1876 before moving on to Denver, where she worked as a maid, according to the 1880 federal census.[28]

Philip and Anna moved on to Crested Butte, Colorado. Perhaps they were interested in seeking a fortune in silver or coal mining, since Crested Butte was a mining boomtown at that time. However, Philip was a shoe and harness maker and practiced this trade in Denver and throughout different communities in Colorado.

The Dere family: (back row L-R) Frank, Christopher, Joseph, and Philip Dere; (front row L-R) not named, Philip Jr., Fredrick, Anna (Stoffer), and Catharine Dere.

He moved to Parachute in the late 1890s because this location was more profitable to his trade. He and his family lived on the Middle Fork of Parachute Creek in the early 1900s.

Anna Dere died in 1923. Philip Sr. lived until the age of eighty-three in Parachute, when he was killed by an automobile while delivering mail on February 22, 1936. Both Anna and Philip are buried in the Russey-Hurlburt Cemetery.

MARGARETHA "MAGGIE" (DERE) LINDAUER | #53

Philip and Anna's first child was Margaretha, or "Maggie" as she was known. She was born in Denver on July 20, 1880, and was baptized in the Catholic Saint Elizabeth Church in Denver. The church was founded by a group of German Catholics in 1878 and is a prominent feature on the Auraria campus in Denver today. As she approached the age of nineteen, she married Peter Joseph Lindauer on March 4, 1899, in Glenwood Springs, Colorado. (Information on Peter can be found in the Peter Joseph Lindauer section.) Peter at that time owned a general merchandise store in Parachute, selling a variety of items plus groceries. They lived in a house behind the store and began their family of six children there. After a couple of years, Peter and Maggie purchased a homestead at the confluence of the three forks that formed Parachute Creek.

---

[28] *US federal census, 1940.*

Maggie was one of the early pioneer women in the Parachute Creek area and lived a hard life as a rancher's wife, bearing six children, about two years apart. Maggie died March 26, 1915, at the age of thirty-five, leaving six children ages eighteen months to fourteen years. She had lost one child and did not want any more. According to her death certificate, she died from acute nephritis, jaundice, and a pelvic infection at the sanitarium in Rifle. She had been taken there suffering with complications of Bright's disease and peritonitis. Margaretha is buried next to her husband Pete in the Russey-Hurlburt Cemetery in Parachute.

CHRISTOPHER C. DERE | #58

The second child was Christopher C. Dere, born in Crested Butte in the early 1880s. By 1910, he had moved to Denver. He married Ida Milner in Garfield County in 1922. In 1930, he and his wife were living in Grand Valley and the federal census[29] reported them with three children: Katherine A., Christopher C., and Charles E. The Dere family lived at the head of Parachute Creek and several of their children attended Granlee School. The family homesteaded 120 acres in the Middle Fork of Parachute Creek next to the Pete Lindauer Ranch.

In 1922, Christopher C. Dere strung a wire as an aerial across the Middle Fork canyon, a distance of some 1,000 feet and was able to hear a concert being played on KFKA, the Western Radio Corporation Denver Post broadcasting station. This was north and adjacent to the Peter Lindauer property. His journey came to an end when Christopher passed away in 1938.

PHILIP DERE JR. | #58

Philip Dere, Jr. was born in 1886 and married Nellie Thompson in 1913 in Denver. He later married Ellen Newell July 24, 1923, in Garfield County. Philip Jr. was an educator and taught in Denver and Idaho and apparently practiced this profession in various other cities. Philip Jr. and Nellie had four children: Loraine, Philip, Ana Belle, and Billy Jean Dere. The 1930 federal census[30] indicated that Philip Jr. was widowed and living in Apache, Arizona. He died from arteriosclerosis in 1966 and is buried in Parachute.

JOSEPH DERE | #58

Joseph Dere was born in 1888 in Parachute and never married. He moved to Oak Creek, where he was involved in the mining of coal. No other information could be found on Joseph.

FRANK DERE | #58

Frank Dere was born in Parachute in 1893 and in the federal census of 1900 was listed as seven years old.[31] He is identified in the World War Draft Registration of 1917-1918 as a farmer living twelve miles north of Grand Valley, Colorado. In 1920, he was listed as an inmate at the Colorado State Hospital in Pueblo, Colorado, where he apparently passed away at the age of twenty-eight.

CATHARINE K. DERE | #58

Catharine K. Dere was born in 1895 in Parachute. She died of typhoid fever at the age of fifteen.

---

[29] *US federal census, 1870-1940.*

[30] Ibid.

[31] Ibid.

CHARLIE DERE FAMILY | #58

According to the 1930 federal census, Charlie Dere was born in 1899 in Parachute.[32] He married Flora Van Pelt on May 12, 1928, and they had two children: Stanford and Beverly. Stanford married Arvella Jean Krabbe October 24, 1965, and they had four daughters: Cherie, Bobbie, Joann, and Tracy. Stanford, usually known as "Bud," graduated from Grand Valley High School and entered the US Army. Following his service, he worked for the Bell Telephone Company and retired after thirty-four years. He and his family live in Grand Junction. Beverly was born October 6, 1934, and also graduated from Grand Valley High School. She married Charles "Sharkey" Jensen in 1952 and worked as a secretary for Mesa Drug Company for some twenty years. Beverly passed away in 2006. Sharkey had died the previous year, in 2005.

Beverly and Stanford "Bud" Dere at Home Ranch, ca. 1939

In 1926, Charlie obtained his father's forty acres at the head of Parachute Creek. He also obtained his brother Frank's forty acres and lived in a cabin built on the former forty acres. He lived there for some five years and then bought the 120 acres in Middle Fork that had been sold to Judd Sipprelle earlier and moved on to his property in 1944. Charlie and Flora lived there until it was sold to the Union Oil Company of California in the early 1950s for future oil shale exploration. He then moved to the Peter Lindauer Ranch that had been sold earlier to the same company. After Charlie's death September 20, 1969, Flora moved to the Van Pelt Ranch that had been her parents' home, located northeast of the town of Parachute.

During the years Charlie lived on Middle Fork, he raised cattle and sheep and farmed the narrow valleys, raising hay to feed his livestock. They survived the summer floods and the rocks that would come down from the cliffs high above their family home. Flora died on February 2, 1988, and is buried with Charlie in the Russey-Hurlburt Cemetery in Parachute. Stanford Dere, who now lives in Grand Junction, retired from the Mountain Bell Phone Company in 1989. He and cousins Charlene Semsack of Arvada, Colorado, and Gloria Jasinowski of Virginia Beach, Virginia, provided much of the Dere family information.

FREDRICK DERE | #58

Philip Dere Sr. and his wife Ann's last child was Fredrick Dere, born in 1903. He is listed in the 1920 federal census at the age of sixteen.[33] Little information could be found on Fredrick Dere; he joined his brother Joseph in Oak Creek and worked there for some time. He never married and passed away in 1950.

---

[32] Ibid.

[33] Ibid.

IRVING AND HALLIE PARKHURST | #56

Hallie and Irving Parkhurst

Everett Tracy, his wife Ida, and a son Everett Jr. came into the Parachute Creek valley in 1893. Everett's two sons by a previous marriage, Irving and Hallie Parkhurst, came with them. They located on land at the Una railroad stop between the Colorado River and the D&RG railroad west of the town of Parachute. The soil was very poor and alkaline. They soon moved to an unknown location on Parachute Creek. As the boys grew up and married, Everett Jr. moved to Battlement Mesa and developed a profitable sheep ranching business. In the 1920s, he and his father moved to Washington to make their home.[34] Irving Parkhurst also went into the sheep ranching business, but moved to the East Fork of Parachute Creek.

In the late 1890s, Irving Parkhurst had purchased a portion of his East Fork homestead from Robert Wheeler of Parachute Creek. He sold his property to Hallie, who had married Madeline (Kramer) Parkhurst. There were two ditches on this property that were used to irrigate four fields of hay. The hay in these fields was used to feed the owners' livestock. The dams that were used to divert water to these ditches were often destroyed by high water in the spring and by periodic floods during the summer. It became a continuing task to keep water in the ditches for irrigating the crops.

Hallie and Madeline Parkhurst sold their interest in the property to Paul and Bessie Lindauer, who took possession of the property on October 15, 1929. A deed of trust from Paul's dad, Peter, in the amount of $1,005 and a note from Paul in the amount of $413.80 had held the property. Upon clearing all encumbrances on the property, Paul and Bessie paid $2,500 as recorded on the deed.[35]

They ranched and farmed the property until 1937, when it was sold to the Union Oil Company of California. Paul, Bessie, and their family moved downstream to the Lloyd Blue property one mile west of Parachute and developed this ranch into a profitable operation. They raised their children at this site.

JOHN DAVENPORT FAMILY | #53

John Davenport was born in Tennessee in May 1833. His father was born in Virginia and his mother in Tennessee. He married Martha (Slate) Davenport in 1856. She was born July 1839 in the state of Georgia, and her parents were both from North Carolina. No children were listed in the 1900 census.[36] John Davenport was one of three who developed homesteads where East Fork, West Fork, and Middle Fork converge to form Parachute Creek. He identified himself as a farmer in the 1900 federal census.[37] He was interested in raising and running sheep, for he combined his herd of sheep with John Hurlburt, Martin Billiter, Watson, Starkey, and Charlie Brown. (Some first names could not be found.)

---

[34] Murray. *Lest We Forget*. 1973.

[35] Garfield County Clerk & Recorder's Office.

[36] *US federal census*, 1870-1940.

[37] Ibid.

John Davenport sold his interest to Peter Lindauer in 1900. He moved to town, where he purchased a general store from Douglas Armstrong.[38] The 1890 census[39] also indicated that John Davenport had residences in both De Beque and Mesa, Colorado. He died in Bayfield, Colorado, on April 4, 1921. Later, Irving Parkhurst, Peter Lindauer, and Philip Dere occupied the Davenport properties at the convergence of West, Middle, and East forks on upper Parachute Creek.

Photo courtesy of Daisy (Shehorn) Looney and Grand Valley Historical Society

First Family of Parachute and the first home they built there. Left to right: Mrs. Hurlburt holding Lottie (Shehorn), Luther and Mark Hurlburt, Minnie (Clarke), Lou (Wayne), Billiter, Joe Trimmer and his wife, Frances, also a daughter. (This photo is from Murray's text *Lest We Forget*, 1973.)

JOE TRIMMER | #53

In the fall of 1882, JB Hurlburt and his partner, Martin Billiter, brought their 2,000 head of sheep from Meeker over the Government Road to Parachute Creek. Hurlburt and Billiter spent the winter of 1882-83 taking care of the sheep and building a cabin for their families that they had left behind. A photo of the Hurlburt cabin is shown above.

The people in this photo established the first settlement on Parachute Creek. The photo shows Joe Trimmer and his wife, Frances, with a daughter of John and Martha Hurlburt, who was born in Pittsville, Shasta County, California, in 1882. Additional information on Joe Trimmer could not be found although he was one of the first three to develop homesteads at the convergence of the East, West, and Middle forks.

---

[38] Murray. *Lest We Forget*. 1973.

[39] *US federal census, 1870-1940*

MORTON T. ROWLEY | #53

Morton T. Rowley was born in Utah Territory in July 1861. His father was from England and his mother from Scotland. Morton identified himself as a farmer. According to the 1900 census[40] of Parachute Creek, Morton married Mary E. Rowley in 1886. Mary was born in Iowa in July 1870 and her maiden name was unknown. They had five daughters and one son: Clara M. (1887), Winnie E. (1889), Frances C. (1892), Alice W. (1894), son Mark J. (1896), and Effie (1898).

Morton Rowley and Joe Trimmer took up homesteads adjoining John Davenport. Morton had an interest in the oil shale of the area and was one of the first men to experiment with the extraction of oil from shale on Parachute Creek.[41] He filed on water and developed a homestead at the junction of East, West, and Middle forks in an effort to establish a sheep and cattle operation. This became the Peter Lindauer ranch in 1902. Morton Rowley was present at a meeting of the original members and officers of the Parachute Mining District that had been by formed in 1890. The mining district was formed by local men to maintain a written record of the laws governing mining and the patenting of oil shale claims. It also provided land descriptions of claims of many of the original signers of Parachute Mining District and others in the region.

Mike Callahan and other early pioneers of Parachute knew from stories told by Ute Indians that the "rock that burns" had a potential value. Mike became a major promoter of the future of oil shale and often told the story of his own cabin with a fireplace constructed from the beautiful blue-grey oil shale found in the area. According to Murray's report[42] Mike had invited friends to a house warming of his new cabin. When he lit the fireplace, it became so hot that it burned the cabin and its contents down. The peak west of the town of Parachute was named after Mike Callahan.

PETER LINDAUER AND FAMILY | #53

One of the earliest pioneers into Western Colorado was Peter "Pete" Joseph Lindauer. He came into the Parachute area in the early 1890s. His father Franz (Francis) Lindauer was born in 1818 in Baden-Württemberg, Germany, and married Monika (Monica) Zoliar in 1848 in Germany. Leaving Le Havre, France, Franz, his wife Monica, and two children, Helena and Michael, immigrated on the ship *President Fillmore* to the United States in 1854. They settled on a farm in Ripley County, Indiana. A third child, Louisa Theresa, was born there in 1855. Louisa died at the age of thirty-three. Peter Joseph was Franz and Monica's fourth child. He was born in Jefferson County, Indiana, December 5, 1859, followed in June 17, 1862, by a younger brother William Ferdinand, known as Ferdinand.

Ferdinand "Fran" married Katherine Ethel Schwendeman in 1895 and they had three children: Francis in 1897, Florence in 1899, and Robert in 1901. After selling his share of their store to his brother Pete, Fran moved to Glenwood Springs, where he managed the Lindauer Hotel for several years. He died in Glenwood Springs of tuberculosis in 1915 and is buried in the Rosebud Cemetery there. Katherine moved back to Ohio with her family and died there December 4, 1933. She is buried in Ripley, Illinois.

Pete Lindauer left his home at the age of seventeen and took a stagecoach west to Kansas City. He spent a number of years there and became proficient in leatherwork. He went to Georgetown, Colorado, working there for a couple of years before moving on to Middle Park, where he obtained work on a cattle ranch feeding cattle and building houses in Kremmling, Colorado. According to his daughter Rose, he spent many hours studying during the long winter evenings since he had only

---

[40] Ibid.

[41] Murray. *Lest We Forget*. 1973.

[42] Ibid.

completed the fourth grade in Indiana. When the Denver & Rio Grande Railroad started to lay tracks from New Castle to Salt Lake City, he was hired with a four-horse team to haul ties. His brother Ferdinand, who came west for health reasons, joined him, and they continued to work with the railroad in the early 1890s.

Pete was a carpenter, and his task was to design and build trestles for the new railroad that crossed the many washouts in western Colorado and eastern Utah. He owned several teams of horses and scrapers that most likely were used in building the rail-bed. As this job ended, they began hauling fruits and vegetables

Margaretha "Maggie" (Dere) 1899   **Peter "Pete" Lindauer 1899**

throughout the Grand Valley and to the higher country using their four-horse teams. Pete apparently liked what he had seen in the Parachute area and returned with his brother Ferdinand and his wife, Katherine, who had come west to join him. Peter continued his carpenter work and in 1898, with the help of his brother, built a store on the northeast corner of Parachute Avenue and First Street. Peter married Margaretha "Maggie" Dere March 4, 1899, in Glenwood Springs. She was the oldest of twelve children born in the Dere family. Peter and Maggie's first son, Paul Lindauer, was born June 30, 1900, in a house behind the store that was believed to have been the first general store in the town of Parachute.

When Pete and Ferdinand decided to sell the store, Pete purchased three claims owned by John Davenport, MT Rowley, and Joe Trimmer along with all water rights at the head of Parachute Creek.[43] At that time, it was known as the John Davenport ranch and was wooded with trees and heavy brush and many washouts. On this property, he created pastureland by moving the streams of the three drainages to the canyon walls with a team and scraper. He eradicated all the trees and brush in the bottomland, created large hay fields, and built ditches to supply adequate water for irrigating his fields.

Peter "Pete" Lindauer ca. late 1930s

Pete and Maggie had five more children: Felix R. (1902), Rose M. (Lindauer) Kramer (1908), Karl (1909), Louis (1912), and Julius (1914). However, Maggie died eighteen months after Julius was born on March 22, 1915. Details about Maggie may be found under the Philip George Dere Family section.

Three and a half miles up West Fork, at the mouth of Light Gulch, Maggie Lindauer had filed on a desert claim that was sold in later years by her husband, Pete. There were mineral springs on Maggie's property and wild game would come fifteen to twenty miles for this water. It was of good quality and 100 percent soft water, plus it had beneficial minerals. Lots of older folks traveled for miles to get a container of this water.

---

[43] Ibid.

Members of the Lindauer and Dere Families, ca. 1910. L to R, Peter Lindauer on horseback, Rose (small girl), Catharine "Katie" Dere, Felix Lindauer, Margaretha "Maggie" holding Karl Lindauer, Paul Lindauer, and Frank Dere on horseback at the Lindauer Ranch.

PETER LINDAUER RANCH | #53

Having sufficient water to irrigate their crops has always been a problem for ranchers on Parachute Creek. Because of the long hard winters when grazing was not available, it was necessary to have enough hay to feed their livestock from late December to mid-May. To overcome this problem, ranchers tried a number of approaches. In 1903, a dozen ranchers started building a reservoir about one-half mile wide and a mile long on West Fork. In the early 1890s, Bill Tanney and a fellow by the name of Scoggins had done much mining at the head of West Fork looking for asphalt deposits that were predicted to be oil shale. When heated by the sun, the oil in the shale runs out of the rock like tar. However, the veins ran out.

During their mining activity, they had observed the flow of the West Fork Creek and thought they could enhance the flow of Parachute Creek, since water went only two-thirds of the way down the valley. There was little or no water for the lower end of the valley, so they started construction of a dam. When they were about two-thirds completed, the Bureau of Reclamation stepped in and construction was stopped. It was deemed unsafe due to the fact that shale rock and dirt being used lacked structural integrity. After that, all the ranchers started irrigating in the early spring with snowmelt water at the head of Parachute Creek. Because of this, much of the water sank into the earth and re-emerged two to five miles downstream in the form of springs. In normal precipitation years, all ranchers on the lower end of Parachute Creek now had sufficient water for irrigation and domestic uses through the summer.

During the early 1900s, Peter and his family of five boys and one girl ran upwards of 1,000 head of cattle. At that time there was plenty of money available through the Federal Land Banks, which readily loaned money to ranches. So most of them had a good string of cattle and lived fairly well for a few years, but with much debt. As WWI ended, many of the ranches lost their cattle and ended up in bankruptcy and foreclosure. They gradually gained back some of their financial stability as the 1920s came to an end, only to again enter a major recession in the early 1930s. The hardships and lack of spending money kept most of the ranchers broke and always seeking other means to support their families.

Pete completed all of the clearings and drainage changes with teams of horses and a scraper that he continued to use well into the 1940s. He spent forty-three years on his ranch with the help of three of his sons, Felix, Karl, and Julius. They built their own homes and supported their families by raising livestock, selling their cattle, raising silver foxes, and guiding hunters.

In 1947, as a result of Pete's advanced age at eighty-eight, and associated infirmities, he felt depressed and of no value to the ranch. His daughter-in-law had taken his gun away, and while all other family members were gone, he ended his own life by hanging in the family barn on December 14, 1947. He is buried in the Russey-Hurlburt Cemetery.

PAUL R. LINDAUER AND FAMILY | #56

Paul R. Lindauer was the oldest of six children born to Peter and Margaretha Lindauer. He was born in 1900 in the town of Parachute. Two years later, the family moved to the head of Parachute Creek where his parents had purchased three claims from homesteaders Joe Trimmer, Morton Rowley, and John Davenport. At the age of three, Paul was lost for half of a day and tracked down by an old bear trapper. He attended the Granlee School for his early education and finished the tenth grade at Grand Valley High School before becoming a full-time cowboy. He lost his mother at the age of fourteen and for a couple of years helped his dad and housekeeper raise the other five children.

Paul Lindauer with his hounds – 1920s

Paul soon became responsible for taking care of their large cattle herd and spent much of his time in the summer on the mountains looking after their cattle and participating in rodeos around the area. For several years he did some farming—mostly ranch work—on several ranches on Parachute Creek. Paul was a trapper, quite a roper, and a cowboy; he was one of the few that used a big loop. He competed in rodeos for years and received several trophies, including spurs and a saddle in recognition of his successes. In 1974, Paul was the oldest native living on Parachute Creek.

He worked in the oil shale initial industry for some time, digging assessment holes for individuals wishing to establish ownership on oil shale claims that had been filed. Paul lived on Parachute Creek for seventy-seven years prior to joining his many cowboy friends in 1977 beyond the Great Divide. Harry Hansen, his friend, the old-time cowboy who was often seen smoking his pipe, also ranched on

Paul and Bessie Lindauer – 50th Anniversary - 1974

Parachute Creek for many years. He ran his cattle on the Old Mountain of the Book Cliff Range. They shared many experiences together. Harry joined Paul beyond the Great Divide in 1989.

Bessie (Shults) Lindauer was born in Coffeeville, Kansas, on February 27, 1902. Her father farmed at several locations in Kansas before leaving for Colorado. She grew up with five brothers and two sisters. After she graduated from the 8th grade, the family traveled in a covered wagon to eastern Colorado where they established a homestead. After a couple years of farming, she saw a financial need for her family and attended Colorado State Teachers College to become a teacher. She taught in eastern Colorado for five years before coming to Parachute Creek in 1924 to visit her parents on the old Benton Ranch. While there, she again saw a need for additional income for her parents and a teaching position was available at the Book Cliff School. She thought this might be a good change, especially since she had met a member of the school board, Paul Lindauer.

Paul and Bessie were married December 20, 1924, in Glenwood Springs and her teaching career ended. Since married teachers were not allowed to teach, she became a ranch wife. In 1925 the newly married couple signed a three-year lease on the Hughes Ranch, where their first son was born. The ranch was small and Paul wanted to start his own herd, plus he had just broken his leg practicing roping. In 1929, they moved about one mile up the East Fork branch of Parachute Creek to a new ranch they had purchased, and ranched there for nearly eight years.

After completing several severe winters on the ranch, Bessie insisted that the family of three boys and one girl move closer to a school near town. The two older boys needed to ride a horse to the one-room school three miles each way, come rain, snow, or shine, and they often had to stay home (more details occur later in the text). In 1937, Paul, Bessie, and the family purchased the Lloyd Blue/Lindauer property, one mile west of the town of Grand Valley. Paul had leased back the East Fork ranch, and both ranches were farmed for several years. The author of this document grew up on Parachute Creek and moved livestock and machinery up and down the valley between the home ranch and the East Fork ranch (eleven miles one way) and became well acquainted with the local residents.

Paul and Bessie looked forward to shipping time and paying bills. Several trainloads of cattle would be shipped by rail to market from Parachute every year. Paul, with other local cowboys, would load the cattle on the train cars, climb into the caboose, and follow the train to Denver. In Denver, the cattlemen were met by Mr. Zietz, owner of the Buckhorn Café, who would take them all down to his restaurant for large porterhouse steak dinners. Paul's main interest was always his family and his cattle. He had built a good herd in the 1920s; however, he lost most of them in the depression of the '30s and was very careful buying cattle for the remainder of his life.

Paul and Bessie were respected in the community, and Paul was honored as Grand Marshal of the Grand Valley Days' Rodeo and Parade in the mid-'70s. He worked in the early days under Frank Squires and Sam Wasson, who were range foremen for the East Fork grazing allotment and Rifle Cattlemen's associations. When these early range foremen retired and sold out, Paul was appointed as their replacement. He held this position on the East Fork allotment for some forty years. He was still in the livestock business in 1977 when he passed away, and was considered the longest (operating) cattleman in business in the area. Paul rode the Book Cliff Range for some sixty-three years. He died of heart problems on June 18, 1977, and is buried in the Russey-Hurlburt Cemetery. Bessie passed away April 11, 1994 at the age of ninety-two and is buried with Paul in the Russey-Hurlburt Cemetery. (More details of Paul and Bessie and their family may be found under the Lloyd Blue/Lindauer ranch.)

In 1910 there were thirty-four families living on Parachute Creek. By 1950, the number had increased to fifty-eight families, and the author knew most of them. In 1974, however, there were approximately eight families left, with four owning their own property. In 2012, only one of the original families still owned their ranch and farmed their property. Oil and gas companies have purchased all of the other properties on Parachute Creek. The Parachute Creek Valley now contains many natural gas wells.

FELIX R. LINDAUER AND FAMILY | #52

Felix R. Lindauer was born in Parachute May 20, 1902, and grew up on the Peter Lindauer ranch. He attended elementary school at the Granlee School and then attended high school at Grand Valley. He married Edith Evans of Holmes Mesa on October 17, 1923, and they celebrated sixty-seven anniversaries together. Edith was born April 6, 1903. Felix and Edith raised two children: Orland, born May 15, 1924, and Mary, born on their ranch May 20, 1926. Mary died October 31, 1942, from an undisclosed illness as she was starting her college career.

Felix was a man of never-ending patience. He had a special ability to fix things on the

Felix Lindauer at Grand Valley Days Parade

ranch, serving as a mechanic and creating new equipment as desired. He helped neighbors and others fix their automobiles as vehicles became more common. Felix went to Denver by train and bought a 1919 Harley Davidson motorcycle with a side-car and drove it back to Grand Valley over 200 miles of dirt roads in the mountains. He later took his wife-to-be on a ride; however, she was not as impressed as he with the new mode of transportation.

Felix used an old forge that the family had bought from the town blacksmith to build parts that were needed on the ranch. He ran the family's sawmill, cutting the necessary lumber for his bride's new home and for a cow camp that was built in Bull Gulch on the East Fork cattle range. He repaired machinery, turning an old truck into a buck rake that ran backwards. All of the controls, including the steering wheel, were turned 180 degrees and the axles and transmission were changed to allow full speed going backwards to pick up hay. The ranch used this buck rake for a number of years until Felix became fascinated with the New Holland bailer that was bought and used until they sold the ranch. Behind his house was a large pen fenced with individual housing for silver foxes that the family raised. They sold furs in order to pay for the boarding of their two children, Orland and Mary, to at-

Felix and Edith Lindauer on their 67th anniversary.

tend Grand Valley High School.

Felix participated in guiding hunters and working on the ranch as needed. He told his grandson, Gerald, when he was a young boy he "witnessed a wagonload of mountain lions taken by government trappers in the nearby West Fork of Parachute Creek as they came by [their] house." Following the lion kill, the deer population increased in the valley. He was considered one of the best shooters in the valley and spent many hours sighting in rifles and pistols for neighbors. Needless to say, he took home many turkeys from the local annual fall turkey shoot. Felix, with his brothers, found a mother bear and cub hibernating up West Fork. When they rousted the large black bear from her den, they found it necessary to kill the mother for their own safety and survival. Bears were considered a threat to any rancher at that time and efforts were made to eliminate them. They roped the cub and it became Felix's pet for several years and was a wrestling partner for him until it broke out of its pen and escaped.

When Felix and Edith sold their portion of the ranch in 1954 to the Union Oil Company of California, they moved their house and home into Grand Valley. During this period he also bought the local Texaco service station and operated it for several years. Later, Felix sold the station to Norman Payton, who was ranching on Parachute Creek at that time.

A few years after moving from their ranch, Felix and Edith bought 120 acres of the original "Doc" Wilson ranch located adjacent to the Book Cliff School on Parachute Creek. Here, Felix, his son Orland and his wife Jody ranched for some twenty years (see Orland Lindauer section for more details). This ranch was eventually sold to the Sinclair Oil & Gas Company. Felix and Edith lived in Grand Valley until Edith passed away in 1988 at the age of eighty-five. Felix spent his last years in the Rifle Nursing Home and passed away on October 10, 1999, at the age of ninety-seven.

ROSE (LINDAUER) KRAMER AND FAMILY | #53

Rose Marie Lindauer was born in Parachute in 1907 and spent her early years on the Peter Lindauer Ranch. She was only seven years old when her mother died. She rode on horseback behind her neighbor Kay Parkhurst to attend grade school with her brothers at the Granlee School. It was difficult for her growing up as the only girl in the family. Many of the neighbors helped her in these early years. In 1919, an oil shale representative visited the ranch and suggested to her father Pete that she needed to go to an all girls' school. Pete sent her to Mount St. Scholastica in Canon City for one year. She then stayed with friends in Grand Valley and attended high school.

Rose Kramer – Registered Nurse - 1930

Rose heard of the nurses' training program at St. Mary's Hospital in Grand Junction, and with the help of neighbors and her brother Julius, she was able to get the uniforms and money to go there. She graduated in 1929 as a registered nurse. She then worked at the D&RG railroad hospital for several years.

On a return trip to Grand Valley to visit family and friends, Rose met Curtis Kramer from Nebraska at a Saturday night dance. Curtis was the brother of Madeline Kramer Parkhurst, who was the wife of Hallie Parkhurst of Grand Valley. Curtis and Rose were married in 1931 in Salida. They returned to Nebraska where Gloria was born in 1933 and Charlene in 1934. The family returned to Glenwood Springs in 1939. Their son Clifford was born in 1946, and in 1949 they moved to Grand Junction, where Clifford lives today. Gloria (Kramer) Jasinowski became a registered nurse and finished her career teaching nursing. Charlene (Kramer) Semack attended Mesa College for two years, then married a CPA and helped him with his career. Clifford has excelled in the real estate business in Grand Junction. Rose continued working at the new St. Mary's Hospital until she retired. She passed away in 1992 and is buried in Grand Junction.

The 1925 Grand Valley girls' basketball team included Rose (Lindauer) Kramer, bottom right, and Winfred Shults, top second from left. Others are not identified.

Rose had many stories to tell of her early life in Parachute, growing up with five brothers. She reported some of this information in an audiotape stored at Grand Junction's Western Colorado Museum.

> My father employed many housekeepers; none seemed to stay long, apparently because of the inconvenience of five children. Baths were unheard of. Sometimes my father would send us up on the small mountain back of Rowley's and tell us to gather the wild flowers that grew there and put them on the small graves that were there while he tilled the fields below. Once he took us to the Grand Valley Cemetery and we would put flowers on our mother's grave. I would ask him why our mother did not have a stone. He would reply, "It is all I can do to care for the living." Years later, I understood what a load he had to bear. I know now how proud he would be if he could have foreseen the future, how those five young children strove for education. In time to come, there would be a registered nurse, a welder, and a cement man. Rose and Curtis's children and family grandchildren would have college degrees and they would become teachers, bankers and welders, computer specialists, and some have doctor degrees.

KARL AND IVA LINDAUER | #54

Karl A. Lindauer was born July 18, 1909, in Grand Valley, Colorado, and died December 6, 1991, in Parachute. He attended elementary school at the Granlee School and attended high school at Grand Valley High School. During World War II, he was drafted into the army, and as a result of his previous experiences with horses and running a remount stallion site at his home ranch, he was assigned to the United States Cavalry, where he doctored and took care of horses at Fort El Reno near Tulsa, Oklahoma. While there, he met his future wife, Iva Taylor, and they were married in 1944 at Fort Reno, prior to his discharge from the service. Iva was born and raised in Indian territory in Oklahoma on a 160-acre prairie farm that had neither fences nor trees. She attended elementary school in a "Masonic home for children." Iva worked for a railroad construction company and for the Blue Cross Hospital in her early years. She remembered the severity of the weather in Oklahoma and recalls one incident where she had to walk eight miles on a railroad track to get to work, for the bridge across the Canadian River was out. The temperature was eight degrees Fahrenheit with the wind chill factor near twenty degrees below zero. Karl and Iva had no children.

When Iva first arrived in Grand Valley, she could not understand why anyone would want to ranch in such a country where the annual precipitation was near twelve inches a year and there was little grass. Of course, she had come from an environment where the annual precipitation was near forty inches and there were hills covered with good grass for cows to graze. However, she learned to love the people of western Colorado and they loved her. She served as the local tax expert and bookkeeper for many individuals within Grand Valley.

Following Karl's time in the service, he returned to the ranch and built a new home in the old horse pasture near his father's house and became a partner in the family ranching operation. During hunting seasons, he and his brothers served as guides for hunters. The Lindauer Ranch was sold in 1954 to the California Union Oil and Gas Company. Karl then bought a ranch some five miles south of the town of Parachute on the southeast side of the Colorado River near Wallace Creek. He ran cows there for a number of years and built saddles. He became very proficient and was sought after by others in the area because of his quality leatherwork.

Orland Lindauer, left, visits his father, center, and Uncle Karl, right, in July 1965

After several years, he decided to leave ranching and sold his ranch. For a number of years, he made his living by building houses, selling them, and moving to another location. During a period of ten to twenty years, he lived in Bayfield, Orchard Mesa, Clifton, Paonia, and Craig, where he managed a motel for several years. He also worked for the government trapping predators.

In his later years Karl lived in Fruita, Morrisania Mesa, and finally an apartment in Parachute, where he died of a heart attack on December 5, 1991, at the age of eighty-two. When Karl died, Iva moved to the Senior Center in Rifle, where she enjoyed many activities. She loved to play cards and was a delight to visit since she had so many stories of hardships as well as fun and pleasure. Iva lived for another thirteen years following Karl's death. She died at the age of ninety-nine. Both are buried in the Russey-Hurlburt Cemetery.

Louis Lindauer with his horses Mercury and Dixie in the 1960s.

LOUIS LINDAUER AND FAMILY | #51

Louis was born January 10, 1911, on the Lindauer Ranch at the head of Parachute Creek. He maintained that he was "born January 7, 1911, and it took three days for the doctor to visit the ranch." He attended the Granlee School and graduated from Grand Valley High School in 1929.

Louis was an excellent athlete. He excelled in boxing, baseball, and as a horse trainer. If he had been training horses in this day and age, he would be known as a true "horse whisperer." He spent several years in the Hayden, Colorado, area working on the Jap Wyman and Coke Roberts ranches, breaking horses that were sold as "remounts" to the United States Cavalry. It was during this time that he interacted with Coke Roberts, who was one of the original quarter horse breeders, establishing the breed. While working for Coke Roberts, Louis cared for one of the foundation studs, "Old Fred," and he used this stallion for breeding mares on a small ranch near Una, Colorado.

It was during this time that he began courting Edna Maude "Midge" Wurts, who lived south of Rifle near the Mamm Peak area. He met Midge at one of the community dances held in a one-room schoolhouse on the mesa south of Rifle. According to one of his sons, "it was not unusual for him to ride horseback from Hayden to the Rifle and Grand Valley area to meet up with his future wife. He often did this on weekends, staying Friday nights at a ranch near Rio Blanco and then riding on to the Wurts Ranch."

Louis and Midge were married on August 3, 1938, and to this marriage four boys were born: Larry (1939), Gary (1949), Leslie (1952), and Carl (1962). Three of the boys were teachers and administrators at different levels in Colorado, and one a city management employee. The youngest, Carl, continues to coach and teach in Las Animas, Colorado. Larry and Leslie both have Ph.D. degrees and served as school superintendents in Colorado.

Over the years and with the help of his sons, Louis raised quarter horses and thoroughbreds and

Louis, 85, and Edna "Midge" Wurts Lindauer, 77, in 1996.

raced them at a number of places throughout the United States. One of his thoroughbreds, "Cantsherun," won the 1970 Colorado Futurity at the Centennial Race Track in Littleton, Colorado. The mare was named Colorado Race Horse of the Year in 1984.

Louis was also a great hunter and trapper. He created his own scent—a secret formula—to use in trapping coyotes and bobcats. Trappers from all over western Colorado would seek him out to get some of his magical scent. He and his brother Karl killed a mule deer that is rated 49th in the Boone and Crocket records at this time. This buckhead hangs in their youngest son's home in Las Animas. In 1940, Louis worked as a government trapper controlling predators of livestock owned by ranchers throughout Garfield, Rio Blanco, and Pitkin Counties. He continued in this job through the end of World War II.

Louis also spent much of the 1940s and 1950s following rodeos throughout the west. He was a calf roper and bulldogger and set some early time records in bulldogging in Utah and Kansas. His wife Midge never missed one of his rodeos and often competed in barrel races. Louis spent many years following the rodeo circuit and retired from rodeos as a well-recognized rodeo hand. He was a lifetime member of the Pro Rodeo Cowboy Association.

After retiring from the rodeo circuit, Louis spent twenty years in a new career as a steel worker and traveled throughout much of the west working on large building construction. He retired from the Colorado Iron Workers in March 1977. During those twenty years and several years after, he raised, trained, and managed several racehorses at tracks in eastern Colorado at Centennial, Arapahoe, Raton, New Mexico, and back east at some Pennsylvania racetracks.

Louis and Midge finally settled on a small ranch in Las Animas, Colorado. He continued his horse breeding, feeding, and racing while in his spare time he trapped predators. Louis Lindauer considered Parachute his lifetime residence. He died in Pueblo January 12, 2000, at the age of eighty-nine. Midge died August 31, 2001, in Evergreen, Colorado. Louis and Midge's ashes were spread over the East Fork Falls.

JULIUS LINDAUER FAMILY | #55

Julius was born in 1914 on the Peter Lindauer Ranch on Parachute Creek. His mother, Margaretha, passed away when he was one and a half years old. For much of his early years, a housekeeper was employed to take care of him. However, the older brothers and his sister Rose did much of the caretaking. He attended Granlee School, and when his sister moved to Grand Junction to study to be

Julius Lindauer on the Peter Lindauer Ranch in the 1940s

a nurse, Julius was sent to be near her and attend high school in Grand Junction for two years. He then moved back to Grand Valley, where he graduated from high school in 1932.

Julius learned to play the guitar in later years and spent many evenings entertaining others. He also performed music for dances at the Woodmen of the World (WOW) hall in Grand Valley. Julius spent much of the summer irrigating and putting up hay. In the fall, he assisted in guiding hunters, and through the winter he kept busy feeding their livestock.

Julius married Betty Baughman February 2, 1945. Betty was a granddaughter of one of the earliest settlers of Parachute Creek, JB Hurlburt, and a daughter of Jessie (Hurlburt) Baughman. Julius and Betty built their home on the east side of Middle Fork across from Karl and Peter's homes. They lived in this house for a few years until the ranch was sold to the Union Oil Company of California in 1954. Julius then moved the house down Parachute Creek to the ranch previously owned by the Benedetti family. It was located two miles west of the town of Parachute. Shortly after he had moved, he came down with polio and died on August 13, 1955. He is buried in the Russey-Hurlburt Cemetery in Parachute.

Julius Lindauer married Betty Baughman February 16, 1945

Julius and Betty had three children: Judy (Lindauer) Gosick, MD, born April 27, 1948, who practiced medicine in the Denver area; Leland, born April 8, 1950, who owned his own structural engineering firm and holds an MS degree in architectural engineering; and Norman, born August 10, 1955, an educator with a master's degree. He and his wife Diane taught in Grand Junction schools for thirty years. Norman was only three days old when he lost his father. They retired to Henderson, Nevada.

Betty sold the ranch after Julius's death and moved to Rifle. She married Loren Mead on June 15, 1956. They had one child, Lance Mead, who was born in June 1957. Betty later owned a motel in Grand Junction and worked for Walker Drugs. She moved to Rifle, where she worked in a flower shop from which she retired. She and Loren spent thirteen winters in Arizona and prized the time they were there with their many friends and family.

Betty suffered a stroke in May 1996 and never fully recovered, yet she retained her wonderful attitude. They moved back to Grand Junction in 2001 and she died there October 6, 2003. Her husband Loren died January 24, 2006.

GEORGE ALFRED GARDNER FAMILY | #50

George Alfred Gardner was born in New Brunswick, Maine, on March 5, 1846, according to the federal census of 1880.[44] He married Mary Elizabeth "Liz" Wayne of Wisconsin on December 28,

---

[44] Murray, *Lest We Forget*, 1973.

The George Gardner family left their sod house in Nebraska to move to Colorado. L to R, unidentified horse rider, George W., George A. (father), Clara "Bertha," (tall boy) Harry, (toddler) Harvey, Mary Elizabeth (mother), Charles A., Mary "Mate," and Walter.

1878, later moving to Custer County Nebraska in 1880. They had eight children together.

George and Liz brought their family by covered wagon from Broken Bow, Nebraska, to Glenwood Springs and then on to a 100-acre homestead just below the confluence of the three forks of upper Parachute Creek. They settled on a portion of the Davenport property adjacent to the Lindauer Ranch in the early 1890s. George, Liz, and their family remained at this location for years. There, they raised four of their children: Clara Bertha born in 1878, George W. in 1885, Harry C. in 1888, and Frank in 1891.

George homesteaded his place in Gardner Gulch, which still bears his name. He had a small farm that included an orchard, where he raised apples. Liz kept busy with an extensive garden. The soils were very fertile in the area and Liz planted well, providing neighbors with fresh vegetables as they became ready for harvest.

An interesting story is told about Liz a few years after they moved to Parachute Creek. She had saved up her money until she was able to buy a team and buggy so that she could go to town once in a while. When she asked her husband George if he wanted to take it for a drive, he took her up on the offer. He drove to the town of Parachute and lost both the matched team and the buggy in an unlucky poker game. When he got home she met him at the door with a shotgun, and he was locked out of the house for a while. They were able to solve the issue, but he was not allowed to drive the team to Parachute again without her.

HUGH RILEY

Hugh B. Riley was born 1867 in Maine and raised there. His parents were Daniel Riley and Mary A. Riley. He married Mary L. "Mate" Gardner in 1899. They were living in Parachute in 1900, apparently on the south side of a major drainage to Parachute Creek, which today is called Riley Gulch. After several years, they sold their property in Riley Gulch. Hugh and Mate filed on a half section of land in the West Fork of Parachute, which they later sold to the Federal Oil Shale Company.

Mate Riley was a sister of Mrs. Cade Benson, both daughters of the pioneer Gardner family. It was reported that she had a still in West Fork that the gentlemen of the valley visited. They apparently homesteaded up Riley Gulch; however, no further information could be found.

The family moved to Canon Creek, Garfield County, Colorado, in 1910. By 1920 they were back in Grand Valley. At that time, they had a daughter Frances Riley, who was fifteen years old. Ten years later, Hugh was living with his married daughter Frances (Riley) Sawyer in Salt Lake City, Utah. He divorced "Mate" and later she married Roslyn Smith.

JOE BELLIS – LIFE STORY AND TRAGEDY

Joe Bellis was born in Washington, DC, in 1871 and left his home to go to Chicago when he was quite young. After spending a few years there, he moved on to Colorado where he worked with various mining activities. He was involved with the development of mines in Gilpin County, Clear Creek County, and Idaho Springs. He gained a lot of experience and knowledge of the mining industry while still fairly young. He teamed up with a Lee Townsend, and the two of them developed mining interests throughout Colorado.

Around 1910, Joe became interested in investing in natural resource development, specifically in oil shale in Garfield County. He and DD Potter of Denver, along with several other western slope men, formed the Federal Oil Shale Company that was combined with Union Oil Company of California. Joe was interested in all types of oil development but ended up in Grand Valley, where oil shale had been recognized as a potential petroleum product. He invested his money and time in the location and development of oil shale. He continued to be active in civic affairs, both within the Grand Valley area and throughout the state. He had a beautiful home in Grand Valley. Joe was considered one of the first individuals and pioneers to investigate oil shale development in Colorado.

Joe Bellis was a very active and energetic individual and was well known all over the state of Colorado. However, in mid-May 1936, Joe was instantly killed on the Parachute Creek road ten miles northeast of Grand Valley and about one mile south of the Lindauer ranch. He was in the process of taking a box of dynamite up to one of the Bellis oil shale claims in Gardner Gulch. Indians and hunters had previously used this route as a trail to the top of the mountain. Joe left Grand Valley early on that morning with Dean and Buck Kerlee of Grand Valley. The three men were headed up the creek to work on one of the claims. When Joe reached the spot where the trail left the road, he dropped off the younger men, who started up the trail, and he went on up the road to a place where he could turn around. That is when the explosion occurred. The jarring of the turn-around may have been the cause that set off the dynamite. Joe was instantly killed and the force of the explosion threw him some fifteen feet into the air and totally demolished the vehicle.

For years after, there was talk in the valley that he had personally set the explosion since it was thought that he had some financial problems and this was an easy way out. He left a widow, Jessie

(Brown) of Grand Valley, and a small adopted daughter, Berna. In 1936 as a young man, the author of this work rode his horse past the wreckage of that automobile each day on his way to the Granlee School, which was about one mile farther down the road.

THE UPPER (GRANLEE) SCHOOL | #49

The Upper Creek School (or Granlee School, as it was commonly called) was built during the years 1892-1894 from logs cut in the area. The date of the organization of the Granlee School could not be found in court records but in the records of county superintendent MVB Blood, the dates given for organizing the school districts at that time were between 1885 and 1890.

According to LaVerne Starbuck's research on original school districts from Parachute to Anvil Points, best evidence from county superintendent records indicates that District #7 was formed August 23, 1886.[45] This district was to cover all of the Parachute Creek drainage, extending from the divide north and west between the White River and the Grand River to the divide from Rifle Creek and Parachute then south and west to the divide between Roan Creek and Parachute Creek and south to the county line.

On May 18, 1895, Doc Wilson was elected president of the school board, JB Hurlburt was elected treasurer, and JW Ward was elected secretary of the newly formed District #7, the Granlee School located nine miles northwest of the town of Parachute. Several months later JB Hurlburt petitioned to form a new District #16 from District #7, that was organized on June 11, 1895. Although District #7 was further divided three more times, the last petition created District #11 on April 4, 1900, called the Book Cliff School. This school was located about five miles west of the town of Parachute. These two districts were the first and third of the earliest country schools created in Garfield County. They held school for some fifty years but both were finally annexed into District #16 on June 24, 1948. All students were then bused into the town of Parachute.

Milton C. Granlee gave the property for the school that was located just across Parachute Creek from his stone home. The local ranchers and their families donated their time, tools, and teams of horses needed to level the ground and build the school. A vestibule was added for the benefit of the children to leave their boots, lunches, and overcoats. They could get a drink from a water bucket that sat on a

Photo courtesy of LaVerne Starbuck

Mrs. Edna Freeland is shown standing in the doorway of the Upper Parachute Creek Granlee School, District 11, created on April 4, 1900.

---

[45] Starbuck, *Children Came: Some from Log Camps Others from Ranches*, 1989.

bench. The school was modern since it had two outhouses, one for girls and one for boys. Teaching materials and library books were sent through the mail. Two large slate blackboards were present in the front of the room where the children practiced their spelling, writing, and math.

Most teachers lasted only one year at the school and local ranch wives filled in as needed. The first year that Leta Ruth Funk taught there, and before she married Charlie Benson, the school had a furnace in the basement that could be stoked with coal and if the dampers were closed the school would be warm the next morning. One night the furnace got too hot and nearly set the building on fire. After that, a pot-bellied stove was installed in the center of the schoolhouse and it was the teacher's duty to get there early and build a fire. Many times, it was the students who ended up building the fire in the winter so they could keep warm during the day.

The school closed in 1947 as the district was officially consolidated in 1948. Roberta "Bobbi" (Benson) Wambolt had attended elementary school (years 1-6) at the Granlee School then moved into the town of Grand Valley in 1946 to live with her grandmother Benson and continue her schooling. Her sisters, Marjorie and Charline, were able to finish the eighth grade in the Granlee School before attending the Grand Valley Schools.

Following the consolidation of the district, all students were bused to the Grand Valley School, District 16. The annexation of District 7 into District 16 was completed on June 24, 1948. The Granlee School then belonged to District 16 and preparations were being made in the 1970-1980s to move the historical building to Parachute. The property on which the building was located was owned by Union Oil and Gas Company of California and the school was burned during this time period, apparently to reduce liability and tax issues, as told by Dee Freeland.[46]

Some of the teachers during the life of the school were reported in an article published by LaVerne Starbuck in the *Valley West Dispatch* in 1989[47] as follows:

Helen Elson, C. M. Osburn, Adella Miller, Jessie Lanzendorf, S. B. Yeoman, Ruth Carter, Minnie Sandusky, Myrtle McKinney, Jeannie Lindsey, Miss Munson, Stella Hayward, Viola Davis, S. G. Ash, Bertha Perham, Mate [sic] Gardner, Flora Perham, Mrs. Louis Brown, Ella Johnson, Gertrude Hilliker, Inez Goode, Doris Crawford, Ruth (Funk) Benson, Roberta Ogden, Maud [sic] Cline, Gladys Pruett, Eleanor Johnson, Reba Da Lee, Margaret Mahoney, Edith Leatherman, Edith Corn, Ruth Burlison, and Edna Freeland.

MILTON GRANLEE FAMILY | #48

Milton C. Granlee was born on a farm in Pennsylvania, February 17, 1860. His parents were Joseph Beach Granlee and Elizabeth Ann Mapel. In 1888 he married Clara Bell Clayton, born in 1870 in the state of Iowa. Her parents were both from Iowa and Milton's were from Indiana.

Clara and Milton raised three children: Ruth born in 1898, Beulah in 1902, and a son Milton (Dean) Granlee in 1908. The Milton Granlee family came to the upper reaches of Parachute Creek in 1895. The previous year of 1894, Milton had secured 176 acres on Parachute Creek from the General Land Office. The land was patented and signed by President Grover Cleveland to Milton E. Granlee.

Milton Granlee, with aid from Tom Glover, Gabriel Crawford, Nelson Good, and JM Sipprelle, provided the financial assistance and work for finishing the new Methodist Church in Parachute that began construction in 1886. The Granlees dutifully drove a horse and buggy from their ranch to the

---

[46] Oral Communication, Dee Freeland and Eilene Bumgardner letter, Parachute, Colorado. 2012
[47] Ibid.

Methodist Church every Sunday when possible. Due to differences and problems between the minister, Passmore, and the church leadership, the church was not finished until 1902. During 1912-1915, a quitclaim deed was provided for lots 8, 9, 10, 11, 12, 13, and 14 in block 2 for the church in the town of Parachute.[48] Today, the church is still in operation and in good condition. It is known as the Grand Valley United Methodist Church.

On March 19, 1918, the Federal Land Office assigned Milton an additional fifty-six acres. Milton built a ditch and a dam for irrigating his property on Parachute Creek with help from his neighbors: the Hughes, Coxes, and Wells. They all benefited from the water in this ditch. Milton assigned twenty-eight acres of his property to the Uintah Basin Producing and Refining Company, interested in developing oil shale. Joseph Bellis was a witness to this warranty deed.

By 1937 the property was transferred to daughter Ruth Granlee, who was living in Los Angeles at that time, and then on to son, Milton (Dean), who was a maintenance operator in California. Dean died in Rancho Cucamonga, San Bernardino, California, on October 23, 1986, at the age of seventy-nine. Their youngest daughter, Beulah, was living with her parents in 1940 in Pasadena, California, and working as a government secretary. The older sister, Ruth, was believed to have continued teaching; however, no additional information could be found for her. The whole family was highly musically inclined and their reputation was widespread in the Parachute Creek area.

The Granlee Trail, just east of the Granlee Ranch, became a major access to the Old Mountain, as it was called. Many ranchers in the valley used this access to take their cattle to the high mountain meadows in the summer. Milton Granlee died in Pasadena on June 14, 1957, at the age of ninety-seven. Clara Granlee died April 16, 1955, at the age of eighty-five in Pasadena.

ARCADIOUS BENSON FAMILY | #46

Arcadious "Cade" Benson was the son of Elvis Harvey Benson and Sarah F. Bigbee. He was born July 5, 1863, in Tennessee. After a time in Pueblo, Elvis, Sarah, and Cade moved on to Parachute Creek as early settlers in this area. Cade homesteaded 160 acres nine miles north of the Colorado River on May 26, 1892, by Certificate of Grant signed by President Benjamin Harrison. Cade married neighbor Clara Bertha Gardner on April 26, 1895. Because Bertha was seventeen at the time, her father George A. Gardner went along to the courthouse in Glenwood Springs to sign permission for her to marry. Cade built a two-room cabin that became his and Bertha's home for over sixty years. In March 1922 Cade homesteaded 320 acres on the Old Mountain, two miles from the Benson Ranch. A trail to connect with the Granlee trail was built as was a cabin where the Benson family spent summers grazing cattle and horses, raising a garden and milking several cows. Milk was separated, and the cream was transported down the trail in five-gallon cans by packhorse. It was then taken to town and sent by train to a dairy. Excess milk was fed to the pigs and chickens.

There were six children in the Cade and Bertha Benson family. Sadie Winifred (Benson) Letson was the oldest and became a long-time resident of Grand Valley. She married Otto Letson, who lived on a Parachute Creek ranch during his early years and later operated a gas station in Grand Valley until his death. Cade and Bertha had five other children: Lloyd Cecil, Merle Elizabeth, Elvis Harvey, Charles Elmer (the second youngest), and Juanita Louise, who attended some high school before marrying and moving to California. Cade died May 24, 1943, and Bertha died the following summer. Both are buried in the Russey-Hurlburt Cemetery in Parachute.

---

[48] Garfield County Clerk & Recorder's Office.

CHARLIE BENSON FAMILY | #46

Charlie Benson was born May 26, 1905, at the Benson Ranch on Parachute Creek. He attended the Granlee School through the eighth grade, then left school to work on the home ranch with his father. Cade had a well-equipped blacksmith shop and taught Charlie the use of the equipment necessary for repairing farm implements and harnesses and for shoeing horses. He used the forge for heating and the anvil to shape shoes to fit a horse's hoof. There was a grinding wheel mounted on a steel structure with a seat and pedals to turn the wheel for sharpening tools such as shovels, hoes, sickles for the mowing machines, household knives, and larger knives used for butchering beef, hogs, and venison. Charlie was a good horseman and broke many work teams and riding horses for use by his family and neighbors. Charlie learned carpentry out of necessity, as did most young ranchers, in order to build the structures needed on their farms or ranches. He and his father built fences on the summer range for keeping their horses and dairy cows enclosed so they did not roam far from their homestead. The cows on the Old Mountain summer pastures were milked, and cream was carried down the trail on packhorses in large cream cans to be shipped by rail to a commercial dairy.

For a number of years, Charlie's family spent summers at the Cade Benson homestead on the Old Mountain. They stayed there until a month or two into the school year when it was time to take their cattle down before snowfall and to prepare those that would be shipped to market. When Charlie and his older brother Elvis were in the early grades, they walked the couple of miles down the trail to the Granlee School on Monday mornings and stayed at the ranch during the week with their sister Merle and her husband. On Friday evening, they hiked back up the trail to the homestead.

Rancher Charlie Benson served as bus driver for Granlee School students.

In 1927 at the age of eighteen, Leta Ruth Funk, a schoolteacher from Boulder, Colorado, and her older sister Roberta (Funk) Ogden, applied and were accepted for teaching positions in Garfield County with the idea that they would be near each other. However, when they arrived in Glenwood Springs, they found that Roberta was assigned to a school in Carbondale and Ruth to the rural Granlee School on Parachute Creek over sixty miles from Roberta's school. Ruth found room and board with Gladys and Albert Allen, who lived about one mile from her school at that time. Albert, driving a team and buckboard, met Ruth at the train depot. After a two hour, nine-mile trip with little to no conversation, she arrived at the Allens' home, where she met Gladys, who became a life-long friend and confidante. At the end of the school year, Ruth was required to return to Boulder to attend classes that would renew her teaching certificate for a second year. Meanwhile, she had met Charlie Benson at a dance held at the Granlee School, and when the second year of her teaching ended, she married Charlie on May 11, 1929.

The Benson Ranch was owned by Cade Benson for a number of years, but eventually sold to Charlie following his marriage to Ruth. They lived for one year in a log house, known as the Cox place, about one mile from the Benson Ranch before moving to the home ranch in 1930 as Cade and Bertha retired to Grand Valley.

During WWII, the call went out for carpenters to help build Camp Hale at Pando near Leadville, Colorado, that would house the 10th Mountain Division of the US Army. Charlie and two neighbors, Red Walters and Harry Hansen, were among the men from the Parachute Creek area that answered the call and worked there until the project was finished.

The marriage of Charlie and Ruth Benson resulted in seven children; all spent some time at the Granlee School and all graduated from Grand Valley High School. Charlie and Ruth raised five girls and two boys as follows:

Roberta "Bobbi" Jeanne Wambolt was born on February 27, 1931, in Rifle and spent most of her life in the Parachute area. She attended Colorado State University for one year but returned home to

Charlie and Leta Ruth (Funk) Benson, June 14, 1975.

allow her younger sisters to go to college. She worked as a telephone operator in Grand Valley for several years until she met Marvin Wambolt. They were married in 1952.

Marjorie Merle Lange was born on May 30, 1932, on the ranch. She attended Colorado State University for two years and worked as a secretary for several years until marrying William Lange in 1960.

Charline June Allen was born on June 13, 1933, on the ranch. She attended Colorado State University for one year and later married Sonny Gibbons. They moved to Denver where she remained until Sonny's death. After Sonny Gibbons took his own life, she worked as a secretary in Boulder for several years but later returned to Grand Junction. She met Ron Allen, a former classmate who had moved with his family to Parachute and graduated with her class. They married, then moved to Montana, where he had been offered a position as superintendent of schools.

Helen Ruth Arnett was born in Grand Valley on September 19, 1940, and worked as a secretary for Grand Valley High School and for the US Postal Service.

Pamela Rose Brock was born on December 7, 1945, in Grand Valley and attended the University of Northern Colorado for one year. She worked as secretary of the Grand Valley schools for some time. She later worked as a mail carrier for the US Postal Service. Pamela died in an automobile accident on Piceance Creek November 1, 2002, while delivering mail.

Cade Lyle was born on July 3, 1939, in Grand Valley and graduated from Colorado State University, where he earned Bachelor and Master's degrees in engineering. After a number of years working in Montana as an engineer, he returned to Colorado and established his own engineering firm in Parker.

Gregory Charles was born in Rifle on January 3, 1948. He attended Colorado State University for one year and entered the

The Benson sisters, L to R, Bobbie Wambolt, Marjorie Lange, Charline Allen, Helen Arnett, and Pamela Brock, in the summer of 1975.

US Army for two years. He worked several years for oil shale research companies in the Grand Valley region and took a job with the British Petroleum Industry at Prudhoe Bay, Alaska, and continued to live and work there. Recently he purchased a home in eastern Colorado and commutes to work.

Charlie and Ruth lived on the ranch until it was sold to Union Oil Company of California in 1955. They leased the ranch for two years, but in 1957, they moved to the Martel Sherwood Ranch. In 1963, Charlie and Ruth retired to a home they had in the town of Parachute, where they spent their last years. Ruth died September 24, 1988, and Charlie passed away on November 10, 1990. Both are buried in the Russey-Hurlburt Cemetery in Parachute.

One of Charlie and Ruth's daughters, Charline June (Benson) Allen, was thought to be a boy before she was born; however, her parents quickly changed Charlie to Charline when she arrived. In the next several paragraphs, Charline expresses her special thoughts on living in an original two-room log house with added bedrooms and an upstairs, when needed, that her grandfather had built and in which her father, she, and Marjorie were born.

> It was a great experience growing up on a farm of fields of hay and grain raised to feed our cattle and horses and a large orchard of dozens of varieties of apples, as well as apricots, pears and plums among other fruits. I don't remember being taught to ride, but a large amount of our time was spent on horseback for both fun and work. I was told that my first ride was at the age of three months when my dad carried me on a pillow on one arm while reining his horse with the other up a steep trail and through the switchbacks and the ledges to our cow camp. My mother rode along behind us. We were to stay overnight there so Dad could check on the cattle the next day.
>
> As my sisters, brothers and I grew older, we rode along with our Dad to trail our cattle out to the summer range and stay overnight in the log cabin that was the cow camp. This was a

co-op cow camp used as needed by several Parachute Creek cattlemen. There were bunk beds firmly built along the walls, and provisions with dishes and a bucket for water that was always left for use by others. We were sure to find coffee, sugar, lard, and flour in tins, and eggs stored in the coolness of the grain bin to be questionably preserved for the next visitor. A spring of pure mountain water ran clear and cold just a few yards from the cabin door. We carried water to the cabin while Dad built a fire in the iron stove and made biscuits and eggs for our lunch. Other times he would cook a fine dinner of French toast, venison (if it were in season) bacon, and boiled cowboy coffee, of course.

On the ranch, Dad planted and cultivated fields of alfalfa, oats, and wheat. He traded work at harvest time with neighboring farmers, who worked their way from the first ripened field to the last, gathering at "haying time" and "threshing time" at each farm. Dad also harvested vast amounts of fruit from orchards planted and nurtured by his father Arcadious. Bushes of apples of several varieties were picked and packed into new bushel baskets and delivered to the train station in Grand Valley to be shipped off to market. There were also cherries, plums, apricots, and pears to be harvested. Whatever fruit which was not made into pies, canned into jars, or made into jams and jellies by Ruth would be distributed to neighbors or sold.

My two older sisters rode Shetland ponies to the one-room Granlee School when they were in the first and second grades in 1938. Since horses were ridden to school during those days, student fathers had built a shed at the school and stocked the manger with hay so the horses would be sheltered and fed while they were tied to the manger all day. The Shetlands were anxious to get home to the farm as soon as school was out for the day and once or twice the girls were left to walk the mile home after their mounts had jumped out from under them and galloped off to the barn. In 1939, I started to school and since there were now three of us and the ponies were uncooperative, Dad made the decision that there would be no more riding to school.

BILL OGDEN FAMILY | #45

Through the years the following families lived on the Ogden place, as it was later called, located across the creek from the Benson home: Claytons, Killians, Albert Allens, Chapmans, Marsh Williams, Lloyd Zedikers, and Ogdens.

William "Bill" Henry Ogden was born in Basalt, Colorado, in 1907 and died in 1978. He married Roberta Funk in 1927. She was born in Russell, Kansas, in 1906 and moved to Boulder, where she finished high school and attended the university to become a teacher. Roberta met Bill while teaching near Carbondale and in 1940 they moved to a ranch owned by Vern Gardner, (who never lived on the ranch) some eight miles up Parachute Creek south of the Cade Benson ranch.

Roberta taught in the Grand Valley schools for a number of years and in Soldier's Summit, Utah, in 1955-1957 while her husband worked on the railroad. She ended her teaching career by teaching English at Adams State College for several years. She died December 28, 1997. Ruth Benson and Roberta Ogden were sisters.

Roberta and Bill spent interesting times in their professions: Bill as a heavy equipment operator, and she as an English teacher who loved to write. One of her articles appeared in the Sunday magazine of *The Daily Sentinel* published October 29, 1972, and titled "A Wilderness Sojourn: A Summer of Railroading."⁴⁹ Bill had been assigned the task of keeping the narrow-gauge railroad open. This was one of the last steam-powered trains and routes open during the summer of 1972 as the trains, a popular tourist attraction, made their way between Durango and Silverton from June 1 until October 5.

Since the tracks were covered with snowdrifts, it was necessary to start work on May 1, for it took about thirty days to remove all the rocks and snow and repair the tracks for the ninety-mile round trip made daily by two tourist trains. During their work, they had to remove a bear from the tracks. This bear kept coming back trying to get their food. What's more, elk would often get on the tracks and deer were plentiful. Bill spent one week with his bulldozer removing a large snow slide that blocked the tracks. During their free time, they fished the Animas River and caught native trout that supplemented their food, often cooked over an open campfire. Roberta cooked for the crew and collected raspberries and chokecherries by the bucketful to take home for canning into jams and jellies. General William Jackson Palmer had built the high mountain railroad between Durango and Silverton (elevation 9,300 feet) in 1881-1882, primarily for the gold and silver mining industry. It remained the only transportation between the two towns for years and today continues as a major tourist-traveled route.

Bill and Roberta had three children: Bill Jr. was born in 1929, Mary Ann in 1934 and Perry in 1945. Mary passed away in 2006. Perry moved to Idaho where he lived for many years raising his family. Bill Jr. moved to Oklahoma where he sold topsoil. He played Santa Claus for the local children since his large white beard was a duplicate to that of St. Nicholas. He moved to assisted living in Oklahoma in 2013 and died there in August 2014.

The Ogden family sold their ranch in 1945 and moved to the town of Grand Valley. Bill was a rancher most of his life but spent a number of years working on the D&RG Railroad. He was one of the first to purchase a large John Deere tractor for his farm and he helped many neighbors plow their fields.

Bill Jr. told an interesting story about finding a golden wedding band while plowing up a garden spot. The name inscribed on the inside of the ring was "Killian" and years after it had been lost he was able to track down the family and return the ring. Killian once owned the property that the Ogden family lived on for several years.

WILLIAM CLAYTON FAMILY | #45

The Claytons operated a dairy and ran range cattle on the Old Mountain. They all worked wherever there was work to be done. The girls, as well, helped put up the hay. Mrs. Granlee was a daughter of the Clayton family. The Clayton family, with seven children (five girls and two boys), moved up on Parachute Creek in the 1890s. They also lived on what is known today as the Zediker place. Additional details of this family could not be found.

JAMES KILLIAN FAMILY |#45

James and Dollie Killian (owner of the ring mentioned above) lived on the Vern Gardner ranch and Ogden property between 1910 and 1920. They ran cattle and summered them on Trappers Creek, a side stream of North Water. Their herd numbered several hundred head of big steers with long horns. Bill Riley was their cowboy and did the riding. The large cattle were shipped to Kansas

---
⁴⁹ Ogden, "A Wilderness Sojourn: A Summer of Railroading," 1972.

City, where they weighed in around thirteen hundred pounds each. They had come from one of the finest summer ranges in this area. Additional details of this family could not be found.

SIG AND ALICE "MA" COX FAMILY | #40

The marriage of Francis Seagal "Sig" Cox (1863-1943) and Alice (Dykes) Cox (1863-1964) may have been one of romance or merely an economic expediency, but it endured for over half a century. Although both were born in Missouri, during their early lives they lived in Atwood, Kansas. Sig had been married only a year when his first wife died, leaving him with a stepson, James. Alice was married to Sig's brother John and had three children, Maude, Nellie, and John, before her husband also died. We know that Sig and Alice were married in 1891.

There are no records to tell us about Sig and Alice's lives in Kansas or why they decided to move to Colorado, but they embarked on a five-week covered wagon trip to Parachute in 1895 with five children: James (1879), Maude (1884), Nellie (1887), John (1889), and Delbert (1893). Two more sons, Frank (1896) and Fred (1898), were born after the Cox family arrived in western Colorado.

The family lived on Battlement Mesa for a while before filing on an abandoned homestead on Parachute Creek. There is still a landmark on maps called Cox Gulch. Sig and Alice lived on that ranch, raising their family for the next twenty-five years until moving into Grand Valley. Alice was reported to be a midwife and is said to have delivered a number of Parachute babies.

Sig died September 3, 1943, after a short illness. Alice, or "Ma Cox" as she was known, survived him by twenty-one years. She was a well-known figure around Grand Valley and told people she was going to live to 100, a rare event in that day. She made good her promise, dying January 9, 1964, at the age of 100 years, 9 months.

John Cox appears to have been the only son who continued to live on Parachute Creek, north of the Crawford Ranch. According to public records he was married to Jacqueline "Jaq" in 1912, and they had two children: Gifford (1913) and Johanna (1916). John was a great musician, playing the violin for country dances and get-togethers on Parachute Creek. His son Gifford played a guitar as well.

Their home burned down in the 1930s and they likely moved to the Sig Cox Ranch further up Parachute Creek. They may also have lived on what was later known as the George Benedetti place. The family spent most of their summers on West Mountain. Dave Crawford remembers going with them for part of one summer. The cabin was quite nice, even having a flagstone floor.

When John Cox started up the Crawford trail he always carried a large sack of peanuts. By following all the shells he discarded along the way, people could easily track him. He joked that was so he could find his way back.

John died unexpectedly of pneumonia on July 28, 1937. Apparently his band of sheep was sold to Gus Morris, who also took over the Cox cabin on top of West Mountain. Jacqueline moved to the Gus Morris house in Grand Valley. There is no record of when she died or where she was buried, so it is possible that she went to live with Johanna later in her life.

GEORGE KERLEE |#43

George Kerlee was born December 22, 1884, in Indian Territory (Oklahoma). When he was about six years old his father Jesse and second wife, Elizabeth (Doby), moved George, his sister Ella, and brother Harrison to Battlement Mesa.

Jesse was a renowned woodsman, who taught his two eldest sons to live off the land. George reported that wild game was very scarce when they arrived, having been killed off in previous years for the many mining camps. If a person found tracks, they would have to follow that trail for as long as it took to kill the game.

George likely started fending for himself at an early age, pushed out of the nest by his nine or ten half-brothers and half-sisters. An amusing side to George was that he never wore a pair of washed Levis, having been made to wear ragged clothes as a child. When the Levis got sufficiently dirty he'd just buy another pair and discard the old one.

George Kerlee

When he was still a young man, George rode a horse all the way to Oregon and back, taking several years. He provided for himself by working at ranches along the way and gambling. According to his stepson, Dave Crawford, "You never wanted to gamble with George because you'd probably end up broke!"

In 1907, he was married to May White and they lived on various ranches in the area where George worked as a ranch hand. Their infant died in 1909 and the couple never had more children. In 1914 he and his brother Harrison each filed on 160 acres high above Battlement Mesa, and this may have been the start of his sheep business.

Tragedy touched George in 1915 when his brother Harrison, a rejected lover, killed a young man who just days before had married a local girl. Harrison was arrested but later broke out of the Garfield County jail and was never seen or heard from again. There was some speculation that George may have played a part in the escape, but it was never proven.

Although George and May didn't buy property on Parachute Creek until the 1920s, they were living on their own land by 1930, and the census listed them as having a sheep ranch. It's unclear from whom they bought the land.[50] It's possible that George ran sheep on West Mountain before that time. He was fond of saying that every time he ran cattle he went broke; every time he ran sheep he made money.

Until his third and final marriage to Doris Crawford, George was fairly unlucky in love. His first wife May divorced him and married the hired hand, Leslie (Hack) Farris, taking part of the ranch property next to the Killian/Ogden place. A few years later George married Ollie Hollenbeck, but that marriage was short-lived. Ollie took another piece of George's property and established her home next to the John Cox ranch. When George and Doris were married in 1946, they built another home on what was left of his land in the middle, and all lived in harmony.

When George developed heart trouble in the late 1940s, he bought a sure-footed mule that he could ride to herd his sheep. He also had a sheep dog that he'd send up the mountain to the ledge to flush the sheep out. The dog would watch for George to wave his hat one way or the other and then he'd move the sheep. By 1950 George's health had deteriorated to the point that he and Doris moved down to the Tom Cline property in Grand Valley. George died on July 8, 1954, and Doris lived there until selling out because of the I-70 project. Doris died in July 1995 and both she and George are buried in the Battlement Mesa Cemetery.

GABRIEL PURDY "PURD" CRAWFORD AND LENA GORDON |#38

Grandson Dave Crawford doesn't have many memories of Gabriel (Purd) Crawford because he was only four years old when his granddad, born in 1857, died in 1932. Gabriel was born in Nova Scotia on March

---
[50] Oral communication, David Crawford, 2012.

The original Crawford family L to R, Gabriel, John, and Lena, 1908.

1, 1857, and moved to Leadville in 1881. His brother Titus had also come to Colorado, but Dave has no memory of him.

Gabriel (or Purd as he was known) Crawford drove a freight wagon from Leadville to Grand Valley. Purd spent some time riding shotgun on the stage from Leadville to Aspen and doing some freighting to the Parachute area. He came to Parachute with his brother, Titus, his wife, Lena (Gordon) Crawford, and her brother, Paul Gordon. Lena Gordon had gone to Leadville from Missouri with her father, Josephus, a coffee merchant, in 1880. Sometime after arriving in Leadville, Josephus went off prospecting and no one knows what happened to him. Lena boarded with a family and worked in a gin joint or a restaurant. Dave remembers her saying that she knew Jack Dempsey. Paul was excellent at tanning leather, braiding, and making all kinds of leather goods. He moved to Arizona at the turn of the century due to ill health. Titus, Purd, and Paul all filed homesteads on Parachute Creek.

Purd and Lena were married in Aspen in 1885. He was twenty-eight and she was sixteen. Dave does not know how or when they moved from Leadville to Aspen but, according to his obituary, they moved to Grand Valley in 1886 and settled on Parachute Creek in 1888. Purd's obituary says that he moved to Aspen in 1884.

When the Crawford family moved to Parachute Creek, there were still teepee poles on their land, the Ute Indians having left only a few years earlier. The family had three homesteads on Parachute Creek. Purd had 160 acres (1892) and Titus had another 160 acres (1902). Paul Gordon (Lena's brother) also filed for 160 acres (1902) adjoining Purd's section. Purd almost lost his homestead because he wasn't a citizen, so he became naturalized in March 1924, at age sixty-seven. He died in April 1932 at age seventy-five.

Purd and Lena had two boys, Oren and John Gordon Crawford. Oren died at the age of eleven in Aspen. This loss had a major impact on Lena's life, causing her to be very protective of her remaining son. They lived the rest of their lives on the creek or in town.

The Crawfords ran range cattle and operated a dairy at their ranch. They summered their cattle on Old Mountain, which was accessed by way of Granlee Trail. This was the same trail that Tom Glover and Doc Wilson had used. However, in the early 1920s Purd Crawford took up a homestead on the West Mountain, which was De Beque cattle range at that time. He then built his own trail known as the Crawford Trail that joined his ranch holdings.

Purd and Lena moved to the Frank Cox house next to Parachute Creek in Grand Valley in the 1920s, where they raised chickens. Lena leased the Parachute Creek property to son John and his wife Doris, but she retained ownership. When he died in Arizona in 1935, Paul Gordon's land apparently passed to Lena because it was part of the land she leased to John and Doris. Lena died in January 1950 at age eighty. The Crawford property then passed to her son, John Gordon Crawford.

JOHN GORDON CRAWFORD FAMILY | #39

John was born on Parachute Creek on February 26, 1894. He was a veteran of World War I. According to his application for Burial Allowance, he was drafted in May 1918 and discharged in February 1919. According to the same application, John was a private in Company E, 35th Infantry Regiment and during the time he was in the army, they were stationed on the Mexico border. Army troops were still being sent to the border in pursuit of bandits and undoubtedly, John was among those troops. Dave thinks that his father came down with meningitis while in the service and lost most of his hearing, which caused him to have a speech impediment for the rest of his life.

In 1920 John married Doris Sutherland, a young schoolteacher from New Castle, who'd come to teach at the Book Cliff School. They met when she boarded with the Crawford family the school year of 1919-1920. They had three children: John "Jack," 1920; Eva Lou, 1923; and David, 1928. As of 2013, Dave and Eva both live in Kamiah, Idaho. Jack is deceased.

John had a wry sense of humor. One time, a neighbor saw him riding and he was wearing only one spur. The neighbor asked him, "John, why are you only wearing one spur?" John replied, "I just figured if I could get one side moving, the other would follow!" Dave recalls that John seemed rather awkward until he mounted a horse, then he seemed to become one with the animal.

There is a story about a 45-70 rifle. The weapon was Gabriel "Purd" Crawford's from when he rode shotgun on the Aspen to Leadville stage, and it was passed on to his son John. Dave remembered a time when he, his dad, his brother Jack Crawford, and Walter Kern Wheeler went hunting. Kern was sporting a brand new forty-dollar Stetson hat. Kern challenged John that he couldn't hit his new hat with the old 45-70 rifle. No one believed he'd be able to do it. Kern threw the hat into the air, just like in the old cowboy movies, and John aimed and put a hole right through the crown of Kern's new hat. No one ever doubted him again.

John applied for a 320-acre homestead in 1921, and although it was approved, there's no record of it ever being patented. Dave does not remember his dad talking about another homestead. There is paperwork on placer mines for both John and Gabriel, dated 1924, but Dave doesn't know anything about these claims. He said when the oil shale boom hit everyone ran out and filed claims. They probably did, as well.

John and Doris were divorced in 1945, and John moved into town, where he built a cabin next door to his mother, Lena. He lived in the cabin until his mother died and then he moved into her log house.

John was sixty-one when he died in 1955. He was working for Tony Long on Holmes Mesa, feeding cattle with a sled. John unharnessed the horses and Tony took them to the corral. When he returned, John was dead. He is buried with all the other Crawfords in the Russey-Hurlburt Cemetery in Parachute.

DORIS (SUTHERLAND) (CRAWFORD) KERLEE | #42, 41

Doris divorced John Crawford in 1945, and then married George Kerlee in June 1946. Dave lived with her and George during his last year of high school. She and her mother, Laura Sutherland, both taught at the Book Cliff School in the 1930s and 1940s.

Doris (Sutherland) Crawford Kerlee

Doris was pretty much a no-nonsense kind of woman. Someone said of her that she was the best bull-raker on Parachute Creek. She was also an excellent hunter. In her late sixties or early seventies, she killed a deer above the East Fork Falls and was packing it down over her shoulders when she slipped on the shale, and fell, breaking several ribs. She was in great pain but wasn't going to let the meat go to waste, so she quartered the deer and packed it out a mile or so to her pickup, making four round trips. She didn't even go to the doctor until the next morning.

As much as she enjoyed the outdoors (especially fishing), Doris was also an accomplished musician, playing the piano and violin, then in later life, the cello. Dave remembers the Saturday nights when families would gather at the Crawford ranch on Parachute Creek to play music and dance. After moving into town, Doris occasionally played for both the Christian and Methodist churches. Perhaps the most devoted of her fans were her children and grandchildren who never tired of hearing her play classical music.

Anyone who knew Doris admired her for her ability to grow just about anything. She had a magic potion that she fed her roses to make them some of the best in town. The secret ingredient was a sucker from the Colorado River, some of the same ones which are now protected.

Doris didn't drive until after she and George Kerlee were married, and it was George that taught her. She was about forty-five or forty-six years old. She would put the truck (a 1951 Ford) in gear, wind it up until it was about to blow, pop the clutch, and finally travel down the road at 20 mph. She really never changed her driving style in all the years that followed. By 1982, when she left Parachute, the old pickup was in sad shape from too many loads of wood, too many poached deer, and too many loads of topsoil, but it was still running.

Doris Kerlee moved to Idaho in 1982 to be near Dave and Eva. She died in July 1995 at the age of ninety-five and is buried along with George Kerlee in the Battlement Mesa Cemetery.

JOHN PURDY (JACK) CRAWFORD FAMILY | #39

John Purdy Crawford was born in 1920. Being a severe diabetic, he died at age fifty-three of a heart attack. His brother, Dave Crawford, born October 23, 1928, supplied much of the Crawford information for this manuscript. He is unsure of when Jack and Vesta (Benedetti) Crawford bought the Crawford property from his family (probably right after WWII) but at one time he owned all their holdings.

In order to make ends meet, Lena had previously sold off some of the property to the Eaton Investment Company, and then Jack sold the remaining Crawford property to Union Oil Company of California around 1949-1950. Dave thinks Jack and Vesta lived in the old original log house when they were first married, and built the "basement" house while living there. After he sold the land, he leased back the house from Union Oil. Jack adopted Vesta's daughter Patty, and they had another daughter, Rita.

EVA LOU (CRAWFORD) SMITH/ HARRIS | #39

Eva Lou graduated from high school in Grand Valley in 1941 and left shortly thereafter for a job in Denver, where she met her first husband, Howard Smith. After World War II, they settled in Washington State and she later moved to Idaho, where she still resides. She has two adopted children: Donny and Susie.

DAVID LYAL CRAWFORD FAMILY #39

David Crawford graduated from Grand Valley High School and married Carol Herwick in 1954. He retired in 1982 after thirty-one years of service with Mountain Bell Telephone Company. They had three children: David, Debra, and Carla. Dave and Carol were divorced in 1974 and Carol married Ed McManus. Dave never remarried. Together they prepared and provided the information on the Crawford and Kerlee families. David resided in Idaho and Carol lives in Grand Junction. David passed away May 1, 2014.

ROSLYN SMITH FAMILY | #30

Ron Elijah "Roslyn" J. Smith was born in 1864 in Kansas. His father Stilman J. Smith was born in Ohio, and his mother Lucy J. Smith was born in Virginia. Roslyn came west and was reported to be single and living in Rifle in the 1910 federal census.[51] He apparently married early but was divorced. He was remarried to Mary Louise "Mate" Gardner and living in Garfield County in 1920, but later moved to Glenwood Springs.

Mate and Roslyn owned some 160 acres near Parachute Creek four miles from the town of Parachute. Mate, however, wanted to sell the property and move up the creek to be nearer her sister, Mrs. Cade Benson. They sold their homestead to Bob Wallace and James Wheeler. Each man bought eighty acres, enabling James to move closer to town and the site where he had started a blacksmith shop. James Wheeler and family built a very nice log home at this site. It remained one of the finer buildings along the creek for years. In later years, the house burned down.[52]

Roslyn Smith was one of the earliest to file on land on Parachute Creek. He was instrumental in the development of the "Low-Cost" ditch that served as a major irrigation ditch for the lower Parachute Creek farming community. Mr. Freeland later bought Mr. Wallace's part of the acreage and it became the home of the Freelands, located five miles west of Parachute. In the federal census of 1930, Roslyn was living in Beckworth, Plumas County, California, at the age of sixty-six, but no wife was listed. He died on December 19, 1945, in Davis, California, at the age of eighty-two.

ROBERT BUMGARDNER FAMILY | #39

Robert "Bob" Allen Bumgardner was born in Roper, Kansas, on December 12, 1891. His father, William Moses Bumgardner, was born in Latona, Kansas. Bob's mother, Maude Myrtle Landreth, was born at Sedan, Kansas. In Kansas, Bob worked for the railroad. He moved to Carbondale in 1902 with his parents and attended school there. In Carbondale, his father worked as railroad agent and telegrapher. While on his job, Bob was given a telegram to take to the president of the United States, Theodore Roosevelt, who was hunting in the McClure pass area, not far from Carbondale.

Robert "Bob" and Cora (Wheeler) Bumgardner, ca. 1920

Bob married Cora Wheeler on May 15, 1915, at the Star Ranch near Rulison, Colorado. Cora had come to Parachute when she was two years old. She was born in Clark, Routt County, Colorado, in 1889. Cora's original name was Clark Ella Wheeler, but when her schoolmates started calling her "Clarky" and "Darky," she changed it to Cora. Cora recalls her father saying they came to Colorado because a gentleman by the name of Pat Burke had gone to Parachute in 1890. He had seen the new orchards that JB Hurlburt had planted and were then beginning to bear fruit. He had brought some apples back with him to show James Wheeler,

---

[51] *US federal census, 1870-1940.*
[52] Murray. *Lest We Forget.* 1973

Bob and Cora Bumgardner pose with their children on the ranch ca. 1920. Bob is holding Joseph, while Maude and James stand in front.

who wondered what they were doing in this snow-covered country when they could raise all kinds of fruits in the Parachute area.

Cora's father, James Ferris Wheeler, was born in Kendall County, Illinois, and moved to National, Iowa, near the Mississippi River in the late 1850s. He moved from there to Red Oak, Missouri, where he met and married Mary Louise Weber, Cora's mother, in 1875. The Weber family owned a blacksmith shop. This is where James learned the blacksmithing trade that he later used in creating one of the first blacksmith shops in Parachute. In 1888, James and Mary moved with their children to Routt County, and on to Parachute in 1891. James Wheeler worked for JB Hurlburt for about six months before settling in Wheeler Gulch. Later, he bought eighty acres from Mary "Mate" Gardner and Roslyn Smith, who had moved farther up the creek. James sought to be nearer to town where he could do blacksmith work. He planted apple trees and built a sturdy log house on this property that remained a landmark for many years until it was destroyed by fire in the 1960s.[53]

From Bob and Cora's marriage there were seven children: Maude Louisa (1911), James "Jim" Robert (1913), Joseph William (1919), Clarence Allen (1921), Calvin Wheeler (1922), Paul Elvin (1927), and Philip Gene (1931). All seven were deceased as of 2011.

Bob Bumgardner was known for his friendliness and good sense of humor. He had many good stories to tell and a strong philosophy that he would impart to anyone. He spent much of his life as a rancher raising cattle and herding sheep. He stayed in the cattle business during the depression, even when banks were calling in all their loans and came to get his cattle. He had been alerted to losing his

---

[53] Ibid.

cattle, so he hid several head in the cottonwoods along the creek, and these were the foundation of a new herd for the next few years.

During the years of 1934 and 1935, Bob worked for Mark Hurlburt and was able to save enough money to buy more sheep. He rode out to near Cisco, Utah, and bought 500 head of pregnant ewes and trailed them back to Parachute. They were sheared in Parachute and then trailed up the creek for several miles when a severe May storm hit. Since the sheep had lost five to ten pounds of wool and were not adjusted to the area, he lost nearly fifty percent of the herd. He ran the remaining herd with Mark Hurlburt's flock and later with the Orland and Felix Lindauer sheep on Long Ridge above the Lindauer ranch. His sheep camp often welcomed strangers and cattlemen riding in the area. He always had a cup of ranch coffee and some sourdough biscuits available.

After several years, Bob Bumgardner sold the sheep. He spent four years during the Second World War working in Cheyenne, Wyoming, repairing airplanes and doing various jobs at the Air Force base. Most of his children ended up on ranches raising their own livestock. Bob passed away March 30, 1979, and his wife, Cora, passed the following year on January 8, 1980. They are both buried in the Russey-Hurlburt Cemetery.

PAUL BUMGARDNER FAMILY | #39

Paul Elvin Bumgardner was born November 17, 1927, on Parachute Creek, most likely at the Cox Ranch. He spent his elementary school years at the Granlee School. Paul grew up on Parachute Creek and helped his father on the ranch for a number of years. He was drafted into the Army in 1945 but was released in 1946. He worked as a ranch hand throughout the community and in both

Bob and Cora Bumgardner in the mid-1970s.

Students pose in front of Book Cliff School on its last day in 1938, L to R, back row: Paul Bumgardner, Sonny Gibbons, Mona Gardener (teacher), Roland Christenson; front row: Anna Cristenson, Edsel Bruckner, Harriet Christenson, and Gene Bumgardner.

Meeker and Roan Creek. He additionally worked in construction at different times. Paul married Julia Rubyette Curtis (Speer) at Grand Valley on November 17, 1959. She had two sons from a previous marriage, and Paul adopted both sons. Together, they had a daughter, Cheryl Linea, born on July 12, 1967. Paul was an excellent farmer and good with horses and teams. He and his family had owned property known as the Vern Gardner place, located just south of the town of Parachute. Paul sold the property during the oil shale boom of the 1980s, just before the boom crashed. He lost everything except the down payment. Consequently, he moved to Missouri and remained there until the fall of 1993, when he developed a blood clot in his leg from an injury while hunting. Paul Bumgardner passed away in Denver October 28, 1993.

GENE BUMGARDNER FAMILY | #39

Gene Bumgardner was one of the last cowboys who ranched on Parachute Creek. He was the youngest of Bob and Cora's children. Gene was born on the old Crawford ranch some five and one-half miles up Parachute Creek on August 22, 1931.

Gene describes his birth as follows:

> Dr. Miller had told my mother that she was not in a family way but rather had a growth of some kind. Two neighbors, Edna Freeland and Thelma Hansen, had come to help my mother. Thelma was a registered nurse and they demanded that he (Dr. Miller) get there and now. My mother was forty-two years old and she had complications with my birth. As a result, I had turned blue before I took on air and my wife says that when I took on air, I have been full of it ever since.

Gene graduated from the eighth grade at the Book Cliff School, where his mother had gone to school, and attended Grand Valley High School before he decided to quit school at the age of sixteen. He recalled his father telling him:

> "I sure can't make you go to school, but I can sure make you do ranch work"—and I did. I also learned to smoke Bull Durham cigarettes.[54]

When he was around twenty years old, Gene married Eileen "Boots" Clarke of Grand Valley, whose great-grandfather was JB Hurlburt, the first pioneer to settle and farm on Parachute Creek. Shortly after his marriage, Gene entered the Korean War, where he served for thirteen months. He returned to Parachute Creek, where he and Boots raised three children of their own: Mike, Rock, and Jeanne May, along with a foster child, Rick. Gene continued to work with his father, but he was persistent on building his own herd of cattle.

Although Gene and Boots lived in the De Beque area during their later years, he helped his father and family on Parachute Creek. They built their ranch herds up and operated over 3,000 acres of land, with each owning his own herd. He is quoted as saying, "I've done a lot of irrigating, and taken care of lots of cows in my lifetime."

Gene, Boots, and their families spent much of their lives ranching on Parachute Creek and some time on Roan Creek, located just over the hill south from their Parachute ranch. During the 20th cen-

---

[54] Witt. *I Remember One Horse....The Last of the Cowboys in the Roaring Fork Valley and Beyond,* 2002.

tury, they spent time raising families and livestock. Their children continue to live in the area. Gene was a cowboy all his life. When he was two years old, his mother placed him on a pillow in front of her on her saddle, and they moved cattle on the West Mountain. He got his first brand, an upside down broken heart, at the age of two, and it is still in the family today. Gene loved working cattle and being his own vet. He is quoted as saying:

> I could handle most health problems. I learned to sew up a prolapsed uterus, take care of pink eye, hoof rot, vaccinations, and most other ailments as needed. If you called a vet for every problem you had, your vet bill would soon be bigger than your grocery bill.[55]

Gene and Eileen "Boots" (Clarke) Bumgardner at their ranch in the 1960s.

Gene died on February 24, 2004, and is buried in the Russey-Hurlburt Cemetery.

TOM GLOVER, 1884 RANCH, AND FAMILY | #33

In 1884, Thomas Glover was one of the earliest settlers to arrive and settle on Parachute Creek. He was born in West Virginia around 1859 and was living there in 1870. He was the second oldest in his parents' family of five. At the age of twenty-four, he married Alice Gates in Leadville and then came west to Parachute from the mining camps with plans to plant an orchard and sell the produce to the miners.

Tom, Alice, and their baby daughter Queenie chose a beautiful spot up near the banks of Parachute Creek about five miles west of the Colorado River. They lived in tents for the first few years until they were able to build a suitable cabin. High mountains on both the north and south sides protected the site. The grass was lush and deer grazed among the big cottonwood trees and oak brush. The creek was clear with an abundance of fish and beavers. The beavers built dams that formed large pools in the creek where the fish thrived. Tom thought the valley would be an eminent place to raise cattle and build a home.

Luckily for Tom, the depression that had hit the mining camps in 1883 affected the cattle market. Cattle became much cheaper, and there was good grazing around his property. Tom purchased some cattle and set up a ranch operation, hiring two individuals to help him. One of these individuals was Marcus Dee Freeland, his cousin who had come west with him. Tom planted an orchard and several crops on his 300-plus acres. He and his helpers cut and hewed cottonwood trees and constructed sev-

---

[55] Ibid.

The Big House. Tom and Alice (Gates) Glover built their home with hewn cottonwood logs.

eral buildings on his property. Before laying the logs, it was necessary to construct a rock foundation to keep the wood away from the damp soil.

Tom was able to patent his property on December 26, 1891, using his Cash Entry No.733 as evidence of purchase. He had selected prime property and continued to enlarge it as opportunities became available. When the railroad traveled through Parachute in the early 1890s, many people came into the valley; however, much of the valley had been filed on and the irrigation water had been adjudicated at that time. [56]

One of the cabins built on this property is believed to be one of the oldest buildings on Parachute Creek. Because of the historical significance of this cabin, Williams Gas and Oil Company, Inc. gave the cabin to the Grand Valley Historical Society in 2007.

George and Nettie Fogel Benton had one daughter, Rose, who, in later years, married Arle Bruckner, also of Parachute Creek. When George Benton died, Rose inherited the Benton Ranch, and she and Arle moved into the Big House – originally built by Tom Glover – which caused Charles and Alice Lewis to move into the Glover Cabin from the Big House. This resulted in Charles's brother, Willard Lewis (1909), vacating the cabin and being forced to find another place to live. The Glover Cabin was one of several buildings that Tom Glover had built. After a few years, the cabin was used as a storage place for apples picked from the large orchard nearby that Tom Glover had established.[57]

Before it was sold, the Glover Cabin, constructed from hand-hewn cottonwood logs, was taken apart log by log and moved north and east across Parachute Creek. Here it was reconstructed and used as a horse barn with a manger, as described by Ella Lewis and observed by the author of this text. Rose Benton Bruckner sold the property to Martel Sherwood in 1947. Williams Production, RMT, Inc. purchased the property from the Union Oil Company of California, who had purchased the property from Martel Sherwood.

The Glover Cabin now stands as a Colorado Historical Site at the Battlement Mesa Historical Society on Battlement Mesa, Colorado, thanks to the generous contribution from Williams Production RMT, Inc. The Historical Society reclaimed the old stone Battlement Mesa Schoolhouse—built in 1897—and wanted to include an original cabin on their property as a model of a rural teacher's cabin. Consequently, as a gift to the community, the Williams Oil and Gas Company, Inc. moved the cabin to the four-acre site on the Battlement school property and rebuilt the structure. This included a new raised foundation, roof, chinking, and general requirements needed to meet codes of the area. The cabin was furnished by local Society volunteers who found appropriate antique furniture for the living quarters of a rural schoolteacher who might have lived in the area. Many tourists visit the reclaimed Glover Cabin today as it depicts what a one-room home for a teacher and a rural school-

---

[56] Murray. *Lest We Forget*. 1973

[57] Oral Communication, Ella (Lewis) Hendrick, Summer 2013.

house were like in the 1890s and early 1900s.

One day, during the first summer when the Glovers were building their cabin and living in a tent, Alice Glover was washing clothes outside in their yard. She had placed her baby, Queenie, on a blanket on the ground nearby. Alice scrubbed and rinsed the clothes by hand. While she was hanging them to dry, she was startled by a noise and turned to see a mountain lion carrying little Queenie into the nearby brush. She screamed, grabbed an axe, and ran after the lion. Apparently the scream caused the lion to drop Queenie and he ran off into the hills. Queenie was not hurt, but neighbors said that she had teeth marks in her temple that were with her all her life.[58]

The Glovers built this cabin with cottonwood logs in the late 1890s.

Queenie grew up on Parachute Creek where she was born in 1886 and a younger sister, Lucinda "Lou" Glover, was born in 1890. Queenie attended elementary school at the Book Cliff School and finished two years of high school in Parachute. By 1910, she had married Samuel S. Shaw who was eleven years older than she. They had two children: Tom, born in 1905; and Alice, born in 1909. By 1920, Queenie was divorced and living in Napa, California, with her two children, Tom and Alice Shaw. She returned to the Grand Valley several times over the years to visit with the friends she had left behind.[59] By 1930 she had married

The Glover Cabin was contributed, reclaimed, and refurbished by Williams Oil and Gas company as a home for a country school teacher, and is now located at the Grand Valley Historical Society school site in Battlement Mesa.

L. L. Steuck in Napa and her son, Tom Shaw, and her parents, Tom and Alice Glover, were living in Napa.[60] Queenie and her family later moved to the Los Angeles area. Queenie May (Glover) Steuck died September 12, 1957, in Napa, California.

Tom Glover was one of the largest ranch operators and cattlemen in the area. He sometimes employed eight to ten men and ran up to 2,000 head of cattle under the brand of T-raised M. He summered his cattle on the Book Cliffs and wintered them on the Colorado River. Glover Park on the

---

[58] Oral Communication with Daniel T. Michael, descendant, August 2008

[59] Murray. *Lest We Forget*. 1973

[60] Ibid.

West Mountain of the Book Cliffs is named after him. The Bureau of Mines at Anvil Points gets its mining water from what is known as the Glover Park Stream.

Hundreds of cattle were trailed up Parachute Creek in the early days of summer to the mountain range, and herds of horses followed the cattle. The federal census of 1900 reported Thomas Glover at the age of forty-one, living in Parachute, Colorado, with his household: his wife, Alice; his two daughters, Queenie, sixteen, and Lucinda, ten; his mother, Harriett Gates, seventy-five; Dee Freeland, twenty-three; and William Murphy, twenty-six.[61] Dee Freeland was a cousin of Tom Glover, and William Murphy was apparently a hired man.

The Glover Ranch is directly south of the Book Cliff School and had many different occupants over the ages. The Glover Cabin served as home for the Lewis family for a number of years. It is thought that the Glover Family owned much of the land later occupied by Enos Yeoman, Earnest Sandstrom, Henry and Viola Stanton, Christenson, Power, Fender, Shults, and Orland Lindauer, who also owned some of the Doc Wilson property. It was one of the largest single ownerships in the valley.

While Tom and his family had a beautiful ranch, there wasn't enough grass for their large herd of cattle, and they decided to move on.[62] When the Glover Family sold their property, the following article announcing the sale of their property was printed in a local newspaper:

Queenie (Glover) Steuck, in Napa, California, in the 1920s or 1930s.

Glover Ranch Sold:

Thos. Glover sold his ranch containing about 300 acres last week to R. O. Watson of Sentinel Butte, North Dakota. This sale included his fine orchard of 35 acres, farm implements, and about 300 head of cattle. The price paid was $15,300. This ranch is considered one of the best ranches in this section of the valley. Mr. Watson will take possession the 1st of May. Mr. Glover has not decided definitely as to where they will locate, but will probably leave here. They were among the first settlers of the valley, locating on Parachute Creek about 23 years ago, and they have a host of friends who will regret very much to see them leave.[63]

This was a real loss to the community since the Glovers were well liked in the area. They had helped fund the first Methodist Church in Parachute that was built in 1886 by local members of the church. Major funding sources from Parachute Creek included "Mr. Glover and Mr. Granlee who financed

[61] *US federal census, 1870-1940.*

[62] *Grand Valley News*, April 3, 1907.

[63] Ibid.

the work for the inside finishing of the building." [64] The local community would not let them leave without a major party. The Glovers were surprised at the band that showed up and the many people who came to their house for a leaving party. Women within the community had planned a grand going-away party and prepared many special dishes. Everyone enjoyed the games, music, and the communion with friends and neighbors. As indicated in an article of the *Grand Valley News*, over sixty people turned out for this bittersweet surprise party.

The 1910 federal census reported Tom Glover and his family living in Twin Falls, Idaho.[65] It further reported that his wife and daughter, Lucinda, were the only family members living with him at that time. He had moved to Napa by 1920 and was residing there in 1930 with his wife, who was sixty-eight years old. He was seventy-one, and his grandson, Thomas, was twenty-five years old. No information on death dates besides Queenie's could be found.

The ranch was advertised for sale again on December 21, 1910, at private auction. Robert O. Watson sold the ranch to Henry Benton on April 15, 1914. Following the death of Henry Benton, the property passed to his daughter, Rose, who leased the property to several different individuals for a number of years. One of the residents on this property was Walter O. Shults, who, on March 1, 1926, leased 310 acres with the obligation of clearing, plowing, and cultivating the property identified as the Benton Ranch. On January 1, 1930, Earnest Sandstrom leased the Hilliker place of 310 acres (thought to be much of the same property). Shults had leased and agreed to farm it for $190. The next year he leased only five ten-acre parcels from Rose Benton, for much of the soil located on the north side of Parachute Creek was alkaline in nature and considered poor. On February 5, 1943, Rose (Benton) Bruckner, the daughter of Henry Benton, sold the property again to Martel Sherwood, a local rancher.

C. W. "DOC" WILSON AND FAMILY | #36

After the bad winter of 1889 nearly put the JQS cattle company out of business, Doc purchased as many cattle as he could of the remaining JQS herd. He moved back to Parachute where, according to Mark Hurlburt, Doc was the second person to settle on Parachute Creek, perhaps in the late 1880s or early 1890s. He continued in the cattle business for himself using the brand 7-4.[66]

According to the 1900 federal census[67] and a news report in the July 21, 1898, *New Castle Nonpareil Newspaper,* Doc married De Etta Arner, who was born in the 1860s. It is believed that she had previously married Frank Gillium of Aspen and they had one child, Beulah, born in 1888. De Etta subsequently divorced Frank Gillium. She came to this marriage at the age of thirty-one with Beulah and later she and Doc had two other children: Charles W. "Billy" Wilson, 1899; and Beryl Wilson, 1902. The Wilsons returned to Parachute from Rifle after they were married and bought the Hilliker place located some four to five miles up Parachute Creek near the Glover ranch operation.

Doc was a major livestock operator in the area, and he sold and bought cattle and horses from local ranchers. He acquired the nickname Doc from neighboring ranchers because he had a great skill in nursing sick livestock back to good health. He sold wagons, harnesses, and some real estate to local residents. Some of the sales were to EF Yeoman, Earnest Sandstrom, Charlie Haley, Edwin Hilliker, Dee Freeland, HC Russey, James and Sig Cox, Joseph Bellis, and Christopher Dere. The records of these

---

[64] Murray, *Lest We Forget*. 1973.

[65] *US federal census, 1910.*

[66] Ibid.

[67] *US federal census, 1870-1940.*

sales and chattel mortgages can be found at the Garfield County Courthouse in Glenwood Springs.[68]

Doc Wilson ran his operation until 1918, but with available grazing declining, he sold his ranch. In the federal census of 1920,[69] he was identified as owning a home—mortgage-free—in Glenwood Springs and living with his family. His family moved to California in the early 1920s, and he joined them in 1925, according to his obituary. The 1930 federal census[70] indicated that he owned a radio set at the age of sixty-two and had no occupation. It was reported that he had moved to Fontana, California, in 1940, and he often visited Palm Springs where his daughter Beulah was now living. She had married David Margolius after working as a private investigator for several years. She and her husband owned the up-scale Ambassador Hotel in Palm Springs, which was demolished in later years. They had no children, and Beulah died March 18, 1986. Doc's other daughter, Beryl, worked as a desk sergeant for the Los Angeles Police Department before marrying Robert Wilson Miner. They had three children. Beryl divorced Robert Miner, and from then on, managed the Ambassador Hotel. Beryl died December 24, 1986, only nine months after her sister's death. Doc died February 15, 1953, in Palm Springs at the age of eighty-five. He is buried in the Montecito Memorial Park Cemetery in Montecito, California.

Doc's son Billy graduated from the University of Colorado with a degree in business in 1923 and married Alyce Jane Ritter in 1939. He was an accountant by profession and died September 28, 1964, in California. Billy Wilson had two sons, Howard and Marshall, who visited Colorado from California in the summer of 2013 and provided the author with additional information on the Wilson family.

Seen here in the early 1900s, the Enos and Ellen Yeoman family included, L to R, back row: George (teacher), Elmo Yeoman, Cora Wheeler, and Blanche Yeoman; middle row: Jesse Yeoman, Bob Dawson, and Clifford Yeoman; front row: Everett (last name unknown), John Crawford, Lula Wheeler, Grace Yeoman, John Wheeler, and unknown.

ENOS F. YEOMAN AND FAMILY | #36

Enos F. Yeoman, one of the earliest settlers on Parachute Creek, left an extensive record, as reported in A. W. Bowen's text *Progressive Men of Western Colorado*. The following information is reported directly from this source:

> After years of storm and danger since reaching man's estate, and enduring hardship and privation in almost every form, Enos F. Yeoman of the Parachute Creek region, Garfield County, has found a peaceful home amid the abundant opportunities and large rewards for systematic labor offered in the state of Colorado.
>
> He was born in 1842 in Fayette County, Ohio, the place of nativity also of his parents, Levi and Mary J. (White) Yeoman, well-to-do farmers of that state. The mother died in 1855 and the father in 1863. Their offspring numbered seven, Enos being the second.
>
> He was reared on the farm and bore his part in its useful labors until the beginning of the

---

[68] Garfield County Clerk & Recorder's Office.

[69] *US federal census, 1870-1940.*

[70] Ibid.

Civil War, when he enlisted in Company K, Forty-Eighth Ohio Infantry, in which he served three years, six months and fifteen days.

Soon after the close of the war he settled at Cheyenne, Wyoming, and found employment as a government scout. He was sent to Fort Bowie in the Chiricahua Mountains in Arizona, where he remained until 1876, then returned to Wyoming and was employed as a scout in the Sioux war of that year under Generals Crook and Merritt and in this campaign saw hard service and had many narrow escapes. He was with Thornburg at the Mill Creek massacre and many others of the noted engagements of the time.

After the close of the war he went to Nebraska in 1880 and married Miss Ellen Shimel of Iowa. He then moved to where he now resides on Parachute Creek and where he has since been engaged in farming and raising stock. He takes an active interest in school affairs, being secretary of the local school board, and in other phases of the public life of his community. He is a social member of the Woodmen of the World.

He and his wife are the parents of eight children, seven of whom are living: Melvin, Elmo, Branch, Clifford, Grace and Lela. Another daughter named Maud died in 1900 at the age of seventeen. Enos Yeoman was diligent and faithful in all the duties of citizenship and no man in his community is more highly or more generally esteemed.[71]

The Yeoman family moved to Parachute Creek in 1896. They settled on a quarter section five miles from the town of Parachute where the Book Cliff Schoolhouse was located. The family raised hay and cattle before they sold to Henry Stanton in 1916. The Yeoman family moved to Arizona, and none are believed to be living. The Stanton family ran shorthorn cattle for a period of years on this property that apparently adjoined the Doc Wilson property. Orland Lindauer lived on the Doc Wilson property and part of Yeoman property for sixteen years. Following Orland's death in 1985, his wife Jody continued to live at this site until it was sold to the Sinclair Oil Company.

ORLAND LINDAUER AND FAMILY | #36

Felix Orland Lindauer was born May 15, 1924, in Grand Junction. His parents were Felix Richard and Edith (Evans) Lindauer. He grew up on Parachute Creek, attended the Granlee School by horseback, and graduated from Grand Valley High School in 1942 along with his sister, Mary Margaret. Orland grew up on the Peter Lindauer family ranch, spending much of his time hunting and being a young cowboy.

Mary was born December 12, 1925. She had taken an advanced high school program that enabled her to graduate early. Following a short stay in a Denver business school, Mary contracted leukemia and passed away in May of 1942.

Orland spent much of his early life working with his father and

Orland Lindauer with a bobcat

---

[71] Bowen. *Progressive Men of Western Colorado.* 1905.

Mary and Orland Lindauer stand in front of the old Grand Valley Bank building, which is now a restaurant.

uncles on the Lindauer Ranch, where they also raised remount horses for the US Army. In July of 1944, he entered the Army and served in the European theater, where he was wounded in the Battle of the Rhine. He was treated in a military hospital in France and later moved to the McGraw General Army Hospital in Walla Walla, Washington. His service awards included the Purple Heart, Good Conduct Medal, Croix de Guerre Medal, and the European African Middle Eastern Service Medal.

Orland and Alice Quinn were united in marriage on December 29, 1944. They raised two children: Mary (Lindauer) Satterfield, born April 15, 1949; and Gerald, born April 24, 1957. They lived on the Granlee Ranch until 1952 when they moved to the Doc Wilson Ranch that Orland and his father, Felix, had purchased, adjacent to the Book Cliff School. Alice died from a brain tumor July 16, 1962.

Felix Lindauer continued to work with his son Orland in their partnership of running the ranch, where they raised hay and cattle. Felix did a variety of gunsmith work, and both he and Orland were great competitors at the local gun and turkey shoots. Orland operated a backhoe for numerous years and worked for various individuals and groups throughout the valley. He spent most of his life on Parachute Creek and was a rancher and rodeo hand. Most of his friends knew him as "Ordy." He was a skilled calf roper and bull rider. In 1949, Orland was recognized as the champion cowboy at the San Miguel Basin Rodeo in Norwood, Colorado. He continued to participate in rodeos as a prominent figure until the mid-1960s.

Orland was a charter member of the Grand Valley Park Association and was involved in its annual rodeo. He started the Grand Valley Gun Club and helped build the Bull Gulch Cabin on the East Fork of Parachute Creek, where Felix and Orland ran cattle. Orland was a pilot and enjoyed flying. This changed when he crashed his plane in Monticello, Utah, on a trip transporting a friend and his daughter to California. No one was seriously injured in this accident, but it did stop his flying. He was a member of the Ward Underwood American Legion Post #114 of Parachute.

Following a short and unsuccessful second marriage, he found a loving companion named Georgia E. "Jody" Marling, and they spent his last sixteen years on the Parachute ranch. He died in Rifle January 23, 1985, from a heart attack. Jody moved to the town of Parachute following Orland's death, where she lived another twenty-two years. Jody died at the age of eighty-three. Both Orland and Jody are buried in the Battlement Mesa Cemetery.

Orland Lindauer was an accomplished bull rider.

HOMES & RANCHES 1-33

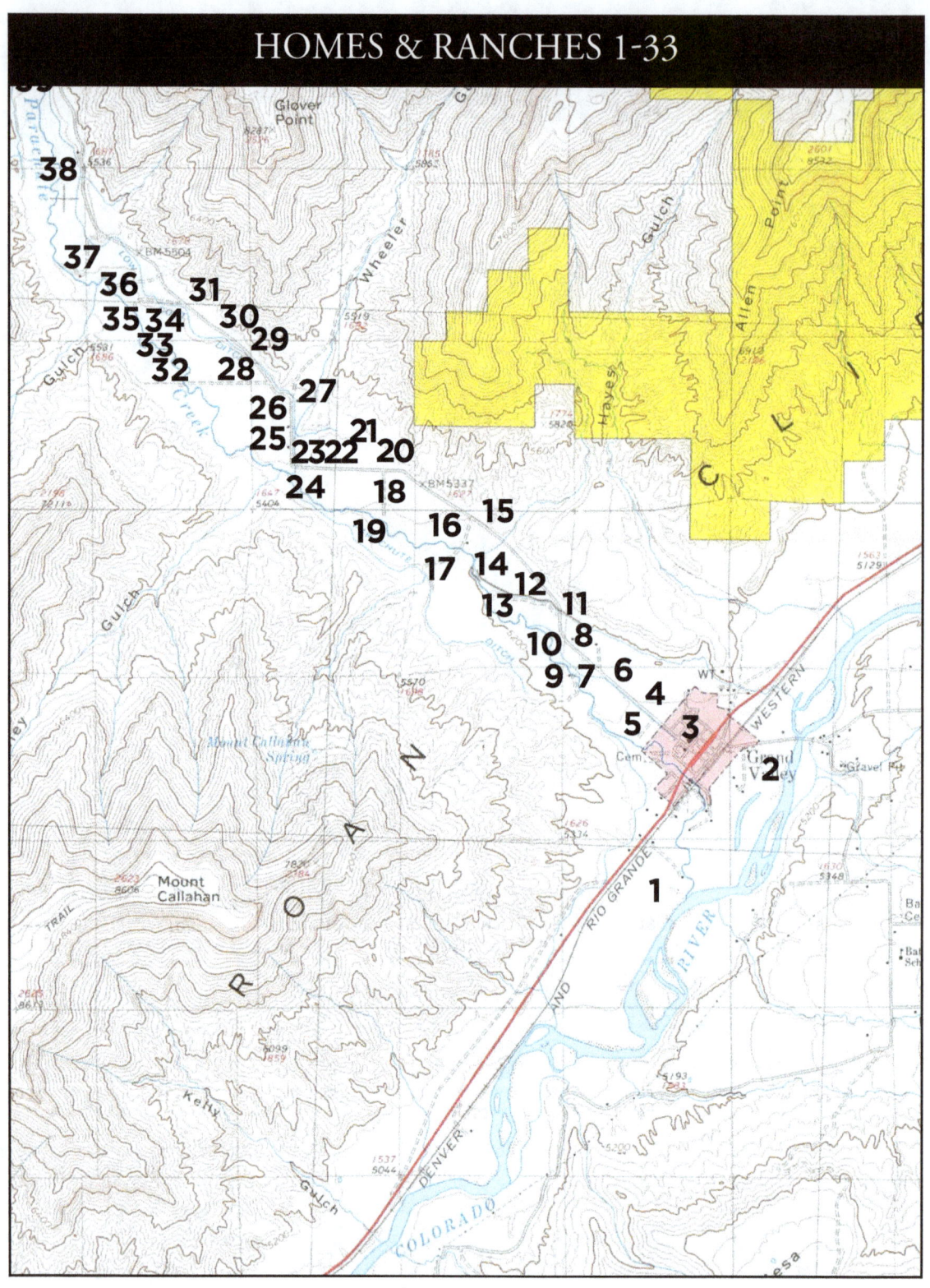

CHAPTER 7

Early Pioneers of the Lower Half of Parachute Creek

THE BOOK CLIFF SCHOOL | #31

Recalling her years at the Book Cliff School, Birdie (Wheeler) DeWitt wrote the following letter for Dee Freeland describing the school. She died in 1970.

I have been wanting to write this ever since you moved the little school house, first my hand didn't work very good, then I got busy, busy doing other things and then last but not least, I run out of writing material; today, I hope to get my speech made. I would like to re-live the good old days of the 90s—not too bad. We knew our neighbors. I still love the little schoolhouse.

When the Wheeler of this family bought a home on Parachute Creek early in 1892, there being four school age children that made enough children for a country school located about five miles from Parachute. The city had outgrown the log house and built a two-room brick house and they moved the little log house to the country.

School started June 26, 1893. Teacher Kate Barthel Smith lived at home on a ranch now known as the Koch place at Grand Valley. She rode a pony to and from school each day. The pupils were Willie and Tom Cline, Queenie Glover, Elmo and Blanche Yeoman, Victor Monks, Florence Cleveland and Steve Barnett. I, Birdie (DeWitt), was the oldest.

We lined up outside each morning and marched to our seats, then repeated the Lord's Prayer before being seated for the day's work. We all went barefoot in summer, so many rocks and brush made getting around rather difficult, never a shade tree. Many happy noon hours and recesses were spent for children playing in the Low Cost ditch. We also had lots of fun on too hot or stormy days to get out, staying inside joking, playing or just visiting.

The house had two rooms on each side and a door and a good shingle roof. There was no ceiling overhead and the logs were bare except for three blackboards. The floorboards were rough, wide, slightly curved and far apart. There was a teacher's desk and chair, a few double seats of various sizes, and recitation seat—second hand with a generous amount of carving by former children, a globe,

Pictured at the Book Cliff School in 1898 are, L to R, Lucinda Glover, Blanche Yeoman, unknown, Jesse Yeoman, Clifford Yeoman, Cora Wheeler, John Wheeler, Isaac Wheeler, John Cline, Cody Cline, Oren Crawford, Queenie Glover, Victor Marks, Bert Hilliker, and Getrude Hilliker (teacher).

dictionary, a class bell that the teacher called the children with, a water bucket and dipper. Children furnished their own books, district furnished ink.

Every day we had special time with reading and writing in copybook, other lessons we heard as time permitted. We carried our lunches in dinner pails or lard buckets. We got our water from the Low Cost Ditch when it wasn't too warm or muddy, other times by a spring near the creek.

About twice a month we would clean up. The boys would carry water in dinner pails, we girls would wash windows, board work, blackboards, desks, erasers, scrub floors, etc. and didn't overlook the yard and the little houses at the end of the well beaten path, we loved our little school house. When fall and cold weather set in, we tried to keep warm by a fire made of brush and shale rocks across the road from the schoolhouse, got rid of a lot of brush before we were donated a pot-bellied old stove and some coal by the parent district at Parachute. Adolph Wheeler attended school a few weeks; school closed early in December.

Next, Mrs. Good taught and she named the school Book Cliff. More children came, some from log camps in Riley, Crawford and Starkey gulches and some more from ranches and the teacher's little girl Nellie. Thirty-two students in all three months. Next year, Mrs. Good taught again for four (4) months.

The next year 1896, a man from Virginia taught, next year Steven Yeoman, a one armed Civil War veteran, taught our first winter school. By then, many changes had been made in school and pupils.

In those good old depression days, we raised what we ate and were glad to get it. Children worked long before and after school, and all too often had to miss school to work at home. There were church and prayer meetings, Christmas trees with homemade decorations, box socials, ditch meetings, and other get-togethers; people taking their coal oil lamps and lanterns from home, some teachers got $35.00 a month. The little log schoolhouse stood by us.

Dee Freeland fell heir to the little old schoolhouse more than a half century ago. Birdie says, Dee can tell you the next chapter, he always liked school moms. You too might add chapter three as you have the much loved little white schoolhouse under your wing and care.[72]

Dee Freeland Jr. moved the schoolhouse to his ranch, where it was rented out for a number of years, but burned in the mid-1980s. He gave the above DeWitt article to Eileen Bumgardner, who had shared it with the author of this text. Similar information was obtained from LaVerne Starbuck. She had gathered information on rural schools in Garfield County while she was an administrator in the Rifle School District. Some of that information follows.

On April 4, 1900, Book Cliff School District 11 was formed out of District 7. Edwin Hilliker was elected secretary, Alice Glover, treasurer, and GP Crawford, president, thus forming the first school board. Other board members in later years included VG Mills, CE Tracy, Samuel Shank, Harry Hansen, Blanche Sandstrom, Doris Crawford, Thelma Hansen, and Mrs. C.I. Lewis. Edna Freeland was a member of the school board continuously from 1909 until 1947 when the school was closed and became part of District 16.

The first teacher of the newly formed district was Gwyneth Floyd, who taught for $50 a month. Other teachers were Lillian Sanderson, Anna Akerman, GP McLaughlin, Alice Tinley, Nina Cherry,

---

[72] Birdie DeWitt. Letter given to Dee Freeland and received from Eilene Bumgardner, 2012.

Clara Green, Doris Sutherland, Ida Zeller, Carol Shinn, Henrietta Sill, Hazel Shank, Bessie Singster, Helen Spears, Lillian Werkel, Laura Lewis, Anna Mae Alber, Lois Sampson, Mary Salatino, Mona Gardner, Helen Patterson, Elizabeth Glover, Letitia Peterson, Laura Sutherland, Lillian Erickson, and Bessie Lindauer.

Some students who attended District 11 Book Cliff School were: Bert Hilliker, Blanche Yeoman, Claude Shults; Willard, Albert, Anna, Glen and Ella Lewis; Joe, Clarence, Paul, and Phillip Bumgardner; Jack, Eva, and David Crawford; Birdie and Martin DeWitt; Ernest and Florence Gibbons; Verda Ferris, Dee Freeland Jr., Walter Wheeler, Clarence Allen, Bill Ogden, Betty Jensen, and Edsel Bruckner.[73]

BIRDIE (WHEELER) DEWITT AND HER FAMILY | #30, 33, 34

Birdie Lena Wheeler was the third child of James Ferris Wheeler (1856-1941) and Mary Louis Weber (1855-1916). Birdie was born on March 3, 1881, in Red Oak, Missouri. She spent her early childhood in Missouri, but moved to Clark, Colorado, with her parents in 1888 for a few years. Her parents then moved to Parachute and homesteaded in Wheeler Gulch some four miles west of Parachute.[74] After a few years, they bought eighty acres from Roslyn Smith on Parachute Creek about one mile east of the Book Cliff School and built a large log home near the road.

On a vacation trip to Washington, Birdie met her future husband, Elmore DeWitt, and was married March 10, 1909. Birdie and Elmore had two children: Elvin, born January 1, 1910, in Adna, Washington; and Mary, born February 4, 1911, on Parachute Creek. Shortly after Elvin was born, the family moved to Parachute Creek, and he attended the Book Cliff School. He spent his early childhood in this area. Birdie and her father had land in Wheeler Gulch. In addition, Birdie had some forty acres just south of the Granlee Place mostly on the east hillside.

Related Family Ladies of Parachute Creek. L to R, Mary (DeWitt) Williams, Maude (Bumgardner) Bruckner, Mable (DeWitt) Powell, Birdie Lena (Wheeler) DeWitt, Cora (Wheeler) Bumgardener, and Sharon DeWitt (child).

Birdie was divorced in 1920 and lived on a small farm on Parachute Creek across the road from the Wheeler log home. She later moved with her son Elvin to a small ranch west of Rifle on the upper portion of Rifle Creek.[75] Elvin joined the Civilian Conservation Corps and was drafted into the military service. He entered World War II and spent three and one-half years in the South Pacific. He was

---

[73] Starbuck. "Children Came, Some from Log Camps Others from Ranches," 1989.
[74] Ancestry.com. Accessed, 2013.
[75] Oral Communication.

discharged October 25, 1945. Elvin never married and lived with his mother for some time. He was a lifetime resident of the Parachute area and nearby Rifle. He died on January 15, 1986, in Rifle and is buried in the Battlement Mesa Cemetery. Birdie died on April 25, 1970, at the age of eighty-nine and is buried in the Russey-Hurlburt Cemetery in Parachute.

Mary DeWitt attended the Book Cliff School followed by two years at Grand Valley High School. She spent most of her life in Garfield and Mesa counties. She married Marsh Williams on July 3, 1928, in Delta, Colorado. Marsh and Mary had no children. Following her husband's death on August 22, 1956, Mary worked at various jobs including the 7-Lakes Resort on the South Fork of the White River east of Meeker. She returned to Battlement Mesa where she died on April 9, 1992. Both Marsh and Mary are buried in the Battlement Mesa Cemetery.

JIM DEWITT FAMILY | #34

Jim Talmer DeWitt was born March 27, 1887 at Hastings, Nebraska, the youngest of seven children born to Fernando and Sarah (Wilson) DeWitt. Jim's older brother, Elmer Ellsworth DeWitt, had moved to Oregon after serving during the Spanish American War in the Philippines. While in Oregon, it appears he met Birdie Wheeler, who was visiting some Wheeler relatives in Washington, and married her shortly

Birdie (Wheeler) DeWitt poses with her children Elvin De Witt and Mary (DeWitt) Williams in 1934.

thereafter. Elmer and Birdie moved to the Parachute area and were living there in 1912 when Jim came to Colorado to visit his brother and sister-in-law. During this visit, Jim met and fell in love with Birdie's little sister, Lulu, and the two were married a short time later at the Star Ranch in March of 1912.

When the first child of Jim and Lula, Mabel, was born in 1914, they were living in Eagle, Colorado. The next child, Bill, was born in Western Kansas in 1915, as was Martin in 1918. In the 1920 federal census report, they had moved back to Grand Valley,[76] [77] and Virginia was born there in 1922.

They moved to Arizona where they can be found in the 1930 federal census. Then in 1933, the twins, Dee and Dean, were born in Parachute. That is the last reference to the family being in the Parachute area. Shortly after the birth of the twins, they made the final move to Rifle. Dee had been named after Dee Freeland, who was a family friend.

Their son, Martin DeWitt, was one of the many casualties of World War II. He enlisted in the Army on November 27, 1940, and was killed in action on June 12, 1944. He is buried in Russey-Hurlburt Cemetery with his parents.

---

[76] Ancestry.com. Accessed, 2013.

[77] *US federal census. 1870-1940.*

MARCUS DEE FREELAND FAMILY | #35

Marcus Dee Freeland Sr. was born in West Virginia in 1877. He arrived on Parachute Creek in 1886 when he was nine years old. In Parachute, he worked as a cowboy for his cousin, Tom Glover. He worked for Tom for several years taking care of the cattle on the Old Mountain. Marcus, or Dee as he was commonly known, was a quiet individual and spoke in a husky voice.

One late fall evening when he was coming off the Old Mountain down Granlee Gulch, Dee became extremely cold and stopped at the Granlee ranch house to warm up. While there, he met Flora Edna Perham, who was a teacher at the Granlee School located just across the creek and roomed with the Granlee family.

Lucinda "Lou" Glover and her father Tom's cousin Dee Freeland at their cabin on the Old Mountain on the Book Cliff Range.

Edna, as she was commonly called, was born in Hays, Kansas, but grew up in Denver. She and Dee were married on June 18, 1904, and were residents of Parachute Creek for fifty-two years. After Edna and Dee were married, she was required to resign from teaching school. Marcus Dee Freelend Sr. lived seventy-two years on Parachute Creek and died on September 23, 1958, at the age of eighty-one.

Dee and Edna had two boys; the first died young and the second, Marcus Dee Freeland Jr., was born on February 9, 1913, and grew up on the ranch. He eventually took over the management of the ranch until the late 1970s when it was sold. Dee Jr. ran his cattle on the Old Mountain and was always willing to help anyone in need. He moved into the town of Parachute prior to selling his ranch.

Dee Jr. participated in many of the Grand Valley Days programs held on Friday nights before the Saturday parade and evening dance. At these community programs, he demonstrated his rope-spinning abilities. He was always interested in guns and ammunition and frequently provided locals with hand-loaded ammunition at a cheap price.

Dee Jr. attended elementary school at Book Cliff School. He did not enjoy school; he was apparently bullied because of his short stature and frequent illnesses. According to comments from individuals who knew Dee, he learned in school to not be very fond of women. However, in later years, he was heard to say that he "wished that he had gotten married and had a family." Dee was always quick to don his western attire and strap on his pistols, boots, and hat to illustrate the old cowboy ways of the West. He spent his last years at the Mesa Assisted Living facility in Battlement Mesa where he died June 8, 2003, at the age of ninety. His mother, Edna, died on August 8, 1956, and both Marcus D. and Edna Freeland are buried in the Russey-Hurlburt Cemetery.

Edna Freeland was an active member in the Parachute Idle Hour Club. She played the guitar and was the owner of a fine small Gibson guitar. She often helped young aspiring guitar players of the area learn to play.

As Erlene Murray reported in her book:

> I believe Mrs. Freeland expressed the feelings of all those living on Parachute Creek, when, on the occasion of their fiftieth wedding anniversary in 1954 she remarked, "I have watched the moon come up over Parachute Creek for fifty years, now, and I know there is no more beautiful sight on earth."

RANSOM WHEELER AND FAMILY | #30

The Wheeler family was one of the first large families to come into the Parachute Creek area in the early 1880s as the Ute Indians were forced to leave. Ransom S. Wheeler, the patriarch of the family, was born in 1822 in either Canada or Vermont. He used both as his birthplace. He married Harriet Ferris in 1844. She was born October 23, 1823, in Vermont. The couple left for the West, settling in Kendall County, Illinois. He purchased land and remained there for thirteen years.

He and Harriet had twelve children: Christiana, born 1845; Charles, 1847; Electra, 1849; James Ferris and Henry (twins), 1851; George, 1855; Ellen, 1860; Isabelle, 1862; William, 1866; and John, 1868. Most of Ransom's family remained in the midwest while several others moved farther west and are described in more detail.

Ransom and Harriet purchased forty acres of land in Dade County, Missouri, and then moved to Red Oak, Missouri, after his Civil War service. At that time, Harriet and Ransom appeared to be separated, and she saw him infrequently during the years following his discharge from the Army. In later years, Harriet left Missouri and moved to Clark, Colorado, to be with her son James and his family.

Ransom was not able to do farm work or hard physical labor because of his war injuries. In 1890, at the age of sixty-eight, he was granted a pension of $12 a month as a Civil War Veteran. He died August 13, 1896, in Parachute and is buried in the Russey-Hurlburt Cemetery. Harriet's burial records were not available.

Twin brothers James and Henry Wheeler

JAMES FERRIS WHEELER | #30

James F. Wheeler lived and grew up in Clayton County, Iowa, from age six until seventeen. His family remained in Iowa during the Civil War years. James met and soon married his wife, Mary Louisa Weber, on November 25, 1875. She was born in Vernon, Indiana, on April 1, 1856. The Weber family introduced James to blacksmithing, which he continued to do for many years. In 1888, he moved his family to Clark, Routt County, Colorado, where he continued his career. His mother Harriet followed him to Clark.

After three years in Clark, Chief Colorow had reported to Hurlburt in the early 1890s that the snow was as deep "as two Ute Indians," and when James had seen the apples grown in Parachute by the Hurlburts, who had brought some to Clark for sale, he decided to move his family to Parachute.

Several of the Wheeler family members, along with James, came to Parachute Creek in 1892. Three of the boys were especially good mechanics and excelled in blacksmith work. Two of the oldest boys were great hunters and had killed several wolves in the early days. James homesteaded in Wheeler Gulch about four miles west of Parachute and soon bought eighty acres at a site nearby. At this location, with the help of his family, James built a sizeable log house on the property and planted apple trees.

From the marriage of James and Mary, eight children were born. The oldest was William Calvin, born September 3, 1876, in Red Oak, Missouri. He died when he was twenty-five years old. The second child was Lemuel Adolf, born in Red Oak, Missouri, who died when he was twenty-two years old. The third child of James and Mary was Birdie (Wheeler) DeWitt. Her story was told in the DeWitt Family section. The other five children whose stories follow below are Robert, Elmer, Clark Ella "Cora," John Albert, and Lulu.

James's wife, Mary Louisa, died February 5, 1916. After Mary Louisa's death, in September 1917 James married Sarah Cline (widowed after John Cline's death) with whom their family had stayed when first

James Ferris Wheeler and his wife Mary Louisa (Weber) were the first Wheelers to settle on Parachute Creek.

James Wheeler owned one of the first automobiles on Parachute Creek. He is seen here with his wife Mary, their daughter Cora Bumgardner and her son Jim.

coming to Parachute in 1891. A story is told that Sarah brought to the new marriage a redwood cupboard that had been made of old flume boards from the abandoned Havemeyer irrigation project of the 1880s, planned by WH Hallet.[78] This cupboard remained in the family for years.

James Wheeler was a skilled carpenter and did excellent work in his blacksmith shop that he operated for years. James died April 13, 1941, and is buried with his first wife, Mary Louisa, in the Russey-Hurlburt Cemetery in Parachute. Sarah (Cline) Wheeler died in October 1931 and is also buried there with her husband John Cline.

Robert "Bob" Wheeler obtained his mule Al Loppy from Gary Bainter.

ROBERT WHEELER | #30, 57

James and Mary's fourth child, Robert, was born on September 4, 1883, in Red Oak, Missouri. He moved with his family to Clark, Colorado, for a couple of years and then on to Parachute. He homesteaded on the East Fork of Parachute Creek in 1918. This property was later sold to Paul Lindauer, who ranched there until 1937 when he sold his ranch and the property to the Union Oil Company of California. The company continued buying up ranches for oil shale exploration.

As reported by Gene Bumgardner, Robert was an excellent cook and very meticulous at whatever he did. In the 1920s, he packed men and equipment to the oil shale country to dig assessment holes and other work. Robert remembers his father, James Ferris Wheeler, as being good with teams of mules and horses.

Robert married Mabel Nelson in December 1914. This marriage led to two children: Lula "Bobbie," born November 5, 1915; and Walter Kern born July 24, 1920, in Grand Valley. Lula worked as a registered nurse in the Parachute/Rifle area and married Vaughn Cameron December 23, 1929. Walter worked for the Dillon County Road Department for thirty years, then retired to De Beque. He married Dede Cox on September 20, 1960. Robert Wheeler died on May 27, 1942.

ELMER WHEELER | #30

Elmer Isaac Wheeler was born in Red Oak, Missouri, June 27, 1887. Shortly after his birth, the family moved to Clark, Colorado. He married Gertrude Smith on May 15, 1910. He died November 8, 1943.

CLARK ELLA "CORA" (WHEELER) BUMGARDNER | #39

The sixth child of James and Mary Wheeler was Ella "Cora" Wheeler. She was born October 18, 1889.

---

[78] Murray. *Lest We Forget.* 1973

The family moved to Parachute Creek where she met and married Robert "Bob" Bumgardner May 15, 1910. They raised a large family on Parachute Creek. Her history is recorded earlier with the Bumgardner family. She died on April 10, 1980, and is buried in the Russey-Hurlburt Cemetery in Parachute.

JOHN ALBERT WHEELER | #30

The seventh child, John Ransom, was born April 13, 1893, in Parachute. He married Jennie Busby, but the date is unknown. They had three children: Ida May, Louise, and Albert. John died March 17, 1940. Albert spent much time in the Parachute Creek and Grand Valley area. He worked as a mechanic much of his life and was recognized as a good one, for he could fix just about anything. He drove the school bus for a number of years, then moved to Rifle in later years.

LULU MAY WHEELER | #30

The last and eighth child was Lulu May Wheeler, born December 31, 1895, in Parachute. She married James DeWitt, who was born in March 1887 and died in March 1955. They had nine children. Lulu May died March 14, 1940, in Grand Valley.

ROY JENSEN FAMILY | #34

Roy J. Jensen was born October 3, 1909, in Stapleton, Nebraska. He spent most of his childhood in the Grand Valley area and was raised by his aunt, Mrs. Thad Mary Bailey. Roy attended the Grand Valley public schools. He married Olive Satterfield on December 30, 1929, in Grand Junction, Colorado.

Roy and his family lived on a small farm near the Wheeler residence about four miles up Parachute Creek. He was a rancher on Parachute Creek for many years and worked out as a ranch hand as needed. Roy also judged horse shows in the Grand Junction region.

Both Roy and Olive spent their last years in Grand Junction, after moving there in 1956. Olive passed away January 3, 1975, from an automobile accident, and Roy lived another nineteen years. He died January 29, 1994, of natural causes in Grand Junction at the age of eighty-four.

Roy and Olive raised two children: Betty Jean, born in 1932 (also listed in the 1940 federal census as Betty Wheeler);[79] and Charles "Sharkey," born in 1933.

Betty married Bud Carr in Denver after finishing high school and they lived in Commerce City north of Denver. Betty was a housewife and provided a home for her family. She attended a school reunion a few years ago but her health was failing, and none of her classmates that were contacted knew her present condition.

Sharkey was born in Grand Valley and attended but did not finish high school. He joined the US Army and was assigned to the 7th Infantry Division. This Army Division participated with the First Marine Division in the Battle of Chosin Reservoir during the Korean War. The battle that lasted for two weeks was the "most violent small unit fighting in the history of American warfare."[80] In this battle, some 35,000 Chinese were killed from a troop list of 120,000 compared to 6,000 US Marine and Army soldiers killed, wounded, or captured and another 6,000 suffered severe frostbite.

Sharkey ended up with a Turkish unit before he was able to find his own. He left the military to work for Mountain Bell Telephone Company in civilian life. Sharkey married Beverly Dere in 1953. They

---

[79] *US federal census, 1940*

[80] Van Pelt, Report on 60th Anniversary of the Chosin Reservoir Battle, Korea—November-December of 1950, 2012.

were divorced in 1968. Sharkey died at Clifton from cancer March 26, 2005. Beverly remarried and lived until the end of 2009. They had two sons: Wayne and Lannie, both deceased.

ERNEST SANDSTROM FAMILY | #29

Ernest "Ole" Sandstrom was born January 1, 1881, in Stockholm, Sweden. He immigrated to the United States as a small child in 1882 and his family settled in Muskegon, Michigan. As a young man he moved to Leadville, Colorado, to seek his fortune during the gold rush days. A few years later, he moved to Parachute. He lived with and worked for Thomas E. Bailey for several years and married Blanche Hurlburt on November 19, 1905, in Parachute. Blanche was born in 1884. A son, Elmer, was born in 1908, but he unfortunately died in 1924 at the age of sixteen.

Ole eventually purchased his own small farm some four miles up Parachute Creek and identified himself as a farmer in the 1940 federal census.[81] He was a member of the Lutheran Church and the Neighbors of Woodcraft.

Blanche sold their farm in 1944 to Bob Davidson as Ole's health had declined, and she and Ole moved into town. He died in 1950 in the town of Grand Valley at the age of sixty-nine, following a three-week illness.

Blanche was very active in the Christian Church in Grand Valley. She was also an active member of the Idle Hour Club of Parachute Creek. She helped Erlene Murray develop the story of the Grand Valley area in her book *Lest We Forget*.

All three members of the family, Ole, Blanche, and Elmer, are buried in the Russey-Hurlburt Cemetery. A special memorial was included on Elmer's headstone, which reads, "A precious one from us has gone, a voice we loved is stilled, a place is vacant in our house, which never can be filled."

Blanche (Yeoman) Johnson, Blanche (Hurlburt) Sandstrom, Chas. Johnson, Ole Sandstrom.

Blanche (Hurlburt) and Ernest "Ole" Sandstrom, ca. late 1930s.

ANDY DAVIDSON FAMILY | #29

Andrew "Andy" Davidson, was born December 2, 1878, in Henrietta, Texas. He arrived on the Texas plains sleeping on a bed made under a wagon. James Jackson "JJ" Davidson and Lydia Sheppard were his parents. They had joined the Mormons in their travels to St. George, Utah, and then on to San Bernardino, California, where they were married. After much traveling, the family finally settled down on a ranch between Craig, Colorado, and Baggs, Wyoming, where they raised horses to sell to the US Army.

Seven children, including Andy, were born to this family in the early 1900s in this area.

---

[81] *US federal census, 1940*

Andy's wife, Olive Alice (Dutton) Davidson was born in Numa, Iowa, in 1879, but moved to Maple Hills, Kansas, where she received her early education and became a teacher. Olive taught school for three years in Kansas until she contracted tuberculosis (TB) from her students. When her brother, Frank Dutton, caught the disease from her, they moved to a home for TB patients in Colorado Springs. After their money ran out, Frank moved to Baggs, Wyoming, and lived with an uncle.

Olive met Andy Davidson in Baggs, and they were married January 1, 1903. They lived there with their family and she home-schooled her children. When it was time in 1924 for their children to go to high school, Olive and the younger children, Velma, Winnie, and Nettie, moved to Grand Valley, since there was not a high school in Baggs. After Andy and his son Bob lost their home in Baggs to a fire, they moved to Grand Valley and rented a farm from Ed Koch. Bob Davidson bought a small farm from Blanche Sandstrom in 1944 on Parachute Creek and built a house at this site.

Olive, Andy, and their son Bob adopted twin daughters in 1939-1940. They were only a few months old at the time. Bob's sister Nita had died, leaving them with their father who was unable to raise them. The Davidsons raised these two joyful and beautiful girls, Sherrill and Sharon Davis. The girls attended Grand Valley schools. Sherrill married Art Powell in 1955, but the marriage lasted only five years or so. Her sister Sharon graduated from Grand Valley High School in 1957 and married Bob Dillon one year later. She died from liver cancer in 1962 at the age of twenty-three. Sherrill worked at a variety of jobs over the years while raising five children alone. Sherrill returned to the Western Slope after some twenty years in New Mexico and married Jimmy La Donne of Rifle. He died two years later in 2000. Sherrill is retired and lives in Clifton.

CHARLES LEWIS FAMILY | #32

Charles Sydney Lewis, the father of Charles Irving and Willard Lewis, was an early resident of Parachute Creek. He was born in Wisconsin May 28, 1870, and died May 6, 1903, of malaria. He was a farmer most of his life. His wife Nettie (Fogel), was born in 1870 and died in 1917. Both parents were residents of Wisconsin. After Charles Sydney died, Nettie moved to a warmer climate—thought to be Missouri—for the benefit of her son Charles Irving's health. After a few years, they moved from Missouri to Colorado.

The two sons, Willard Lewis and Charles Irving, lived on Parachute Creek most of their lives. Charles Irving was born March 11, 1898, in Allen's Grove, Wisconsin. He married Alice May Johnson on December 9, 1924, in Rifle. Alice was born on December 9, 1905, in Littleton. Her parents were Fred A. Johnson and Jennie Johnson of Delta, Colorado. Following the marriage of Charles and Alice Lewis, they moved to the Big House on the original Glover ranch, known in 1927 as the Benton Place. The ranch included the lower portions of Starkey Gulch and the Bruckner Place. Charles's wife,

Charles Irving Lewis family ca. 1940. L to R back row: Albert, Charles Irving holding Ethel, and Charles; front row: Ella, Anna, and Glen.

Governor John C. Vivian visited the Book Cliff School in 1944. L to R, Glen and Ella Lewis, Governor Vivian, Mrs. Lewis (teacher – no relation to Lewis family), Anna Lewis, Mike Arnold, Gary Fender, and Charles "Sharky" Jensen.

Alice May, died July 21, 1978, in Grand Junction, Colorado and is buried at the Battlement Mesa Cemetery. Charles died from injuries received from a falling tree on February 6, 1951, and is also buried in the Battlement Mesa Cemetery.

Charles Irving's brother Willard was an irrigator and worked for many ranches on Parachute Creek over the years. He never married, and when he retired, he moved into the town of Parachute. Willard died July 29, 1959, a few years after his brother had passed away.

Charles Irving and Alice Lewis had seven children who are identified as follows.

The oldest child was Charles Irving Lewis Jr. born in 1926 in Vernal, Utah, but moved with his family to Parachute when he was six months old. Charles Jr. attended Grand Valley High School but left early to help his father on the farm. He worked as a farmhand and farmed several ranches over the years, but he still remained close to Parachute Creek. He managed property on the upper portion of Parachute Creek and helped others in his later years. When the ranch was sold to the Union Oil and Gas Company of California, Charles Jr. moved up the creek to the old May and Hack Ferris home and ranch. The original house had burned, so Charles Jr. moved into a relatively new log home that had been built by Red Walters in 1947. Charles had his primary residence

Charles Irving Lewis family 1996. L to R, Ethel, Ella, Albert, Anna May, Glen, and Charles.

on Parachute Creek for some eighty-six years, but moved to an assisted living facility in Battlement Mesa in 2013. He passed away in March of 2015.

Albert Wayne Lewis was born in 1928 in the Big House. He graduated from Grand Valley High School and spent the greater part of his life as a mechanic. He worked in California but spent most of his life in Oregon. Albert died in 2012 at the age of eighty-four in Idaho Falls, Idaho.

Anna May (Lewis) Wiltsey was born in the Big House in 1930 and graduated from Grand Valley High School in 1948. She then graduated from nursing training. She lives in Clifton.

Glen Andrew Lewis was born 1933 in the Glover Cabin. He attended the Book Cliff School and graduated from Grand Valley High School in 1952. He worked for the mine at Gilman, Colorado, and was trained in heavy equipment operation. He was a large equipment operator and worked for

Hinsdale County and various construction companies. Glen had a stroke in 2013 and spent several months in a home before passing away on January 3, 2014.

Ella Marie (Lewis) Hedrick was born in 1934 in the Glover Cabin. She attended the Book Cliff School and graduated from Grand Valley High School. Following high school, Ella married Duane Hittle in 1954, but they later divorced. She then married George Hedrick who worked for the police department in Gunnison. While there, she was the secretary for the local gas company. They moved back to the Grand Valley/Rulison area in 1996, and George passed away in 2011. Ella has been the primary source of information, providing the photos for this family and was able to describe the early history of the Glover Cabin.

Charles Irving Lewis Sr. farmed the Starkey Gulch area until it was sold to Mary Bailey. The family then moved to Battlement Mesa in the mid-1930s where Thad Bailey employed Charles Sr. for several years. In 1938, the Lewis family moved back to the farm on Parachute Creek and into the Big House. The children then could walk to the Book Cliff School, a distance of two miles. The school districts consolidated in 1947, and from that date on all children were bused to Grand Valley schools. The last living child of Charles Irving Sr. and Mary was Ethel Jane (Lewis) Gardner. She was born March 23, 1938, on Battlement Mesa while her family lived there. The family moved to Parachute Creek, and she attended the Book Cliff School followed by Grand Valley High School. She married Fred Gardner who is now deceased. Ethel now lives in Parachute.

Edward Loren Lewis was born on December 4, 1949 in Glenwood Springs but lived only two days.

Siblings Charles Lewis Jr., 88, and Ella (Lewis) Hedrick, 80, in summer 2014.

THE BRUCKNER FAMILY | #28

Samuel Fredrick Bruckner was born October 18, 1867, in New Chester, Wisconsin. He was thirty-two years old when he married Hannah Elmira Beals on March 30, 1900, in New Chester. Hannah was born July 26, 1883, in Turquoise, South Dakota. They had four children, all born on the farm in Wisconsin. The children are as follows: Helen Ann (Bruckner) Warp, 1901; Fredrick "Fred," 1903; Samuel "Floyd," 1905; and Arle Harry Bruckner, 1907.

Samuel and Hannah were divorced in 1910 and Samuel never remarried. In 1919, he sold his Wisconsin farm and moved to Briggsdale,

L to R, back row: Samuel "Floyd" Bruckner, Maude (Bumgardner) Bruckner, Samuel Fredrick Bruckner; front row: Floyd and Maude's children Edsel, John, and Eyer.

Colorado, with his three sons. Helen stayed in Nebraska with her mother and stepfather until she remarried in 1919. Samuel was not a successful dry land farmer, so he moved to western Colorado and homesteaded in the Piceance Creek Basin in 1920. Shortly thereafter he moved to Parachute. He died in 1944 in Glenwood Springs and is buried in the Russey-Hurlburt Cemetery in Parachute.

Floyd Bruckner worked with his father on the Piceance Creek farm for a short while and returned to Grand Valley where his older brother Fred was located. He worked for room and board that first winter. He was a happy-go-lucky person in his early teens and twenties. George Kerlee called him the "Happy Hooligan." Floyd worked for a number of ranchers on Parachute Creek, including Harry Hansen and Theo Gibbons. He also ran a grain thresher for Robert Nelson.

Floyd was always interested in mechanical items and especially in airplanes. He bought a Tommy Morse Scout airplane engine and started building his own airplane when he moved to Grand Valley. However, new regulations, the lack of money, illness, and the depression all kept him from finishing the plane. He even went to Love Field in Dallas, Texas, to learn how to fly and earned his pilot's license in November 1929.

The Bruckner and Bumgardner cousins are seen in 1938. L to R, back row: Joe, Jim, Floyd, Clarence, and Calvin Bumgardner; front row: Edsel Bruckner, Gene Bumgardner, and Eyer Bruckner.

While Floyd was working for John Wheeler, he met Maude L. Bumgardner, and they were married in the Methodist minister's home in Glenwood Springs, March 21, 1930, a few days after she turned eighteen. Floyd gave the minister a $5 gold piece for doing the wedding. Maude and Floyd had three children: Edsel, Eyer, and John. In 1933, with the help of his father Sam, Floyd built a house along the Parachute Creek road on what is believed to have been part of the Benton Farm. Their oldest son, Edsel, was born in 1931 and graduated from Grand Valley High School. He worked in construction for a number of years before he was killed in 1959 when he fell down a mineshaft in eastern Utah.

Eyer, born in 1935, also graduated from Grand Valley High School. Shortly after graduating, he joined the US Air Force in January of 1954, and this became his career for the next twenty years. Eyer married Betty Marlene Clarke, a Grand Valley native, June 5, 1958, and their son Paul was born the next year. Their daughter Mary Arlene was born in 1960, and nine years later, in 1969, Peggy Sue was born.

Eyer served at a variety of Air Force bases, including two years in Germany, one year in Korea, and one year in California, but most of his service time was on the East Coast. When he retired from the Air Force, Eyer and his family moved back to Parachute Creek on a farm one mile west of Grand Valley and farmed for several years. Following his stay in Parachute, the family decided to move to Missouri and raise quarter horses. Eyer and his family now live in Clifton, Colorado. Although retired, he continues to raise quarter horses.

John, the youngest son of the Floyd Bruckner family, was born in 1938 and attended Grand Valley High School until his junior year (ca. 1954) when he drowned in the Colorado River while swimming with companions.

In November 1945, Janice Bruckner, daughter of Floyd's brother Arle Bruckner and Rose Benton, came to live with Maude and Floyd, who wanted a girl in their family. She proved immensely helpful to the family and was a delight for everyone. Janice graduated from Grand Valley High School in 1951 and married John Anderson Jr. a career US Air Force airman. Janice died in 2011.

In 1958, Floyd worked for the Union Carbide Company, emptying uranium trucks hauling mining products (mined uranium materials) from Uravan, Colorado, to a vanadium plant in Rifle. He worked at the vanadium plant until 1965 when he became ill with lung cancer. Many in the area attributed the development of the cancer to the dust he inhaled while unloading the trucks carrying radioactive uranium ore.

In 1970, Floyd and Maude sold their home and farm on Parachute Creek and bought a home down in Parachute. Floyd died in 1977 from cancer and Maude died in 1998. They are both buried in the Russey-Hurlburt Cemetery. The Parachute Creek community recounts Maude as a memorable lady who was continually a help to her neighbors.

Maude (Bumgardner) Bruckner was 49 when this photo was taken in 1950.

RICHARD "DICK" HAYES FAMILY | #32

Dick Hayes was born in western Colorado on December 20, 1905, and lived until July 1975. He and his family lived about four miles up Parachute Creek, near the stream. At different times, they were also residents of De Beque. His father, Jim Hayes, was from Virginia, and his mother was from Colorado. They lived in Collbran, Colorado, for a time. Dick married Anna E. Barreith in 1929. He was twenty-four years old and she was sixteen years old at that time. Anna's parents, Fred and Aloisia Barreith, homesteaded on the mountain south of the Book Cliff School and above the valley near the top of Starkey Gulch.

Dick passed away in 1975 and Anna died in 1976. They are both buried in the De Beque Cemetery. Seven children were born to this marriage as follows: Richard Buryl, 1930;

Dick and Anna Hayes

Fred Orlanda, 1932; Henry Howard, 1936; Effie May, 1938; Margaret Marie, 1940; Julie Elizabeth 1942; and John William, 1945. Henry, Fred, Effie, and Julie are all retired and living in the Grand Junction area. Effie provided the photos and history of the Hayes family.

Dick was a farm laborer and sheep rancher. He raised sheep most of his life and spent many years herding them and taking care of other ranchers' sheep. He ran sheep with Orland Lindauer on the East Fork Range in the 1940s and 1950s. Dick was a quiet man and always willing to assist anyone in need of help. He was well known in the valley but spent most of his life in the mountains.

HARLAND "ARCH" SHERWOOD FAMILY | #27

Harland Archie Sherwood (called "Arch") was born at Republic City, Kansas, May 9, 1881. Mr. Sherwood spent his early life in Kansas and Oklahoma. He married Zula "Madge" Zediker March 5, 1902, at Wewoka, Oklahoma. She was born in Mapleton, Iowa, March 25, 1885, and moved with her parents to Oklahoma, where she met her future husband, Arch.

In the early 1900s they traveled for several months by covered wagon headed for Colorado, where Madge's parents were located. Their oldest son, Martel, was on horseback at the age of seven or eight driving the family's herd of cattle. The wagon was loaded down with all of the family's belongings plus

Harland "Arch" Sherwood, right, is saddled up with fellow cowboys, L to R, Martel Sherwood, Reuben Nelson, and Marcus "Dee" Freeland Sr. to check their cattle on the Old Mountain in the Book Cliff Range.

a coop of chickens attached to the back. Also, on board were a one-year-old brother, Lester "Irish" Lloyd, born in 1910, and two very young sisters, Viola, born in 1907, and Emma, born in 1909.

They stopped in southeastern Colorado, where Arch was involved in farming for some ten years. After the Sherwood family arrived in Bent County near Lamar, Colorado, in 1911, they lived in a dugout for some time. Viola (Sherwood) Walters remembers her mother Madge telling her how she killed centipedes under candlelight as they made noises crawling along the rock walls, and later how a tornado sucked the roof off the newly built cabin and took all their belongings. To save her family, she placed the children and herself under a steel bed and they all survived. They ended up being very frightened yet thankful that no one was injured.

The family headed on to Grand Valley in 1923. Mr. Sherwood had purchased some property near the mouth of Wheeler Gulch west of Grand Valley. It was their desire to be closer to Madge's parents, the Zedikers, and they were hoping to be out of drought-stricken southern Colorado and the area that had tornados.

Arch and Madge had four children to whom they gave land and who became active citizens of the

Parachute community. Details of the children are reported below. Arch Sherwood died October 25, 1951. Zula Madge (Zediker) Sherwood had died a year earlier on December 24, 1950. Both are buried in the Russey-Hurlburt Cemetery in Parachute. The daughters, Viola and Emma, and their families are identified under the Walters and Stanton family headings.

MARTEL AND MAE SHERWOOD | #27

Archie Martel Sherwood was born in Rowden, Oklahoma, in 1904 and traveled with his parents to Colorado. After Martel's

Martel and Mae (Phillips) Sherwood at their ranch.

first marriage failed, he married Mae (Phillips) Sherwood in Green River, Utah, in 1933. Mae was born March 22, 1901, in Cherokee County, Missouri. She graduated from Columbus High School in 1918 and entered the university at Pittsburg, Kansas, working her way through and receiving her teacher certification. Mae taught business and typing at Clinton, Missouri; Granville, New Mexico; Thermopolis, Wyoming; and eventually in Grand Valley. There, she met her future husband, Martel. After they were married, Mae was not allowed to continue to teach until some years later when that rule changed. She and Martel had no children. Mae helped her husband with cattle and farming on Parachute Creek.

Mae (Phillips) Sherwood

When WWII broke out, she was asked to teach again. She continued teaching until retiring in New Castle in 1958. They grazed their livestock on the Old Mountain during the summer. With the help of neighbors Harry Hansen, Winfield Nelson, Dee Freeland, and a couple other cowboys, they built a cabin on the mountain where Martel spent a lot of time looking after the cattle in the summer. He bought the Benton Place during this time and hired Dan Stanton to irrigate, raise the crops, and feed the cattle in the winter.

During WWII, Reuben "Windy" Nelson, a neighbor and local rancher, entered the service, and Martel took care of his cattle until he returned as a wounded veteran. This helped Windy with a new head start in cattle ranching after he left the hospital.

Martel was a prominent rancher on Parachute Creek for many years. He sold his ranch to the gas companies in the late 1950s and moved to another ranch on Divide Creek near New Castle. He lived the life of a true cowboy, was always available to help neighbors in need, and was well thought of in the community.

Martel died in November 1965 in a farm accident. His good friend and helper Dan Stanton found him on the ranch where he had apparently gotten caught in the power takeoff of a tractor and machinery that he was using. Martel was a cowboy who loved music, dancing, and cattle, but hated farming—a necessary part of raising cattle in western Colorado. He is buried in the Russey-Hurlburt Cemetery in Parachute.

After Reuben "Windy" Nelson sold his ranch on Parachute Creek, he worked for other ranchers

Martel Sherwood takes a break with fellow cowboys.

Martel and Mae Sherwood's ranch home was at the mouth of Wheeler Gulch.

for several years. Following Martel's death, he quit his job and took care of Martel's new ranch and cattle until Mae could get everything sold.

Mae returned to Columbus, Missouri, a couple of years after losing her husband so she could be near her mother and sister. After their deaths, Mae lived alone for a number of years. On the advice of her doctor and her niece, at the age of 100, she moved to an assisted living home near her niece, Mrs. Pauline (Walters) Threlkeld, who would visit her and take her for long rides. Mae would recite from memory many poems that she had loved over the years during her rides. In later years, she became a great fan of pro wrestling and never missed a match on TV. She lived there until her death in 2005 at the age of 103.

Many thanks are extended to Pauline Threlkeld and to Marlene Trent for their help in gathering information on the Sherwoods, Walters, and the Hansens.[82] This historical report would probably not have been prepared and typed without the special typing instruction from Mae to the author in 1947 and 1948. The author, as well, roped calves during branding season for her husband Martel.

LESTER "IRISH" SHERWOOD | #27

Lester "Irish" Sherwood, the youngest of the Arch Sherwood family, was born July 3, 1910, in Woodward, Oklahoma, and came to Colorado with his family in a covered wagon when he was six months old. He attended school in Grand Valley and entered the Army in WWII. He served in the Quartermaster Corps with Company C, 77th Armored Medical Battalion. During his deployment, he observed much suffering that he could never block out of his mind and he often turned to liquor to help.

Irish was always interested in horses and loved to work with them. He had a string of horses that

---

[82] Oral report from daughters, Pauline Threlkeld and Marlene (Hansen) Trent, ca 2013.

were used on a dude ranch at Snowmass Creek. Billy Stanton, his nephew, worked with him and Billy's parents, Francis and Emma Stanton, cooking and helping with the base camp. Irish, Billy, and Arch were in a jeep accident on their way home from Aspen, and Billy was killed. His death drove Irish further into depression.

Irish, at the age of fifty-one, was found dead in the ruins of his residence that burned to the ground on February 8, 1962. County Corner Jack Farnum listed the cause of death as asphyxiation due to smoke inhalation. It is suspected that Irish fell asleep and his house caught on fire. Irish is buried in the Russey-Hurlburt Cemetery.

ROBERT "HARRY" HANSEN FAMILY | #26

Peter Hansen was born in 1864. He and his parents were natives of Germany. Peter had emigrated from Germany to Illinois in 1882. His wife Mary was born in Illinois in 1869. They were married in 1889. Peter and Mary had two children: Gertrude Caroline "Carrie," born in Colorado in 1890, and Robert "Harry," as he was often called, born in Westcliffe May 5, 1892.

Peter and his family moved from Illinois to Huerfano County, Colorado, in 1910 and then to Grand Valley in 1913 where they had purchased the Grant Mills/Frank DeWitt ranch at the mouth of Wheeler Gulch, some four miles up Parachute Creek. In the early days, Peter Hansen's cattle were sold to Eric Clubine of Piceance Creek and were trailed up Parachute Creek and over the mountains to Piceance Creek.

Following the deaths of Peter and Mary, their ranch was divided between their two children, Harry, who married Thelma Zediker, and Carrie (Hansen) Gibbons, who had married Theo Gibbons. The children and spouses maintained their ranch and lived in two separate homes a short distance from each other. Theo operated a modern, well-kept dairy of prime Holstein cows and maintained a beautiful orchard. In later years, Harry operated a beautiful herd of range cattle on their ranch along with his quality orchard.

Harry Hansen spent his early childhood and school years in Westcliffe. In 1902, he and his father moved to Grand Valley and in 1913 moved to the farm home on Parachute Creek. Harry served with the US Army under the command of General John "Black Jack" Pershing in World War I. He was thought to be the last of the early settlers in the Parachute area to have served in WW I. In his earlier years, Harry worked on digging assessment holes for various oil shale claims. The owners of the claims are required to show a certain amount of work on each claim in order

Robert "Harry" Hansen was a farmer and rancher much of his life.

Harry Hansen, right, and a member of the Wheeler family by the cabin at the top of Wheeler Gulch on the Old Mountain. The cabin was shared by the Bensons, Hansens, Freelands, and Nelsons.

to qualify the claim for patent and ownership. Harry spent most of his life as a rancher and farmer but worked away from the farm on many occasions. He worked with Bruce "Red" Walters and others as a carpenter at Camp Hale near Leadville during World War II.

Harry Hansen and Thelma Zediker were married on May 30, 1922, in Meeker. They had one daughter, Marlene, who married Robert Trent. Marlene and Robert had two daughters: Jokay Carmenati of Missouri and Jean Oakley of Idaho. Harry loved to walk each day to visit with his neighbors up and down the valley. As mentioned earlier, he would stop on his morning walk at the Paul Lindauer ranch one mile up Parachute Creek for coffee and to reminisce about the old days with Paul. During his last ten years, Harry lived with his daughter Marlene in Longmont, Colorado. He passed away on September 14, 1989, at the age of ninety-seven in Longmont and is buried in the Russey-Hurlburt Cemetery.

Thelma Zediker was the daughter of Thomas Jefferson Zediker and Lucretia (Alexander) Zediker. She was born on November 19, 1900, in Garber, Oklahoma. She came to Lamar, Colorado, with her parents in 1907, where she grew up and attended school. In 1919, the family moved to Grand Valley. Thelma attended nursing school in Pueblo and became a registered nurse in 1921. After she married Harry Hansen, they lived on Parachute Creek. Thelma followed her nursing career for a number of years and applied her skills to assist doctors and those of the community that needed her help. She passed away in the Rifle Claggett Hospital January 20, 1970, and is buried in the Russey-Hurlburt Cemetery.

GRANT V. MILLS FAMILY | #25

Grant V. Mills' parents were born in Ohio in 1869. His father was from New York and mother from Kentucky. His wife, Mary E. Mills, was born in Illinois in 1871. The dates of their arrival in Colorado and their marriage are unknown. Grant was a farmer, and he and Frank DeWitt were partners in a ranch known as the "Mile High Ranch" or the Grant Mills Ranch located at the mouth of Wheeler Gulch.

Grant and his wife raised a son, Lawrence, who was born in 1895 in Colorado. Grant is listed as living in Parachute in the 1910 federal census.[83] They also had two stepdaughters and two stepsons: Katherine McKinny, born in 1899; Emily, 1900; John, 1903; and Kenneth, 1907.

Coda Cline served as the hired man and was living with the Grant Mills family. He was born in 1889 and his wife, Stella (Cravens), in 1895. They had a daughter, Gladys, who was only two months old when the census was taken in 1910.[84]

Frank DeWitt had earlier built a big red barn on the ranch and a beautiful two-story house with an extensive apple orchard adjacent to the house. He had a feed-grinding operation within the barn that neighbors relied on for their needs. Frank Dewitt was an excellent painter and the ranch was kept in fine repair. Many tons of apples were shipped from the ranch over the years. This "Showcase Ranch" was sold to Peter Hansen in 1913 and he continued to raise apples along with his cattle operation.

In a 1940 census, Grant Mills was apparently retired and living in La Veta, Colorado.[85] He was identified as Virgil G. Mills, age seventy-three, and married to Mary E. Mills, seventy. They had one daughter living in their household whose name was Katherine McKinny, age forty-one.

---

[83] *US federal census, 1870-1940.*

[84] Ibid.

[85] Ibid.

THEODORE "THEO" GIBBONS FAMILY | #25

Theodore "Theo" Gibbons was born on June 6, 1886, in Denver. His wife, Gertrude Caroline "Carrie" Hansen, was also born in Colorado, in 1890. She was the daughter of Peter Hansen who had emigrated from Germany in 1882 and eventually moved to Colorado in the late 1890s. Theo was in the hardware business with his brother in La Veta before he moved in 1917 to a ranch in western Colorado. He met his future wife in La Veta and they were married on July 5, 1911. They established their home on Parachute Creek at the Mile High Ranch.

Three children resulted from the marriage of Theo and Carrie. William Ernest was born in 1913; Florence (Gibbons) Bleil was born July 17, 1920; and Harry Arthur "Sonny" was born January 17, 1927. All were born in Grand Valley.

Ernest Gibbons was one of the first airplane pilots in Grand Valley. He built a small landing strip on the Gibbons Ranch on Parachute Creek and another on Allen's property near the town of Grand Valley. He used these two sites for several years. Ernest worked in CCC camps during the early 1930s. He moved to California, where he was employed as a design engineer for Douglas Aircraft Corporation. He retired from this position and remained in California.

Florence Gibbons grew up on the ranch and attended the Book Cliff School for her elementary schooling. She then attended and graduated from Grand Valley High School in 1938. She married Marvin Bleil, whose career was in the US Air Force. Florence and Marvin retired from the Air Force and moved to Albuquerque for the remaining period of their life.

Harry "Sonny" grew up on the ranch and attended elementary school in Grand Valley. He graduated from Grand Valley High School in 1944. After graduation he was drafted into the US Army during World War II. Sonny served in Japan for several months and, following the end of the war, was discharged in 1946. He attended Mesa College for one year and earned his private pilot's license under the GI bill. In 1950, during the Korean conflict, Sonny re-enlisted as a reservist and was immediately inducted into the US Army Signal Corps. He was sent to Valdez, Alaska, for one year where his unit was building telephone lines across a remote area of the state. He married Charline Benson August 24, 1952, and they had two children: Scott and Chardelle. While the family was living in Denver, Sonny took his own life on May 9, 1962, at the age of thirty-five.

As the family grew, Theo Gibbons continued to operate the dairy and feed-grinding business as well as raising poultry. In later years he and Carrie moved to Grand Valley, where he operated a Texaco service station and a liquor store. Theo died on April 2, 1955.

EDWIN HILLIKER FAMILY | #33

The Hilliker Ranch and Cline Place were adjacent to and west of the DeWitt Ranch. Edwin Hilliker was the first depot agent in Parachute before buying the ranch. The family apparently came to Parachute from Kansas before 1890. Among their children were Gertrude, born 1879, and Adelbert "Bert," born 1884. They were among the first pupils at the Book Cliff School. Between 1910 and 1920 the Hillikers sold their ranch to Doc Wilson and moved to eastern Colorado. Details of the Hilliker Ranch are identified under several other landowners and in particular, Doc Wilson.

THEODORE (TED) MCQUISTON FAMILY | #26

Ted McQuiston was born September 10, 1910, in Indiana where he spent his early years. He left home at a young age and was a drifter for several years. He spent time in Missouri and eventually ended up as a ranch hand in eastern Colorado.

Ted married Nita Cummings in 1934. She was from Graham, Texas. Ted ranched in eastern Colorado for a few years and moved to Parachute Creek to the Zediker/Tucker ranch home and then on to the Harry Hansen home in 1951. They ranched there until 1955 when they moved to Grand Valley where Ted had bought the Texaco Station from Norman Payton. He rebuilt and operated the station until 1959, when he sold the station to Stanley McKay. He worked in construction for years, and after he retired he moved to Grand Junction and raised mules. He was very proud of the colts that he raised and was successful in selling them. The colts were the result of a cross between Caledonia Jack mules and quarter horse mares.

Ted and Nita raised five children, several of whom married individuals from Grand Valley.

Jody, the oldest, was born January 22, 1935, and married Jean Hillesland in 1961; he is retired and lives in Grand Junction. He owns a leather shop and does all types of custom leatherwork. He is excellent at putting zippers in cowboy boots for owners who do not buy boots large enough.

Richard was born in July 1937 and married Betty Allen, a nurse. Both she and Richard worked for Union Carbide in Uravan, Colorado. Then, Betty worked as a nurse in a variety of places including China, Ecuador, and the Veteran's Hospital in Grand Junction, from which she retired. Following this retirement she continued to work for an internal medicine office until retiring again. Richard retired and is now living in Nucla, Colorado.

Louise was born in August of 1938 and married Joe Waddell, who retired from the Bell Telephone Company.

Shirley, born in 1939, married George Allen in 1955. George was killed three years later in a truck/train accident.

William "Ted" Jr. was born in 1942 and married Janice Hutton from Rifle. He worked as a welder for the Grand Junction Steel Company and lives in Grand Junction.

HENRY F. STANTON FAMILY | #36

Henry F. Stanton, the patriarch of the Stanton family, came to the Grand Valley/Parachute area in April of 1914. Henry, the son of Harry and Martha Stanton, was born October 19, 1864, in the St. Clare Parish, Cornwall Province, England. He and his parents immigrated to America in 1865. They settled in New Jersey, and when Henry was twelve years old the family moved to Silver Plume, Colorado. Five years later, Henry moved to Hayden, Colorado, where he met and married Viola Bunker on October 2, 1890. Henry and Viola had eleven children. Much of the information on this family came from Vera (Stanton) Madden, of Rifle, a granddaughter of Henry F. Stanton.

Henry Stanton spent most of his life in the Grand Valley area, from 1914 until he died on January 9, 1935. His children, mentioned below, were born in other locations within Colorado.

The oldest child, Amy Selina, was born May 23, 1892, in Silver Plume and married John F. Severson in Glenwood Springs, August 25, 1910. She lived until September of 1941 and is thought to have spent most of her life in Collbran.

The next, child, Bessie Ellen, was born September 17, 1893. She married George H. Grainger. They lived in Maricopa County, Arizona, but spent some time on the West Coast between California and Oregon. Bessie passed away February 2, 1988, at the age of ninety-five. She is buried in Goshen, Indiana.

The third child, Henry Clements, was born in 1895, but lived only eighteen months. Two of the younger children of Henry and Martha spent some time on Parachute Creek; however, no additional information about them could be located.

Viola Mary Martha Stanton, born March 1, 1906, in Collbran, attended Grand Valley public schools. She married Frank Gardner in 1952, who was a cousin of Vern Gardner, a prominent citizen of the Parachute Creek and Grand Valley area. They were later divorced, and she married Melvin S. Larson on April 2, 1938, in Yuma, Arizona.

Clifford Marion Stanton was born on September 7, 1909, in Collbran, but attended school in the Grand Valley area. He married Mary Walters November 3, 1949, in Aztec, New Mexico, and apparently remained in that area.

GUY STANTON FAMILY | #36

Guy Stanton, a well-known cowboy and range rider for the East Fork Cattlemen and Rifle's Book Cliff Association was born January 29, 1897, in Hayden. He had lost the thumb on his right hand when he dallied a roped animal and caught his thumb between the rope and saddle horn. Many young cowboys were taught the correct way to dally from Guy's experience: to always keep their thumbs up when they wrap the rope around the saddle horn.

Guy married Ortha Robertson October 14, 1925, in Eagle. Guy and Ortha had two children: Roberta M. in 1926 and Phyllis in 1928. Guy spent much of his life as a range rider for the Rifle and Grand Valley livestock men. Guy died July 9, 1976, and is buried in Rifle.

Guy Stanton working as a range rider in the 1940s.

CLYDE STANTON | #36

Clyde was born in Steamboat Springs, Colorado, on November 2, 1898. He spent three years with his parents in Collbran before moving to Rifle and then on to Grand Valley in the spring of 1913. Clyde attended Grand Valley public schools and made the valley his home until his untimely death on July 24, 1932. He apparently had suffered an attack of typhoid fever, and as his condition grew worse he was moved to St. Mary's Hospital, where he failed to respond to treatment. Clyde Stanton never married and spent most of his adult life working in construction and in the oil shale industry. He is buried in the Russey-Hurlburt Cemetery in Parachute.

DANIEL STANTON FAMILY | #36

Daniel Benjamin "Dan" Stanton was born October 10, 1900, in Hayden. He moved with his family to a ranch on Parachute Creek in 1914. He attended Grand Valley public schools and graduated in 1921 according to school records.

Dan married Olive Cline October 13, 1934. (See details of Olive Stanton in Maud Bailey section). Dan and Olive divided their time between Los Angeles and Grand Valley for a number of years and raised four children as follows: Vera (Stanton) Madden who was born in 1935; Terry in 1936; Wayne in 1938; and Verna in 1943.

They returned to Grand Valley in 1946, where Dan served as town marshal and public works superintendent before moving to Rifle in 1960. The oldest, Vera (Stanton) Madden, was born in Grand Valley while the other children, Terry (Barnhill), Verna (Reed), and Wayne were born in California. They attended elementary school in California and in Grand Valley. Vera graduated in 1953 from Grand Valley High School.

Francis and Emma (Sherwood) Stanton

FRANCIS STANTON FAMILY | #23

Francis Stanton was born in Collbran July 11, 1902. He grew up on Parachute Creek and attended Grand Valley schools. He married Emma Sherwood on June 11, 1929, in Glenwood Springs soon after she had graduated from Grand Valley High School. A son, Billy, was born September 22, 1930, in Grand Valley. He attended Grand Valley schools and graduated in 1948.

Francis and his family lived on a small ten-acre tract located about four miles up Parachute Creek that Emma's father, Arch Sherwood, had given them. Arch had given his other daughter, Viola Walters, the adjacent ten acres. The Stantons and Walters were close families and did many things together over the years.

Francis spent most of his life on Parachute Creek, but moved to Arizona in later years when he and Emma retired. He worked as a ranch hand, in construction, and did other jobs including working for the oil shale industry in the Grand Valley area.

Emma died July 29, 1978, at the age of seventy. She spent most of her life as a housewife supporting her family. Francis died at the age of eighty-five, July 3, 1987, in Florence, Arizona. He had been living with his niece, Pauline (Walters) Threlkeld in Phoenix for three years prior to his death. Francis was a friend to everyone. His cremains are buried in the Russey-Hurlburt Cemetery, marked by a bench donated by his niece Pauline. Their son Billy was killed in an automobile (jeep) accident when he and his uncle Irish Sherwood were working as guides for a tourist/hunting outfit near Aspen, August 3, 1951.

FAY "BUCK" STANTON | #36

The last child of Henry and Martha Stanton, Fay Wayne "Buck" Stanton, was born February 11, 1912, in Rifle. Buck, as he was known in the community, moved with his parents to Grand Valley in 1914 and attended elementary school at the Book Cliff School on Parachute Creek, near where his parents lived. He then attended and graduated from Grand Valley High School.

During WWII, Buck served four years in the South Pacific and was awarded the Purple Heart for injuries received during the war. Following his service time, he returned to Grand Valley and established himself as a rancher in the community. He ran cattle on the East Fork allotment of the Book Cliff Range.

Buck purchased a ranch just east of the town of Grand Valley near the river. He never married. He passed away at the age of sixty on June 20, 1972, at his home. Jerry Satterfield, a local cowboy and rancher, had driven past his house near the Colorado River Bridge and noticed that his horse was still in his pickup truck. An hour later, when Jerry returned on the same road, he noticed again that Buck's horse was still in the pickup and thought something must be wrong. He stopped to investigate and found Buck dead on the ground next to his pickup. The Colorado Department of Health reported the cause of death as a coronary occlusion (heart attack). He apparently had just returned from checking on his forty to fifty head of cattle in the Book Cliff Mountains, where he had a grazing permit on the East Fork cattle allotment. He is buried in the Russey-Hurlburt Cemetery.

ROBERT NELSON FAMILY | #24

Robert Grant Nelson was born in Pennsylvania in 1885, and spent his first fifteen years in that state before going out on his own. He headed west at the age of fifteen with the intention of reaching California and settling there. He traveled through Meeker, Colorado, as a young man and met and married Anna Leona Reynolds. Anna was born in Kansas in 1886 and traveled to Meeker as a small child in a covered wagon. Her family settled in the Meeker Valley. For a few years after they were married, Robert worked in the local area. It is not known when Robert came to Meeker, but in 1918 he registered for the draft in Meeker at the age of thirty-three. Robert and Anna had three children: Mary Gertrude (Plowman), Reuben Winfield "Windy," 1919, and Sarah Kathleen (Ridgeway).

In the 1930 US Census, Robert and family were living in Rifle, Colorado.[86] He had moved his family from Meeker to Rifle to find work on ranches up Rifle Creek. From there the family moved to a farm about four miles up Parachute Creek.

Robert was a hard worker and could be seen from time to time running from one task to another to keep things going well. He ran a threshing machine and spent time during the summer months threshing wheat and other grains as needed for local ranchers and farmers throughout the Parachute Creek Valley.

Robert continued to ranch there until he retired and sold his ranch to his only son, Reuben "Windy" in 1948. He and his wife Anna moved to Grand Junction in 1948. He died in 1976 and was buried in the Reynolds Plot in Meeker. Leona died in Meeker in 1982 and is also buried in the Reynolds Plot in Meeker.

REUBEN "WINDY" NELSON FAMILY | #24

Reuben "Windy" Nelson attended Grand Valley public schools through the eighth grade. As a young man, he worked with his father on the Parachute Creek ranch. In February of 1942, he enlisted in First Cavalry Division, Second Squadron, 8th Cavalry Troop of the US Army and after basic training was sent to Brisbane, Australia, to learn how to fight in the jungle. According to Reuben, they spent more time fighting mosquitoes than anything else.

From Brisbane, they traveled to several islands and ended up in the Philippines. They never stopped, day or night. According to a report received from Gwen Stephenson, the director of Colorado Mountain College Senior Programs of Garfield County, Reuben was among the first American Troops in Manila. His squadron had raced 100 miles in sixty-six hours to be the first to enter Manila. On February 13, 1945, they were also the first group to reach Santo Tomas University to free 3,700 allied internees being held by the Japanese who had turned the University into a concentration camp.

---

[86] *US federal census, 1870-1940.*

Reuben noted that he was the second man through the gate and reported that he had "never been so scared in all of my life . . . There were Japanese Soldiers in windows and on the rooftops all around and they were pointing guns at us. I'll never know why they didn't attack us –but there were never any shots fired. We freed all of those international students who had been held by the Japanese for three years."

Stephenson's report notes that T.Sgt. Reuben Nelson continued to fight and was eventually shot in the left leg. Her report further quoted him:

That [gunshot] put me in a hospital tent in Manila for two months. From there, they sent me to Fitzsimmons Army Hospital in Denver—it took me two months to get there. To get ready for the trip, they wrapped me up in plaster of paris from my armpits to my toes—it was not very comfortable. At Fitzsimmons, they put me in traction and from there I went to rehab.[87]

Reuben "Windy" Nelson on horseback at the Sherwood Ranch.

Reuben received the Purple Heart for this injury and was honorably discharged from the army on February 13, 1946. He returned home to the family farm on Parachute Creek. He agrees that he is very fortunate to be alive and remembers and honors his friends who were not so fortunate.

On his return home, Reuben met Leila Ogden, daughter of Charlie Ogden, who was also ranching on Parachute Creek. After four months they decided to "tie the knot." The couple were married December 18, 1948. She was the only girl he ever dated.

In 1948, he and Leila bought the ranch from his parents and remained there for nine years until deciding to sell to the Union Oil Company of California in 1957. Reuben and Leila moved to Meeker with their family of three girls: Iva M. (Osburn); Ruby F. (Wolfe), deceased in 1996; and Dena G. (Thompson). Dena, now of Grand Junction, provided much of the information for the Nelson family.

In Meeker, Reuben worked as a hired hand for Harold Amick for two years. They lived there until 1959 when they went to Mesa, Colorado, where Reuben worked for his wife's aunt and uncle. In 1960, they moved to Rifle, where Reuben worked for Dick Gross on the old Hahnewald Place. In 1962, the family moved to Eagle, where Reuben worked for Homer Jackson on the Newcomer Homestead. He always wanted to buy another ranch but never did.

Wanting to provide more stability for his family, he quit ranching and moved to Gypsum, where he went to work for the US Forest Service. He retired in 1981 after sixteen years of service. Seeking a warmer

---

[87] Oral report by daughter, Dena G. (Nelson) Thompson, 2012, Grand Junction, CO.

climate, they moved to Hotchkiss and remained there until 1991 when they moved on to Grand Junction.

Leila Nelson died in 1993 and is buried in the Russey-Hurlburt Cemetery in Parachute. After her death, Reuben moved back to Rifle and later became a resident of Crossroads Assisted Living in Rifle, where he died October 27, 2012. He is buried with his wife in Parachute.

BRUCE "RED" WALTERS FAMILY | #22

Charles Bruce "Red" Walters was born in 1901 in the town of Moffat, Colorado. His father was Charles Wesley Walters, born in Weston, Ohio, June 23, 1861. His mother was Laura Bell Smith born October 7, 1875, in Friend, Nebraska. Charles and Laura Bell were married in Ridgeway, Colorado, on September 28, 1892. Charles worked as a telegrapher and they lived in many railroad towns including Lake City, Ridgeway, Ouray, Moffat, and Paonia.

Bruce Walters, "Red" as he was often called, had a beautiful head of red hair. He attended school through the eighth grade in many different railroad towns where his family lived. Bruce obtained his first job as a water boy at the Camp Bird Mine in Ouray at the age of twelve. As soon as he was old enough, he took a job with the railroad. There, he worked on a bridge building gang and learned the carpentry trade. As he traveled from job to job through several towns in Western Colorado, he came to Grand Valley, where he met his future wife, Minnie Viola Sherwood.

Viola was born in Seminole County, Oklahoma, Indian Territory in 1906. Her father, Harlan Archie Sherwood, and her mother, Zula Madge Zediker, were both from the Indian Territory. Her great-grandfather, TJ Zediker, and his sons were in the land rush for the Cherokee Strip and homesteaded there.

Bruce "Red" Walters ca. 1930s

Viola, along with her parents and her siblings Martel, Irish, and sister Emma (Stanton), left Oklahoma in 1911 and came to Colorado in a covered wagon. They settled near Lamar and lived in a dugout for some time. Viola, her mother, and her older brother Martel, both very young, learned to drive a six-horse team and do fieldwork. It was a difficult life, and they moved on in an effort to find a better living. They came to Grand Valley in 1923, where Viola entered school. However she was left-handed

Red and Viola (Sherwood) Walters built their first home on Parachute Creek.

and was punished in school for her poor writing; this experience became a lifelong problem. She may

Red, Viola and Pauline Waters.

have finished only the eighth grade.

Viola met her future husband, Bruce Red Walters, in Grand Valley, and they were married December 30, 1926, in Glenwood Springs. Harry and Thelma Hansen, lifelong friends and neighbors of Viola and Red, were the witnesses at their wedding.

Viola's father, Harlan Arch Sherwood, gave them a ten-acre parcel of land about four miles up Parachute Creek, where they built a two-room cabin and planted a grape vineyard. Red and Viola continued to move wherever the railroad sent them for some time. After a few years, they set up housekeeping in their small cabin. A major flood came down Wheeler Gulch and scattered rocks all over their property. After the rocks were picked up and rock fences built, Red began carpenter work in the valley. During WWII, he worked as a carpenter, building barracks and other work at Camp Hale on Tennessee Pass, a military base located about five miles southeast of Redcliff, Colorado. Harry Hansen and Charlie Benson also worked with him.

Their only child, Pauline (Walters) Threlkeld, born February 20, 1940, now lives in Phoenix, Arizona. She remembers living in a one-room cabin that Red had built in Minturn. Following this project, they returned to Parachute Creek and, with the help of Harry Hansen, built a beautiful new home on their property that had been increased in size by another ten-plus acres.

Red Walters was an excellent carpenter who built or rebuilt many houses in the area. He also worked for the Bureau of Mines, building houses at the new government camp called Anvil Points. During this time, he stocked his small farm with milk cows, chickens, pigs, and horses to work and ride. He made a small tractor from an old vehicle that he had used to pull a trailer for water. This vehicle had to be hauled from town.

Red died February 10, 1958, at the age of fifty-seven from a brain tumor that had eventually caused disfiguration of his facial features. He is buried in Rifle. Viola died on July 29, 1978, and is buried in Mesa, Arizona.

DAVID HOFFMAN FAMILY | #20

David J. Hoffman was born in Michigan and had come to Leadville in 1887, apparently searching for his fortune in the gold and silver rush. He was listed as a miner in the 1880 US Census for Summit County.[88]

David was a GAR veteran who moved from Leadville to Parachute. He located on what was later called the Zediker/Tucker Farm about three miles up Parachute Creek. He opened and operated a feed and secondhand store in the town of Parachute. However, he is listed in the 1900 US Census as being a farmer at the age of 61.[89]

Sarah and David Hoffman married later in life. They had only been married thirteen years when she died in July of 1904. No additional information could be found on the Hoffmans that was signif-

---

[88] *US federal census, 1870-1940.*

[89] Ibid.

In this ca. 1910 photo, Bailey family members include, L to R, back row: Maud, Pearl, Martha (mother), Olive, and LaVern; front row: George, Earl, Thomas (father), Iva, and Daniel "Bivian."

icant to their life on Parachute Creek other than providing store goods for the locals.[90] In 1911 at the age of 72, David was admitted to the US National Homes for Disabled Volunteer Soldiers in Sawtelle, California.

THOMAS EWING BAILEY FAMILY | #19

Thomas Ewing Bailey was born on March 15, 1861, in Columbus, Ohio, and married Martha Alice Jessup, who was born August 23, 1863, in Vincennes, Indiana. Tom and Alice, as they were called, were married September 23, 1883, in Phillipsburg, Kansas.

The young couple traveled by covered wagon in 1887 to Iowa. They moved on, staying for a short time in the Piceance Creek area. They moved again to Kansas, Cripple Creek, Meeker, New Castle, and finally to Parachute in 1898. They had a wonderful family of eight children: Maud, Pearl, Olive, George, Bivian, Earl, Lavern, and Iva.

Tom filed a homestead entry on property that included Hanging Lake near Glenwood Springs. He also bought ranch property several miles up Parachute Creek. When the Federal Act of 1910 was passed, allowing cities to purchase federal lands for use as city parks, the city of Glenwood Springs won the right to apply for purchase of these lands and bought them for a city park. Tom and Alice lost the Hanging Lake property. When he moved to his farm on Parachute Creek, he developed a

---

[90] Ibid.

beautiful orchard, which was known for the best-flavored peaches in the state.

In the late 1890s, Tom rented the Tanney Mercantile Store and purchased its stock in Parachute. The building was located across the street from the stockyards. He operated the store for several years before building a new store in 1902 on the corner of First Street and Parachute Avenue. This building later housed one of the first drug stores in the town of Parachute.[91]

Tom developed an early interest in oil shale and was one of the first to build a retort on the West Fork of Parachute Creek. It extracted the kerogen (a complex petroleum product) from oil shale, the "rubber rock," as it was first called, since it had many characteristics of rubber. He sent a sample of the mineral rubber to a Chicago chemist who reported "it was like nothing he had ever seen before." Tom thought it was anthracite coal.

The publicity of this adventure brought many new people to the Parachute Creek area, and the promise of oil and the associated riches from the shale created a great interest in filing claims on unclaimed lands. By the year 1928, there were some 50,000 acres of claims (160 acres each) filed within the county and state and an additional 12,000 acres unpatented in the district. In the spring of 1890, the Parachute Mining District was formed, and Tom was a charter member of the organization. He was active with this organization for many years, first as secretary, then as vice-president from 1890 until 1926. He was elected president from that date until no future oil shale development plans were made. Tom's son, Thomas Earl, helped him with this effort and maintained the historical documents for years. A copy of the minutes of the final meeting on April 19, 1935, was filed with the Garfield County Clerk and Recorder's Office.[92]

Most of Tom and Alice's eight children remained in Parachute with four graduating from Grand Valley High School. Alice died on April 13, 1940, and is buried in the Battlement Mesa Cemetery in Parachute. Tom died July 11, 1940, at the age of seventy-nine and is also buried in Battlement Mesa Cemetery. The children of Thomas and Alice Bailey follow:

MAUD (BAILEY) CLINE FAMILY | #17

Maud Alice Bailey was born in Phillipsburg, Kansas, in 1884. After her family moved to western Colorado, she attended and graduated from the Grand Valley schools. Maud married Tom Cline in 1912 (both were twenty-seven years of age) in the town of Grand Valley. Tom's parents were from Virginia but he was born in Colorado. Details of Tom Cline may be found under the John Wesley Cline Family section.

Tom and Maud (Bailey) Cline with children Erward and Olive.

Maud taught school in the Parachute area for many years. She passed away in August of 1981, at the age of ninety-six, and is buried in Glenwood Springs. Their daughter Olive attended school in Grand Valley and was the class valedictorian when she graduated in 1932. She married Dan Stanton on October 13, 1934,

---

[91] Murray. *Lest We Forget*. 1973.

[92] Ibid.

and they raised four children: Vera, 1935; Teresa "Terry," 1936; Wayne, 1938; and Verna, 1943. Olive worked for a number of years at the Rifle E. D. Moore Nursing Home. She died January 14, 2011.

Maud and Tom's son, Erward Cline, also attended Grand Valley schools, and married Opal Downen in 1939. They had two children: Larry Leon, January 28, 1940; and Donald Dean, November 8, 1942. Erward was working for the Agricultural Stabilization and Conservation Service when he was killed in an automobile accident February 12, 1972. He is buried in the Rosebud Cemetery in Glenwood Springs.

EMMA "PEARL" (BAILEY) ANDERSON | #3

Pearl, as she was known, was born October 3, 1886, in Kansas. She moved with her parents to Parachute and married Benjamin Anderson in 1911. Ben was a barber in Parachute for some fifty years. He was the brother of Thelma H. Anderson, who later married Thomas Earl Bailey. Pearl and Ben had no children. Pearl was an invalid for twenty-five years before her death in 1944 at the age of fifty-eight. Ben was devoted to her. She and Ben are both buried in the Russey-Hurlburt Cemetery.

DANIEL "BIVIAN" BAILEY FAMILY | #3

Daniel "Bivian" Bailey, called Bivian, was born in 1888 and married Margaret Watson. They had one son, Robert. Bivian and his brother George Bailey both enlisted to serve in WWI. Robert Bailey never married. He was identified in the 1920 federal census as a farmer at the age of thirty-one living in Grand Valley.[93] No other information was available.

OLIVE (BAILEY) SHOULTS FAMILY | #3

Olive was born in November 4, 1890, in Kansas and grew up in Parachute. She was one of two students in the first graduating class from Grand Valley High School in 1912. The other was Gladys Patterson. At the age of twenty-nine she married James A. Shoults. By 1930, they had four children and were living in Guernsey, Wyoming.

GEORGE BAILEY | #3

George was born February 21, 1893, on Piceance Creek, Garfield County, and enlisted in the Army on June 5, 1917. He was one of the first victims of the Spanish influenza, dying February 1, 1918, at Fort Riley, Kansas.

EARL BAILEY FAMILY | #3

Thomas Earl Bailey was born in Colorado in 1898 and married Thelma Anderson, who came with her family from Iowa. They were married in 1918 and lived about three miles up Parachute Creek. Earl moved his family into the town of Grand Valley in the late 1930s and worked as a carpenter for many years in the Grand Valley area.

From this marriage, six children were born, and all were raised in the

Earl and Thelma (Anderson) Bailey, ca. 1920s.

---

[93] *US federal census, 1870-1940.*

Parachute area. Donald Burdette was born in 1921 and attended Grand Valley public schools. Bertha (Lindstrom) was born in 1920 and graduated from Grand Valley High School in 1938. Betty (Arnold) was born in 1921 and graduated in 1939. Thelma Mildred (Richardson) was born in 1925 and attended Grand Valley schools. George Wilbur was born in 1927 and graduated in 1945. Wilbur died in February 1969 as a result of a car accident. Ruth Marie (Cutter- Roberts) was born in 1932 and graduated from Grand Valley High School in 1950. Ruth worked in the superintendent's office of the Grand Valley schools, District 16, from 1983 until 1998. She now resides in Denver. Her husband Joe passed away in the spring of 2015.

Earl and Thelma Bailey spent most of their lives in Grand Valley. Thelma died August 20, 1977, and Earl died November 1, 1992. They are both buried in Rifle.

IVA (BAILEY) WETZEL FAMILY | #3

Iva I. Bailey was born in Parachute in 1902 and spent her early childhood in this community. There is a photo in *Lest We Forget*[94] of her being held by her father T. E. Bailey in front of the family store, along with three of her sisters. Iva was married to Joseph E. Wetzel January 3, 1920, and they moved to San Diego, California. They had one child whose name was Rheo. Her husband died in 1967 and Iva (Bailey) Wetzel died on February 2, 1988, in San Diego.

LaVern and Frances (Zediker) Bailey

LAVERN BAILEY FAMILY | #19, 21

LaVern Bailey was the youngest child of Thomas E. and Martha Alice Bailey. He was born on January 20, 1904, in the town of Parachute and was a brother to Earl. He attended schools there and married Frances Zediker, born in 1911. She died August 1959.

LaVern and Frances lived on the south side of Parachute Creek some four miles up and across the creek next to the Mount Callahan Foothills on the north side and adjacent to the Nelson property. They moved after a short time across the valley into the vicinity of the Zediker Place. Beech Zediker had given LaVern and Frances a ten-acre parcel located next to their property and east of the Walters' property. The couple built a small house and remained there for some time before moving into the Zediker home. Later, LaVern and Frances moved into the town of Grand Valley.

LaVern and Frances had one daughter, Joy, born 1928 while the family lived on the south side of Parachute Creek. Joy attended Grand Valley schools while the family lived near the Zediker place. She remembers walking some three miles to school when she was very young. Upon graduating from high school in 1946, Joy married Jack Stone. Joy passed away July 30, 2012, in a Grand Junction nursing home.

EARL STONE FAMILY

Earl Stone was from Oklahoma and his wife Rosa (Willhite) Stone was from Arkansas. They came

---

[94] Murray. *Lest We Forget. 1973.*

to Parachute in 1941 from Kim, Colorado. Following Earl and Rosa's stay on the Patterson Farm, they moved to the Lenhart farm one mile northwest of Grand Valley on Parachute Creek. They bought this small farm with a sizeable apple orchard from Mr. and Mrs. Rookstool. They lived there for a couple of years before moving to a ranch on the Colorado River floodplain about two miles south of the town of Grand Valley.

There were five children in the Earl Stone family. Theo, the oldest, married Shirley Kemper. Shirley was a sister of Mona Gardner, whose husband, Albert, had rented the Nelson ranch property on Parachute Creek along with other acreages that the gas companies had purchased. Albert farmed these properties for a number of years and summered his cattle on permits located on the adjacent mountains.

The next two daughters were Thelma and Audrey. Thelma married Lloyd Thompson, a heavy equipment operator, one of the best and one of a few who was adept at building roads on the steep shale mountains of the Parachute Creek Valley. Audrey married Earl Moore, and they raised their family on Battlement Mesa. After their children graduated from high school in Grand Valley, they moved to Oregon with their children, but did return to Grand Valley for special reunions.

Jack Stone, the second son of Earl and Rosa Stone, married Joy Bailey, daughter of LaVern and Frances Bailey. Jack was born January 26, 1923, and came to the Grand Valley area in 1941. He lived for a while with his parents on the Patterson farm where they raised chickens, pigs, and fruit. They also had a miniature dairy. In 1942, Jack entered the US Navy and served in the Pacific Theater during WWII. He was discharged in 1946 and returned to Grand Valley. After Jack and Joy were married, they lived on the Zediker place for several years. From there they moved into Grand Valley, where they lived for another three years before moving to Grand Junction. Jack worked on various construction jobs before becoming employed with the Mountain Bell Telephone Company, from which he retired after thirty years. While living in a retirement home in Grand Junction, Jack provided information on his family and the time he had spent on Parachute Creek.

The last child was Betty Sue who, upon graduating from Grand Valley High School, married Lyman Van Horn. He owned the Island Ranch at the mouth of Parachute Creek. This ranch was later sold to Paul Lindauer. After the ranch was sold, Lyman and Betty Sue moved to Los Angeles, California, and remained there until they passed away.

JOHN WESLEY CLINE FAMILY | #17

John Wesley Cline was born in Virginia in September of 1841. His father and mother were born in West Virginia. John grew up in West Virginia where he met his future wife, Sarah E. Benedum. Her parents were William Benedum and Catharine Winters.

John and Sarah were married February 18, 1875, in West Virginia. In 1880 they had one child named Myrtle and were living in Grant, West Virginia. Myrtle died that same year near Leadville, Colorado. The family came farther west to Parachute in 1884, where they homesteaded. The 1900 Parachute Creek Census identified four living children: Willie M., born in 1883; Thomas Edison, 1886; Coda, 1889; and John, 1891.[95] A baby named Frank was born in 1884; however, he and another infant both died soon after their birth from scarlet fever. The second infant was the son of Mrs. Marx (no first name was found). Both ladies were early pioneers of Parachute Creek and were friends. The two ladies became pregnant at the same time and had named their recently born boys with the same name, "Frank." With their loss and no cemetery available at that time, the infants were buried

---

[95] *US federal census, 1870-1940.*

Tom Cline at the west end of Grand Valley in May 1942.

on the banks of Parachute Creek. Their tiny caskets were soon washed away in the spring runoff and never recovered.[96]

John Wesley Cline died December 8, 1906, and was buried in the Russey-Hurlburt Cemetery. His wife Sarah later married James Wheeler, who had lost his wife in 1916.

Willie Cline married Charlie Haley and they had two daughters: Alice, born in 1901; and Ida, born in 1905. Willie moved to the Los Angeles area and lived there until she passed away April 6, 1955, after a short illness. Charlie was a prominent figure around Parachute during the 1940s and 1950s, but additional information on his passing could not be found.

John Henry Cline was listed as head of household and a farmer in the 1910 Grand Valley Census. In 1920, John was living with his sister and brother-in-law Willie and Charles Haley in Grand Junction and later at Rio Blanco in 1930. He appears to have gone wherever there was ranch work. He never married and died in Grand Junction in June 1972.

TOM AND CODA CLINE (BROTHERS) AND FAMILIES | #17

Thomas Edison Cline attended elementary school at the Book Cliff School and lived most of his life in the Grand Valley area as a rancher and farmer. He married a local girl, Maud Bailey, in 1912

---

[96] Ibid.

and they lived on Parachute Creek for many years, taking up a homestead on Mt. Callahan. They had two children: Olive and Erward. The family moved to the Tomlin Place on the edge of Grand Valley, leaving there around 1953. John played the violin for many dances in the area. (See more under Maud Bailey).

Coda Cline spent his life working for other farmers and ranchers. In the 1910 census he was shown living at the Grant Mills Ranch on Parachute Creek where he was the hired man.[97] Fifteen-year-old Stella (Cravens), his wife, was a servant and they had baby Gladys, who was only two months old when the census was taken. He and Stella had five children: Gladys, 1910; Wilbur, 1912 (died at 22 days); Vera, 1913 (died at 3 months); Edna, 1914; and Robert, 1916. Coda was a great banjo player and, along with his brother John, played for many area dances in the early 1900s. He and Stella separated and Coda moved to the Meeker area for some years. He died in Parachute in March 1960.

TJ ZEDIKER FAMILY | #20

Thomas Jefferson "TJ" Zediker was born in Bellevue, Iowa, on May 12, 1856. He apparently grew up in that area and married Lucretia Alexander on November 25, 1880, in Spragueville, Iowa. TJ was a retired teacher and made the "run for land" when the Cherokee Strip in western Oklahoma was opened for homesteading September 16, 1893. He ran with Judge Garber, who founded the town of Garber, Oklahoma.[98]

Eleven children resulted from the marriage of TJ and Lucretia, of which nine survived into adulthood: Reil H., born in 1882; Earl, 1883; Zula Madge, 1885; Glen, 1887; Allen, 1889; Florence, 1891; Edna, 1893; Genevieve, 1895; and Ida, 1897. The last two children were born in Oklahoma where the family had moved in the mid-1890s. Most of the children grew up in Iowa.

TJ and his family had moved to Bent-Prowers County in eastern Colorado by 1910 and stayed there for some ten years. In the early 1920s, they moved on to Parachute where some of their family had settled. TJ leased the Benton/Glover place where he raised large crops of apples and used irrigation to grow crops. He was through with dryland farming and had a reputation as a successful farmer. Some of the family, the Sherwoods, had also been dryland farmers in Bent and Prowers counties in southeastern Colorado before moving on to the Western Slope of Colorado. They all became long-time residents of Parachute Creek.

Reil H. Zediker apparently stayed in Bent County when the family came to Parachute Creek. He married Beulah and had two children: Eva and Clyde. Between 1930 and 1940, however, he moved to Grand Valley where he managed the creamery. He could be seen pushing his two-wheeled cart to and from the depot every day, meeting the trains. He later moved to Grand Junction where he died in 1982.

Zula Madge Zediker was TJ and Lucretia's third child. Zula married Arch Sherwood October 5, 1905, in Oklahoma. This marriage resulted in four children who traveled with their teams, wagon, and livestock to southeastern Colorado where they lived on a dryland farm for several years before moving to Parachute. The four Sherwood children were Martel, Viola Walters, Emma Stanton, and Lester "Irish." All four are identified in other sections of this document. They were prominent citizens of the Grand Valley/Parachute Creek area for most of their lives (See Sherwood section).

---

[97] Ibid.
[98] Murray. *Lest We Forget*. 1973.

WILLIAM GLEN "BEECH" ZEDIKER & FAMILY | #20

William Glen Zediker, "Beech" as he was called, was the fourth child of TJ and Lucretia Zediker. He was born January 14, 1887, in Iowa. He moved with his parents to Oklahoma and then to southeastern Colorado and married Alpha Sloan on February 7, 1907, in Shawnee, Oklahoma. Beech Zediker and Arch Sherwood were friends in Oklahoma and each traveled to southern Colorado and several years later on to western Colorado.

Beech followed his parents to Parachute where he opened a butcher shop that he operated for several years. Beech later bought the property known as the Hoffman place, about three miles up Parachute Creek, where they lived for years.[99] This place became known in later years as the Zediker place. The family settled into a nice home adjacent to the county road. Alpha and Beech had four children: Frances (Bailey), Allen Lloyd, Madge (Valentine), and Alvin (who later committed suicide).

Frances (Zediker) Bailey was the oldest child of Beech and Alpha. She was born in 1911 and married LaVern Bailey in the mid-1920s. They lived on Parachute Creek about four miles west of Parachute and at different times on both the south and the north sides of the Parachute Creek (See Bailey section). Their only child was Joy (Bailey) Stone who is discussed earlier in this document. Frances passed away at the age of forty-eight, August 13, 1959.

Allen "Lloyd" Zediker, known as Lloyd, was born April 16, 1919, in Lamar and came with his parents to Parachute when he was one year old. Lloyd grew up on Parachute Creek, graduated from Grand Valley High School in 1937, and attended Mesa College. He farmed with his father for a while and enlisted in the US Army on March 25, 1942, for the duration of WWII. During his time in the service, Lloyd received a battlefield commission in the European Theater. He served in the 36th Cavalry and was discharged as a 1st Lieutenant. Following his discharge from military service, Lloyd continued as a cattle rancher and real estate broker in the community of Grand Valley. In 1952, Lloyd married Marie Surette, a teacher at Grand Valley High School, and they lived on the Parachute Creek Ranch known later as the Ogden Ranch. They had two children: Glen and Diane. Lloyd died in 1968 of a heart attack at the age of forty-eight while attending a basketball game in Grand Valley (Parachute) and is buried in the Russey-Hurlburt Cemetery.

Iola "Madge" (Zediker) Valentine was the third child of Beech and Alpha. She was born on May 5, 1921, and grew up in the Parachute Creek area. She attended Grand Valley High School in the late 1930s. Madge joined the US Army and married LC Valentine while serving in the Army. They were later divorced. Following Madge's discharge from the Army, she returned to Parachute Creek and worked at the Grand Valley Drug Store in the 1940s and 1950s. She also worked for the US Government at Anvil Points on their oil shale project and was later transferred to Salida where she worked for the Bureau of Land Management as a supply clerk for twenty-two years. She retired from this job and lived the remaining years of her life in Salida. Madge passed away August 4, 2004, and is buried in the Russey-Hurlburt Cemetery in Parachute.

THE CHESTER ARTHUR "ART" PAYTON FAMILY | #17

Chester Arthur Payton, known as Arthur, was born in 1885 in Norton, Kansas, and grew up working on family farms. In 1900, his family moved to Minturn, Colorado. He worked on a variety of farms between Minturn and Kansas but spent most of his time in Kansas where he met Mabel Rasmussen/Peak in 1919. They were married in December of that year.

---

[99] Ibid.

Mabel Catherine Rasmussen was born in Red Feather, Nebraska, in a "soddy" in 1890. Her mother Mary died, apparently from an asthma attack, when Mabel was three years old. Her father, George Rasmussen, knew he could not raise their four children, so the two older children were taken in by a neighbor. A couple from Stonington, Illinois—Charles and Flora Hartsock—adopted Mabel. The youngest, baby Jimmy, only four months old, went with relatives, but died eight months later.

When Mabel was twenty-two, she married a man named Alonso "Lon" Peak in 1912. A few years later he drowned in a boat accident on the Snake River in Idaho. Lon and Mabel had two children and one on the way when Alonso drowned. Mabel had no alternative but to sell everything and return home to live with her adoptive family again.[100]

Arthur Payton worked at a variety of jobs until 1939 when he bought a farm near Loma, Colorado, toward the end of the depression. On Dec. 3, 1919, Arthur and Mabel were married in Kansas City, MO. They raised a family of six children, born over the next twenty years.

Chester "Art" and Mabel (Rasmussen) Payton in 1955.

Arthur and his family worked the farm for a few years before he sold the farm in Loma. They bought a farm about two and one-half miles up Parachute Creek. Shortly after they had moved to the Parachute Creek farm, WWII began. Arthur sought work in California where an income was insured and the pay was good. Clarence Bumgardner agreed to look after Arthur's farm while he was working in California. Arthur and Mabel with their two youngest boys, Wayne and Binks, moved to Oakland, California, where money was to be made in the shipyards. Arthur worked as a carpenter until near the end of the war; then he and his family returned to the farm on Parachute Creek. The seventy-acre Payton ranch on Parachute Creek was sold to Union Oil Company of California for $15,000 in the early 1950s.

DOROTHY ELLEN PAYTON | #17

Dorothy was born in 1920. She was an elementary teacher for over thirty years. She died in Grand Junction in 1995.

DALE ARTHUR PAYTON | #17

Dale Arthur attended school in Loma and helped his father on the farm. He was born in 1922, and following their move to Parachute, worked as a ranch hand on Parachute Creek and in Meeker for over twenty-five years. Dale married Viola Christian on February 1, 1947, in Rifle and they had five children: Carol, Jerry, Cindy, Dorothy, and Christie. All Dale and Viola's children have homes in Colorado and live from Grand Junction to Meeker and Parachute. Dale died in Meeker in 2006 and is buried there.

---

[100] Williams, *No Market for 'em,* 2012.

LILY MARIE PAYTON | #17

Lily Marie, who was born in 1923, attended schools in Loma and left Colorado before her other family members left, to work in the shipyards during World War II. Following the war, she remained in California and was last known to be living in San Jose.

NORMAN PAYTON | #17

Norman Charles was born in 1925 and worked on ranches along Parachute Creek and at the oil shale plant at Anvil Points. He also owned the Texaco Station in Grand Valley for a number of years until he moved to New Mexico, California, and then Texas. He moved to Corpus Christi where he worked as an equipment operator. Norman married Irene Williams but they divorced several years later and Irene married Norman's brother "Binks."

CLARENCE WAYNE PAYTON FAMILY | #17

Clarence Wayne, usually called Wayne, was born in 1926 and worked on ranches in the Parachute Creek area during the 1940s and '50s. Wayne worked in the California shipyards until he was drafted in the Army in 1944 along with a group of other men from Parachute. Wayne returned to Parachute in 1946 and worked on various ranches while continuing his education at Grand Valley High School (by then he was twenty and had gone back to high school). Since he had the GI Bill to help pay the cost of more education, he entered Mesa Junior College where he earned an associate's degree in agriculture. Wayne spent most of his life in Parachute and was an active member in the Battlement Mesa community and the Grand Valley Historical Society.

Wayne was a proficient hunter. He often took off on his horse for extended trips. On one such trip he went up on to the East Fork Range to hunt elk. After five days and not hearing anything, the community became concerned and a group was being formed to go look for him. That evening, Wayne showed up at a rancher's home late in the evening having just returned from the mountain and after traveling many miles from where he began. Wayne described this trip as traveling from the East Fork Range across to the Piceance Creek drainages and continuing west around the Middle Fork of Parachute Creek until he came across a bull elk, which he killed. Not knowing what to do with such a large animal that far from home, he gave the animal to two hunters from the Meeker area who were hunting nearby. They in turn provided a cabin, a place for him to sleep, and food. Wayne left these hunters and continued south around the head of West Fork and headed toward the Book Cliff rims seeking a trail off the mountain. He eventually found the old Joe Bellis trail just before dark of the fifth day and traveled off the mountain having just completely circled the three forks of Parachute Creek and ending up at the site on Parachute Creek where Joe Bellis was killed (described earlier) and without an elk.

Clarence Wayne and Alberta (Gardner) Payton, ca. 1950.

Wayne married Alberta Gardner, a native of Parachute who was a graduate of Grand Valley High School. She had a teaching BA degree from Western State College. While Wayne was seeking a job that had a continuous paycheck coming in, they moved to Pueblo where he worked for the Colorado Fuel and Iron Company. He retired after thirty years and returned to Parachute. Alberta worked as a secretary at Southern Colorado University at Pueblo. Following their retirement they built a home on Battlement Mesa and ranched for the next thirty years. Wayne and Alberta provided much of the Payton information used in this document. He passed away December 1, 2012, at the age of eighty-six and is buried in the Battement Mesa Cemetery.

Alberta's father, Albert Gardner, ran cattle up Parachute Creek on the East Fork cattle allotment. He also taught on Battlement Mesa and was a teacher and a principal at Grand Valley High School for a number of years. Albert's wife, Mona Gardner, taught at the Book Cliff School on Parachute Creek and most of the other schools in the Parachute District.

WARREN "BINKS" RAY PAYTON FAMILY | #17

Warren "Binks" was born in 1929 and grew up in Loma and Parachute. He attended Grand Valley High School. Warren married Irene (Williams) Payton following her divorce from his brother Norman. He and Irene moved to Roan Creek where they lived for many years. They both passed away in 2011. Warren was cremated and his remains are with the family. After selling the farm, Warren's parents, Arthur and Mabel, lived in various places before Mabel passed away in 1961 and Arthur in 1972. Both are buried in Rifle.

GEORGE BENEDETTI FAMILY | #16

George Martin Benedetti was born in Kentucky, September 26, 1896, and spent his early childhood at several different locations within the state of Kentucky. Both of his parents were also born in Kentucky. George arrived in Colorado from Kentucky around 1920. He spent time in Meeker before coming to Grand Valley. He worked as a farmer but was much more successful as a caterpillar tractor operator.

George met his wife Estella "Faye" Armstrong, born 1903, in Grand Valley area and they were married in Glenwood Springs October 14, 1920. Faye's parents were John and Agnes Armstrong of De Beque, Colorado. George and Faye lived on a farm across the creek from the Payton ranch that was later purchased by Julius and Betty (Baughman) Lindauer.

Vesta E. was their first child, born May 20, 1921. She married Jack, a son of John G. and Doris Crawford. Jack and Vesta bought the ranch from his father, John Crawford, and lived in the original Crawford log house following WWII. Jack died in November 1973 from complications associated with diabetes. Vesta remarried but came back to Grand Valley to live after her second husband's death. She remained there until she moved to her daughter's place in Lehi, Utah, where she died June 7, 2004.

Vera M. was born March 19, 1923. She attended Grand Valley High School and married Charles "Chuck" Quinn, a local man. They raised their three sons in Grand Valley before Chuck became a mine inspector. Later they left the area for some years. Following Chuck's retirement, they moved to Grand Junction where they remained until their deaths. Vera died in 1993 and Chuck in 2011.

Georgie E., the youngest, was born October 14, 1924. She attended and graduated from Grand Valley High School. She married a local boy, Harold Williams, son of Charley Williams, foreman of the railroad section crew. After the post-war oil shale boom went bust, their family moved to California where they remained until their deaths. Georgie died February 17, 2011, in Norwalk, California. Harold died in 2001.

In the 1940s, during the summers, George could commonly be found driving a team of four to six horses pulling a road grader up and down Parachute Creek. While George drove the team, Francis Stanton handled the large wheel that controlled the grader and its ten-foot blade. Periodic flooding brought tons of soil down from the mountain slopes, overflowing the gulches that crossed the gravel road and covering them with thick mud, debris, and water. To keep the roads passable, frequent clearing and grading of the road was required, and George and Francis did a good job of keeping the roads open. George died in 1957.

The ranches and farms on this lower section of Parachute Creek are smaller in acreage and since the canyon narrows upstream they tend to extend longer often with smaller fields and located further from their neighbors.

CHARLES PATTERSON FAMILY | #15

Charles H. Patterson was born December 25, 1865, near Guthrie Center, Iowa, and spent his childhood there. His father was from Indiana and his mother from Ohio. Charles married Ellen Gertrude Wilson March 3, 1894. Gertrude's mother was born in Ohio and her father in Indiana. Charles and Gertrude had two children: Gladys Elizabeth, born March 21, 1895; and Charlton "Chella," born September of 1899. Charles moved his family to Glenwood Springs in 1900. Gertrude's mother was living with the Pattersons while they were in Glenwood Springs. Shortly thereafter they moved on, trading their Glenwood Springs property for a ranch on Parachute Creek. The 1910, 1920, and 1930 federal censuses list the family as present in Grand Valley and on Parachute Creek.[101]

Gladys was one of the first students to graduate from Grand Valley High School. She and Olive (Bailey) Shoults were the only graduating seniors in 1912. According to the 1910 federal census, Gladys was living in Grand Valley with her parents.[102] Although there are no Grand Valley burial records for Charlton "Chella," it is possible that he died young. He does not show up in any other census of that year. Gladys was married in 1913 to Albert A. Allen and their story is told under the Allen Family section.

Charles Patterson was a dairyman and a farmer. He had a productive orchard where he raised apples and a variety of other fruits. He sold milk products, eggs, and fruit to local markets. His farm was located about two miles up Parachute Creek adjacent to the main road and the foothills to the north. Mrs. Vervig previously owned the Patterson Farm.[103]

Charles Patterson died in 1950 at the age of eighty-five. His wife Gertrude had died previously on August 8, 1945. It is believed that both are buried in Glenwood Springs. After the Pattersons passed away, the farm remained stagnant for some time until it was finally owned and operated by Lou Tuck and his sons of Littleton, Colorado. They raised good crops on this property, but the property was eventually set aside for natural gas exploration and production.

WILLIAM SEAMENS AND FAMILY | #14

William Wesley Seamens was born in 1853 in Ohio. His father was born in England and apparently immigrated to Ohio where he met his future wife, Julia Allcock. William W. Seamens died in 1921. Julia Wiley Allcock was born in Ohio in 1853 and died in 1926 at the age of seventy-three in

---

[101] *US federal census, 1870-1940.*

[102] Ibid.

[103] Murray. *Lest We Forget.* 1973.

the town of Grand Valley. William and Julia are both buried in the Battlement Mesa Cemetery.

Kenneth Seamens was William and Julia's oldest son. He was born in 1875, and the 1910 Census shows Kenneth, his wife Mae, and their two small daughters living on Battlement Mesa.[104] He died in December of 1917 and is buried in the Battlement Mesa Cemetery.

Darrell L. Seamens was born November 22, 1884, in Kansas and died in Grand Valley in 1970. He married Myrtle L. Sill who was born in Kansas in 1882. Her mother, Mary L. Sill, died in December of 1947 and had been living with Myrtle and Darrell in Parachute for the last six years of her life. Myrtle's sister was Henrietta, a teacher, who married Fred Gardner of Battlement Mesa. Erlene Murray described the Seamenses as early residents of Parachute Creek:

> W. W. Seamens, his wife, Julia, and two sons, Darrell and Kenneth, had come from Kansas in 1888 after the father had located land near what is now Rifle, Colorado, in 1886. They made their home here until sometime after 1900. They came farther west, locating in Hayes Gulch above Parachute. They later bought the Cornell place from Mr. Willis who was a retired railroad man, and lived here until Mr. and Mrs. Seamens and Kenneth died; then Darrell still kept the place for many years until he and his wife Myrtle moved into town.[105]

The Seamens family's well-built rock home on lower Parachute Creek was located on the north side of the creek, but over the years it has deteriorated. Most of the ranch was located on the south side some two miles west of the town of Parachute. David Cornell had built the two-story stone house on the property and it remained for many years. In the 1960s, the Powell Family lived on this ranch by moving a trailer house next to the old home. The old two-story house was falling in disrepair and no one wanted to tackle the problem of rebuilding it. They farmed several properties in the area and raised their children at this site. An irrigation ditch and dam were built nearby, known as the Cornell Ditch, supplying irrigation to several ranches downstream and to the town of Grand Valley.

In 1942, Carl Alber Sr. bought the Darrell Seamens Ranch. Later, Lou Tuck and his sons from Littleton, Colorado, farmed a portion of the ranch as one part of their large cattle operation on Parachute Creek in anticipation of a coming oil and gas industry.

Bob Coddington and Dr. Miller built the second hotel in Grand Valley in 1908. Several different people managed it until 1927 when Darrell and Myrtle Seamens purchased the hotel and changed its name to the Country Club Hotel. The Seamenses reported, "We have efficiently and pleasantly served the public with excellent meals and comfortable rooms," until Mr. Seamens' death." [106]

RAY AND IRIS HUBER | #13

Ray Huber was Myrtle Seamens' son from a former marriage. He was born April 30, 1909, in Kansas and came to Colorado with his mother while in his teens. He and his wife, Iris (Wasson) Huber, married in 1928. They farmed a number of acres of the Seamens ranch located at the base of Mt. Callahan. Their ranch was not very productive and was offered for sale for $1,500 in the late 1930s, but money was scarce during those times and apparently there were no buyers. They lived there and farmed the property until it was sold to Carl Jr. "Bud" Alber in the 1940s. Following the

---

[104] *US federal census, 1870-1940.*

[105] Murray. *Lest We Forget.* 1973.

[106] Ibid.

Ray and Iris (Wasson) Huber, ca. 1978

sale of their Parachute ranch, Ray and Iris moved to Fruita, Colorado, where they had bought a farm. They lived there for some twenty years and sold the farm but retained a portion upon which they could put a trailer. Ray and Iris lived there until Ray passed away on May 23, 2000. Iris continued to live in a trailer home in Fruita until she passed away in 2006. Both are buried in the Battlement Mesa cemetery.

THE ALBER FAMILY | #14

John "Henry" Alber, was born in Germany and immigrated to the United States when he was twelve years old. He became an apprentice meat cutter for the Cudahy Packing Company in Omaha, Nebraska, and rose to become the head meat cutter at the age of twenty-one. He established his own meat company in Johnstown, Colorado, and later moved to Breckenridge. He married Hulda Frick, a Swedish immigrant, on September 8, 1897. Henry, as he was commonly called, was elected mayor of Breckenridge and president of the Breckenridge school board.

Henry and Hulda bought the best house in Breckenridge, owned by the famous run-away slave from Virginia, Barney Ford, who had become a powerful influence on the Colorado legislature. This Breckenridge house is now the Barney Ford Museum and has been furnished with early day furnishings.

In 1921, Henry traded his holdings in Breckenridge to Thad C. Bailey of Grand Valley for ownership of the famous Clark-Jenny Ranch on Battlement Mesa. This ranch covered most of the present-day community of Battlement Mesa. He was influenced by the Holly Sugar Company to plant sugar beets for their factory in Grand Junction. This turned out to be a financial disaster, for the price of sugar dropped so drastically that the Holly Sugar Company collapsed.

Henry then opened a meat company in Grand Valley and prospered until the crash in October 1929. With the accumulation of large charge accounts and people unable to pay their bills, he closed his doors and bought the famous Morrisania Ranch. On this ranch, he established a Grade-A Dairy and he and Hulda raised ten children on this farm and dairy.

They were able to be successful in spite of the Great Depression. They introduced many improvements and new strategies in the dairy and farming business. They gave food to needy families and distributed fruit and vegetables up and down the valley. For years, the local people would talk about how Henry Alber saved their lives during those desperate winters.

Doll Brothers and Smith built a general store in Parachute around 1903, after their original store had been robbed and burned. They operated this new store for a number of years, until it was sold to several different individuals: O. C. Tidwell, to Thad C. Bailey, and to Philip Waterman, who sold it to Ray Eaken. Ray operated the store in the 1930s as a grocery store and sold it in the late 1930s to Carl and Edna Alber. The parents, Henry and Hulda Alber, remained in Parachute.

One of Henry and Hulda's sons, Carl Henry Alber, continued the meat cutting and store business following his marriage to Edna Mae. Carl was born in Breckenridge in 1898. He served in the United States Infantry during World War I in 1917-18. In 1918, Carl married Edna Mae Goble, who was

Carl and Edna Mae (Goble) Alber, shortly after their marriage in 1918.

Carl and Edna Mae Alber owned and managed a mercantile/grocery store, ca. 1960s.

born in Leavenworth, Kansas, on February 22, 1897. Her family had moved to Denver in 1900, and she spent much of her early years taking care of her younger sisters and working at various jobs to help her father feed the family while also attending school. She entered Denver University and graduated *cum laude* in three years with a degree in chemistry. Carl and Edna were married one year after she graduated. Carl and Edna had four children and raised them in Grand Valley: Anna Mae (1921), Carl "Bud" Jr. (1922), Fred (1928), and Tom (1934).

Edna, in addition to working in the store and raising a family, was elected president of the Grand Valley school board and was responsible for hiring Dr. Paul B. Baum as the superintendent. Dr. Baum created a great school system for Grand Valley schools. She also taught school at Mamm Creek and Grand Valley High School.

Edna was popular in the community for teaching the women how to can fruits, vegetables, and meat. The Colorado A&M Extension Service promoted household practices for women and their families and selected Edna to be the volunteer leader.

All of Edna Mae and Carl's children graduated from college in the following areas: Carl Jr. worked in the fields of soil conservation; Fred became a county farm extension agent in Colorado and New Mexico; Tom worked with the Farmer's Home Administration/Real Estate; and Anna Mae, the only girl, received her degree in teacher education and taught at Grand Valley High School in the 1940s.

During all these years, Carl Sr. continued to be interested in ranching and raising cattle. In 1942, he bought the Darrell Seamens ranch on Parachute Creek. With the help of his sons Bud, Fred, and Tommy, he raised hay on this property and ran cattle on the East Fork allotment. They wintered their cattle on both the Parachute Creek ranch and on their Morrisania Mesa ranch.

Carl Sr. died of gall bladder cancer in December 1974. His wife Edna Mae lived another eight years. Both are buried in the Russey-Hurlburt Cemetery. The Alber Store in Parachute was removed in 1977 to allow for the construction of Interstate 70.

Fred Alber provided the details of the Alber family. He died during the summer of 2013 in Denver. Tommy Alber, a veteran naval officer, lives in Denver and was recovering from cancer surgery as of the fall of 2014.

Anna Mae and Bud holding Fred, children of Carl and Edna Alber ca. 1930, at the Wasson cabin on the upper East Fork Creek above the falls at the mouth of Grassy Gulch.

CARL "BUD" JR. AND LEONA ALBER FAMILY | #13

Bud attended the Grand Valley Schools and graduated from Colorado State University with a degree in soil science and agriculture. He served as an officer in the US Navy and, upon discharge, married Leona Rickstrew of De Beque, Colorado. They moved to the Huber ranch where the first of their five children (Vaughn, John, Pamela, Ricky, and Terry) was born.

Bud and his wife purchased the Ray Huber Ranch just south of his father's ranch and lived on and operated this ranch in the 1940s until it was sold to Union Oil Company of California in 1984. From there, Bud took a position with the Colorado Soil Conservation Service and worked throughout Colorado as a soil scientist. He was very bright and was committed to the western way of life, often having some cattle to look after. His son said, "Dad always wanted a ranch large enough that anything within a mile of the borders was women's work."

Most of Bud's soil conservation work was with Limon, Burlington, Alamosa, and Cortez offices. He bought a farm in White Water, Colorado, and was raising cattle there until a fall from a horse apparently severely injured one of his lungs. He died at St. Mary's Hospital from an infection following surgery.

JONATHAN "YONE" AND JESSIE BAUGHMAN FAMILY | #12

Jonathan Baughman's father, David Baughman, was born in 1854, in Wisconsin. He moved to Aspen in 1878 to pursue his interest in mining. He was married in 1884 to Mary Lynch, who was born in 1864, in Michigan. David apparently worked in the mining business for some twenty years while he and Mary raised six children. David did not find the riches that he'd sought, and after some conflicts (perhaps involving gambling) in Aspen, he moved the family to Grand Valley in 1908. David lived and worked in the Grand Valley area and took care of his apple orchard on Morrisania Mesa until 1933 when his wife Mary passed away. He then moved with his daughter, Mayme Richie, to San Pedro, California, where he lived until he passed away in 1939.

David's son, Jonathan "Yone," was born April 6, 1887, in Aspen, Colorado, but spent most of his life in Parachute. He was remembered as the first person to build a bridge over Parachute Creek that withstood many summer floods and spring high waters. The bridge was supported by large rock foundations on both sides and was still in use some fifty years later.

Yone courted Jessie Hurlburt, the daughter of JB Hurlburt, a prominent citizen of Grand Valley, and they had plans for marriage. JB wasn't happy that Jessie was going to marry Yone because of David Baughman's reputation that had followed him from Aspen. The future prospects of Yone and Jessie's potential success in marriage looked grim. So JB and the town marshal followed the couple to Rifle and tried to convince Jessie not to board the train and get married. She and Yone did get married, however, on May 13, 1912, in Grand Junction. Following this marriage, Yone's sister, Alice Pearl Baughman, married Jessie's brother, Fred Hurlburt, in August of that same year.

Betty (Baughman) Lindauer Mead was a Parachute Creek resident for many years.

Yone and Jessie had seven children, of whom Jessie was justly proud.[107] Their two daughters were Juanita Evelyn "Neta" Rector (1916-1997) and Betty Lindauer Mead (1925-2005). Betty lived on several ranches during her thirty-year stay on Parachute Creek. (See more about Betty under Julius Lindauer.)

The five sons of Yone and Jessie were Luther David (1913-1984), Norman Mark (1915-1954), George Woodman (1921-1993), John Curtis (1927–2001), and Alfred Orville (1929-1986). Although most lived a full life, strokes and vascular problems shortened some of their lives, as reported by relatives.

Jessie lost her husband Yone, who died of a stroke in 1929, leaving her to support six children at home and expecting a seventh. Her brothers, Mark and Luther, helped her to raise and feed the family over the years. When Jessie sold her place on Parachute Creek, she moved to the town of Grand Valley across the street from one of the Grand Valley schools. She later lived with her daughter Betty in Rifle for some eight years. Jessie passed away January 7, 1977, in Rifle and both she and her husband Yone are buried in the Russey-Hurlburt Cemetery in Parachute.

STANLEY MCKAY FAMILY, PLACE AND PRIOR OWNERS | #11

In an effort to understand the numerous owners of their various properties over the past 100-plus years, the abstract of the McKay property was found. Evalee (McKay) Gifford, the daughter of Evelyn McKay (1917-2008) and Stanley McKay (1915-1979), retained the abstract and shared it with the author. As one can see below, the property changed ownership many times with foreclosures and bank sales, not uncommon during the very difficult depression years. The following is one example of what happened with properties on Parachute Creek:

Philip Dere patented what was to become the Stanley McKay Place on December 12, 1891. It is located about one mile up Parachute Creek west of the town of Parachute on the north side of County Road 215. The deed to this seventeen-plus-acre parcel was recorded in 1896. But in 1892, the property had been sold for $447 to John B. Hurlburt who was in the real estate business; he sold it to Sam Pratt in 1894. Pratt sold the property to Ida M. Tracy in August of 1899. The Wilcox Canal Company purchased a portion of the property. Messrs. Buck, Pratt, and Tracy then owned the property. In 1902, the construction and the development of a large canal out of the Colorado River, called the Havemeyer Ditch, was underway from Rifle to Parachute. Just before the ditch was finished, a

---

[107] Murray. *Lest We Forget.* 1973.

major flood on the river destroyed the dam and it was never repaired.

Gladys Allen, whose parents lived nearby, and her husband Albert Allen purchased the property from Guy Wolverton on April 10, 1919. They sold it in April 1921 to Jabez F. Davidson. Davidson, who died in 1924, had named Albert Allen as administrator of the estate. He, in turn, sold the property to Mr. McIntyre in 1925.

The property was sold to FJ Lenhart in 1936. Lenhart kept the property for seven years and sold it to Thomas Brasher in 1943. Thomas Brasher then sold it in 1947 to a Scarrow family member who then sold the property to the Stanley McKay family in 1948. They kept the property for thirty-two years until 1980 when a portion was sold to the Union Oil Company of California. Another portion of the property was sold to Boots Corn of Grand Junction. In 2011, the property was sold to the Williams Gas Company, Inc. for its gas drilling and development headquarters and main Parachute Creek office, now transferred to WPX Energy. With the exception of the McKay family, the property exchanged hands many times over the course of a few years.

Stanley McKay's grandfather, Hugh Richard McKay, came into the region in the early late 1890s bringing some 700 head of cattle to De Beque, eleven miles south of Parachute. He opened a store and ran cattle on the Book Cliff and De Beque ranges for several years, but was not known to own any property in the Parachute Creek drainage. Stanley and Evelyn Wasson McKay had three children: David, 1938; Evalee, 1943; and Michael, 1949. All three attended and graduated from Grand Valley High School. Stanley and his wife Evelyn spent most of their lives in the Parachute Creek area, finally moving into the Wasson home near the railroad tracks in the 1970s, after they had sold their lodge in Marble, Colorado. Evelyn (Wasson) McKay was the daughter of Sam B. Wasson and Eva F. (Hunter) Wasson.

After Stanley McKay passed away in 1979, Evelyn continued to live in the Wasson home near the railroad tracks in Parachute. She lived another twenty-seven years until her death on December 14, 2006. Their beautiful stone home and adjacent land was sold to the town of Parachute in recognition of the work that the two families had done over the years for the town of Parachute. The home and adjacent lot is called the Wasson/McKay Park and presently houses the Parachute Parks and Recreation District office.

Sam B. Wasson was born in Virginia on June 4, 1865, and spent his boyhood in Iowa. He married Eva September 5, 1894, in Denver and after several years in Kansas and southeastern Colorado they came to the Grand Valley area in 1907. They ran cattle on the Parachute Creek East Fork range during the summer and wintered along the Colorado River near Grand Valley. Sam and Eva were prominent citizens and were well liked in the community of Grand Valley. Mr. Wasson was appointed postmaster on June 1, 1921, and retired in 1930 as the result of ill health. He died on January 15, 1931, at the age of sixty-five. His wife Eva continued to work as an assistant postmaster after his death. She retired in 1937 after seventeen years with the postal service. Their granddaughter, Evalee (McKay) Gifford, kept the family records and provided the information for this section.

AL AND MILDRED MABEE | #10

Alfred "Al" L. Mabee was born in Picton, Ontario, Canada, April 28, 1879, and immigrated with his family to the United States in 1880. They traveled to Denver during the late 1880s or early 1890s. Al had three sisters: Eva, born in 1878; Pearl, born 1882; and Ethel (Conner), born in 1889. His parents were Wineet A. Mabee, born in Canada in 1845, and Susannah, born in 1856. According to the 1900 federal census records, Al was one year old when he arrived with his parents in the

United States in 1880.[108] [109] His father was a hotelkeeper in the 1880s through the 1890s. In 1900, the family was living in Duff (Arapahoe County), Colorado, and Al was with them at that time as a farm laborer.

Al spent time in Leadville in 1907 where he worked as a miner and also as a contractor and fireman. He was married to Myra L. Mabee, as was identified in his WWI draft registration listing his age as 38.[110] Myra was born in Pennsylvania in 1872 and was living in Denver in 1926. At the age of fifty-four, she was living as the wife of Alfred Mabee. Beyond that date, no additional information could be located for Myra. The best estimates for dates and events for Al and Myra have been listed here.

Later, Al married Mildred H. Radtke in Greeley, Colorado. She was born in Illinois in 1900 and lived in several states before arriving in Colorado. When Al and Mildred moved to Grand Valley in 1947, they bought a seventeen-acre ranch about one mile up Parachute Creek where they lived for the remainder of their lives. The couple, who had no children, raised hay for sale on their ranch. In addition to being a housewife, Mildred worked at a variety of part-time jobs, from picking cherries at a large commercial orchard to other odd jobs around the community. She was a friend to everyone in the community. She passed away in 1958 at the age of fifty-eight.

Al lived another three years and died at the age of eighty-two in 1961. He was found at his home on Parachute Creek by a neighbor, Paul Lindauer. He apparently was preparing breakfast when he was stricken with a heart attack. His body was slumped over the kitchen table when discovered some twelve hours later. Both Al and his wife are buried in the Russey-Hurlburt Cemetery in Parachute.

LLOYD BLUE/PAUL & BESSIE LINDAUER RANCH AND FAMILY | #9

In late 1919 and the early 1920s, Paul spent his spare time working with Harry Hansen, digging assessment holes for various oil shale interests. Also, during and following this time period Paul was the principal cowboy for the family and spent much of the summers riding the range and taking care of cattle for the family and others. Following their marriage in 1924, Paul and Bessie moved to the Hughes Ranch, located some nine miles up Parachute Creek. The Hughes brothers owned a little over 100 acres in the valley; however, little of this land was suitable for farming. They remained there for several years before moving to the East Fork Ranch in 1929, where Paul farmed the property and began to build their herd of cattle.

In the early 1930s, Paul and Bessie had only a few head of cattle, having lost most of their herd during the depression. In 1936, the family had grown to four children on the East Fork Ranch and the only school, the Granlee School, was three miles away by horseback. At an elevation of over 6,000 feet, the snow came early and lasted long, and the winters were cold in the bottom of the canyon. Paul and Bessie knew they needed to move the children closer to a school where the weather was less severe and where the children might receive a better education.

Paul had ranched at several locations up and down Parachute Creek and finally found a ranch just one mile from the town of Grand Valley. From this site, his children could walk to school if necessary. The earliest known owner of this ranch was RW McGuirk, who was born in Illinois and came to Leadville in 1880, apparently with his parents. He was an engineer, married to Bertha McGuirk in 1895, and was living in Parachute in 1900 with his wife, two children, and his brother. He had gone

---

[108] Ancestry.com.

[109] *US federal census, 1870-1940.*

[110] Ancestry.com.

to Leadville with his father, John McGuirk, before moving on to Parachute. RW McGuirk was the owner of the thirty-three-acre Blue/Lindauer Ranch on October 16, 1918, when it was sold to Lloyd J. and Alta E. Blue.[111] On March 18, 1926, Lloyd Blue transferred the deed of this property to Thelma Alta and Lloyd George Blue Jr. On June 2, 1940, by agreement of the parties involved, the purchase was confirmed from Lloyd J. Blue Jr. to Bessie E. Lindauer. The thirty acres south of this property were in the estate of Elmer E. and Lucia A. Wheatley. Following Elmer Wheatley's death, his wife sold this acreage to Bessie on October 5, 1943. Paul and Bessie transferred their cattle permit on the East Fork range to this property and added another forty acres further south that gave the ranch a total of some 103 acres. This was deeded land located adjacent to Mt. Callahan, where he had a second spring grazing permit. Following the birth of another child, Paul and Bessie raised their family on this ranch that has continued to remain in the family.

Paul and Bessie's first son, Zelmo, was born on the Hughes Ranch on March 11, 1926, and attended Granlee Elementary School by horseback. He graduated after three years at Grand Valley High School. Following a short college experience, he entered the US Navy during WWII. After his tour of duty was completed, he married Virginia Marchi of Martinez, California, and remained there working for the government at Port Chicago, California. Zelmo had been trained in munitions while in the Navy. He began his career as a munitions specialist soon after his military service had ended and at the end of WWII. Zelmo and Virginia raised a boy, Michael, and a girl, Janelle, who remain in California. He passed away in 1993 from a heart attack. Paul and Bessie's next child, Lola, died at the age of three days due to sudden infant death syndrome (SIDS).

Ivo was born April 7, 1931, and following graduation from Grand Valley High School and a BS degree from Colorado State University, he entered the US Marine Corps for three years. After his release from the service, he married Betty JoAnn "BJ" Barstow of Palisade, Colorado, and they entered the University of Northern Colorado where they both obtained MA degrees and later doctoral degrees, but at different universities. Ivo was hired by the University of Northern Colorado as a botanist. BJ spent thirty-six years in administration and teaching at all levels before retiring while Ivo retired after thirty-seven years of teaching and research. Preceding his retirement, Ivo moved back to ranching in Parachute and continued consulting for the National Science Foundation and other organizations. They live on Battlement Mesa. From the marriage of Betty JoAnn and Ivo, two girls were born. Julia, the oldest, was born August 13, 1961, and lives in Greeley, Colorado, where she has been teaching for twenty years. Julie has one son, Dylan Ivo Lindauer. He lives in Grand Junction and is working to become a "landman." Sarah (Lindauer) Orona, born February 20, 1964, lives in Parachute with her husband and two children. She married Howard Orona on October 26, 1991, and after several years in Ft. Collins, they moved to Parachute. Their oldest child is Cordero, born May 20, 1996, and attends Fort Lewis College. He hopes to become a petroleum engineer. Delcia, born December 10, 1997, is a senior at Grand Valley High School and plans to attend college in California after graduation.

Lorraine was born September 11, 1934, and graduated from Grand Valley High School. Following graduation, she married John Brown of the US Navy in Hawaii. After his service in the Navy, they moved back to Colorado for a few years and then on to Hyampom, California, where they raised two children, Colene and Johnny. Colene was born on April 9, 1954, and Johnny on May 18, 1956, both in Parachute. Both are retired; Colene was a teacher in Hayfork, California, and Johnny was a postmaster in Hyampom, California. Lorraine and John were later divorced and Lorraine married Jack

---

[111] Garfield County Clerk & Recorder's Office.

Weston. They both remained there with her family until her husband Jack died in 2013. Lorraine passed away June 6, 2015, at the age of 81 in Redding, California.

Sydney was born March 21, 1936, and graduated from Grand Valley High School. He married Ruth Bennett in 1957 and worked as a surveyor for several years while raising two boys, Robin and Sandy and one girl Mindy; He then obtained a degree in physical sciences from Fort Lewis College in Durango. He later established a mineral analysis laboratory and spent most of his life in Nevada. Following his retirement and the sale of his assaying business, Sydney and Ruth returned to Parachute and joined a partnership with Ivo on the home ranch until 1988, when it was terminated. They remain in Parachute.

Lynda was born October 2, 1938, and graduated from Grand Valley High School and continued her education through an MA degree at Western State College. She met and married Kenneth MacLennan in 1957. They spent their careers in Gunnison. She taught elementary school until she retired. She and her husband, who was a faculty member and ski coach at Western State College, remained in Gunnison. Kenneth and Lynda had one son, Kevin, who is the registrar at the University of Colorado, Boulder. Kenneth died January 9, 2011.

During WWII, Paul purchased the Lyman Van Horn Island Ranch next to Parachute Creek where it entered the Colorado River and adjacent to the Hurlburt ranch. This added several hundred more acres to the ranch and was an ideal location to winter and calve his herd. The river ranch was purchased by Ivo and Sydney from their parents in the late 1970s and later sold in the late 1980s after being incorporated into the city of Parachute. As of 2015, the home ranch property remains in the ownership of Ivo and BJ Lindauer and a daughter and son-in-law, Sarah and Howie Orona.

FREEMAN "FJ" LENHART APPLE RANCH AND FAMILY | #7

Freeman J. Lenhart was born in 1859 in Pennsylvania. His father was F. Ludwick Lenhart, born in 1830, and his mother, Elizabeth S. Howard, born in 1833. Both parents were residents of Pennsylvania. Elizabeth and Ludwick had four children as follows: Ellen M. in 1854, William A. in 1856, Freeman J. in 1859, and Malone H. in 1864. All were living in Jefferson, Pennsylvania, in the 1880s and 1890s.

FJ as he was sometimes called, was married in 1892 to Emma Lenhart, as reported in the 1900 federal census. He was living in Leadville, working as a locomotive fireman. The census reported that he had been married for eight years. Emma died in 1907. The 1910 federal census listed FJ as living in Grand Valley, Colorado, and married to Katie Lenhart (age thirty-one) who was born in 1879 and had a nine-year-old son by the name of Forrest Drake.[112]

By 1920, according to the Grand Valley census, FJ was divorced and was keeping a live-in servant by the name of Amanda Brown, age twenty-two.[113] She had two children: Agnes, two, and a six-month-old infant. They were living on the farm with FJ, who identified himself as a fruit grower. In later years his apple orchard, located about a half mile up Parachute Creek from the town of Grand Valley, was known as having some of the best red delicious apples in the area.

In the 1930 and 1940 federal census and at the age of seventy and eighty years he was listed as widowed.[114] He passed away in 1944 and both he and his first wife are buried in the Russey-Hurlburt Cemetery in Parachute. Sam Williams, a close friend of FJ, and his wife Laura lived on this property

---

[112] *US federal census, 1900–1910.*

[113] Ibid.

[114] Ibid.

after Mr. Lenhart passed away. The dates of occupancy are unknown. Sam and Laura also lived for a period of time on the ranch across the road and north of the Lenhart property.

ELMER WHEATLEY FAMILY | #7

Elmer E. Wheatley was born in Du Quoin, Illinois, November 1, 1867, and grew up there. He came to Colorado at the age of twenty-one and settled in Longmont, where he entered the newspaper business at the age of twenty-six. He moved to Denver where he met his wife Lucia, and they were married in Boulder, August 26, 1897. Lucia E. Wheatley, was born in Ohio in 1871. Twin daughters, Lucia and Lois, were born in 1900. Their daughter Lucia died when she was a teenager.

The family left Cripple Creek in 1913, after Lucia had passed away. They moved to Grand Valley where he had purchased the *Grand Valley News*.[115] He became the postmaster and held this position for many years. As a dedicated Democrat, he continued publishing this newspaper while acting as postmaster until his death July 23, 1937, at the age of sixty-three. He had been ill at home for several months before being taken to St. Mary's Hospital in Grand Junction. A leg was removed to stop the spread of an infection; however, he failed to respond to surgery and died several days later. His daughter, Lois (Wheatley) Franzel, had come from Buena Vista to be with her father in his final days. He had been engaged in the newspaper business for 54 years. Following his death, his wife, Lucia, managed the post office for a number of years.

The Daily Sentinel[116] reported Elmer E. Wheatley as one of the state's veteran editors having served in this profession for fifty-four years.[117] Elmer and daughter Lois are buried in the Russey-Hurlburt Cemetery in Parachute.

ED POWER FAMILY | #8, 45

George Edward "Ed" Power, the father of Lloyd Power, was born in Carney, Oklahoma, June 26, 1878. He married Hattie Marley December 21, 1901. Hattie and Ed had two boys: Alva, born December 13, 1902; and Leslie R., born October 10, 1904. Hattie died in 1906 in Crescent City, Iowa. Leslie died before the family came to Colorado.

Ed (a widower) married Adeline "Addie" Osborn July 4, 1907. Addie was born July 22, 1887, near Douglas, Kansas, and moved with her parents to Lincoln County, Oklahoma. She spent her early years on the family farm. After Ed and Addie were married they continued living on the farm until 1917.

George Edward "Ed" and Adeline "Addie" (Osborn) Power at their wedding.

Ed, Addie, and their three sons—Edward G., often called Granville, born February 12, 1909; W. Glen, September 30, 1910; and Lloyd Alfred, May 5, 1911—traveled west to Colorado, working on farms along the way to provide funds for travel to Grand Valley and Parachute Creek. They traveled in a Model T Ford and camped out on their way to visit Addie's sister, Laura (Osborn) Gardner, and her husband, James Gardner, who lived on Parachute Creek. It was thought that they lived on a ranch later called the Ogden Ranch.

James's brother Vern Gardner owned property in the area and ran cattle on the East Fork allot-

---

[115] Grand Junction. *Daily Sentinel*. 1913.

[116] Murray. *Lest We Forget*. 1973

[117] Grand Junction. *Daily Sentinel*. 1937.

ment. James and Vern also owned a small farm south of the town of Grand Valley that he later sold to Edward's son, Glen Power, in 1934. Ed Power's son and family lived on this property until the property was purchased by the US Government as a needed right-of-way for the development of Interstate Highway I-70.

Ed and his family returned to Oklahoma in 1918 where he became a mail carrier and also worked on farms. In 1921, Ed and his family moved to Drumright, Oklahoma, where he obtained employment with Tidal Oil Company. Lexie Ruth Power was born there June 27, 1921. Her sister Velma soon followed on September 8, 1924. Lexie passed away January 20, 2006.

In 1925, they moved back to Grand Valley, but returned to Oklahoma the next year where Ralph was born March 18, 1927. Ed was anxious that all six of their children would be born in Oklahoma.

Ed and his family returned to Grand Valley in 1927. He worked on farms and remained here until he was killed in 1940 when crossing the railroad track. His wagon got hung up on the tracks causing the tongue to swing and hit Ed in the head. He never recovered from the injury. He died June 11, 1940, at the age of sixty-two and is buried in the Russey-Hurlburt Cemetery in Parachute. Addie spent most of her last years with her family in Grand Valley and passed away in Van Nuys, California, March 7, 1974. She is buried with her husband Ed in the Russey-Hurlburt Cemetery.

The Powers take friends for a ride in their 1916 Model T Ford in 1918. L to R, back seat: Lloyd Alfred St., Glen Wright, Leslie Riley, and Edward Granville (standing); front seat: Adeline and George Edward Power.

Ed and Adeline Power with Mr. and Mrs. Gardner in 1918. L to R, back row: Alva Washington, Adeline, George Edward, Evelyn, baby Walter, and Mr. and Mrs. Gardner; front row: Lloyd, Glen, Granville, and Leslie Power.

LLOYD POWER FAMILY | #8

Lloyd Alfred Power, the third son of Ed and Addie, was born on May 5, 1911, near Carney, Oklahoma. He married Velma Margaret Davidson May 27, 1934, in Rifle, Colorado. Velma was born in Maple Hills, Kansas, on November 13, 1912. Her mother and father were Olive and Andy Davidson of Baggs, Wyoming. Their history is described under the Davidson Family History.

Lloyd and Velma (Davidson) Power, May 27, 1934.

Lloyd and Velma Power lived on rented farms on Parachute Creek for several years. Lloyd worked in construction and on the Denver & Rio Grande Railroad. During these years, five children were born: Shirley Lavonne (Brackett) who was born in 1935 at Grand Valley and Mary Alice (Miracle) was born two years later. Lois Lorene (Hurla) was born December 21, 1940, and Lloyd Alfred Jr. was born February 3, 1945. Their last child, Robert Joe, was born November 12, 1947. Three of their children, Shirley, Mary Alice, and Lois, attended and graduated from Grand Valley High School.

Lloyd Alfred Jr. moved to Collbran with his dad, who was working on the Vega Dam project. He graduated from Collbran High School. The other son, Robert, graduated from Grand Junction Central High School. All have spent much of their life within fifty miles of Parachute.

Lloyd and Velma purchased a ten-acre parcel of land from Sam Williamson. The property, once owned by Lloyd's brother Glen was located one mile west of the town of Parachute on the north side of Parachute Creek and County Road 215. They farmed several small farms in the area, but Lloyd continued to work on the railroad and finally at Anvil Point's Oil Shale facility to meet the needs of the family.

Lloyd's brother Glen and his wife Marjorie (Armstrong) Power took over the farm in 1938 while Glen worked for James Gardner. Apparently that same year, while all the family were out in the field putting up hay and the women were preparing dinner, their brother Granville and his wife Hazel's six-year-old daughter Betty Lou ran across an old cistern that had a faulty top and when it gave way, she fell in and drowned. This brought much sorrow to the community.

When the Anvil Points Oil Shale operation shut down, Lloyd sold the place to Ralph and Edith (Hoagland) Power in 1958 and he and some family members moved to Dutch John, Utah. Lloyd and Velma retired to Grand Junction where they lived out their lives. Lloyd died February 5, 2000, and Velma passed away on March 7, 2002. They are both buried in the Russey-Hurlburt Cemetery. Lois Power Hurla provided much of the information for the Power family with the help of her sister Shirley.

ALBERT ALLEN FAMILY | #5

Albert Adolph Allen was born May 3, 1887, in Roseville, Kansas. He was the son of John and Hannah Allen, both Swedish immigrants. Albert spent time in Nebraska, living with his brother-in-law before heading to Colorado with Jim Getty, on whose ranch he worked for some time. He met Gladys Elizabeth Patterson in Grand Valley. They were married on October 11, 1913, in Glenwood Springs. (More about Gladys is under Charles Patterson Family.) Gladys was widely known around the town of Grand Valley as a great cook who specialized in angel food cakes. Consequently, whenever there was a celebration around Grand Valley and a cake was needed, Gladys was asked to bake an angel food cake for the occasion. She mentored many 4-H girls as well.

After Albert and Gladys's marriage, they moved to Missouri for three years where Albert was a self-employed farmer. Their daughter, Helen (Vail), was born there in 1917. Shortly after Helen's birth, they moved to Lyndon, Kansas. While there, Albert registered for the draft at the age of thirty and was listed in the 1917 federal census report as being married with one child.[118] Following the birth of their second child, Albert and Gladys moved from Kansas to Grand Valley to be closer to Gladys' parents, Charles and Ellen Patterson. Albert and Gladys may have been living at the Ogden Ranch at the head of Parachute Creek at that time. Sometime later, they moved just west of the town of Grand Valley to a place previously owned by Marion O. Aplin.

Helen, the oldest child of Albert and Gladys, graduated from Grand Valley High School and went on for additional education to become a nurse's aide. She married Carl Vail who was a career military officer. They traveled much of the world, and when Carl retired as a Major from the US Air Force, he attended the University of Colorado and earned a PhD in economics. He later taught economics at Colorado State University and retired from that position.

Front, Helen (Allen) Vail, daughter of Albert and Gladys Allen, talks with BJ Lindauer. Rear, unknown woman talks with Helen's husband Carl Vail.

John was born May 1, 1918, and attended schools in Grand Valley. He graduated from high school in 1937 and married Lola Margaret Linin. She was born in Republic, Kansas, May 18, 1919, and moved to Colorado in 1935. Her parents were Henry and Ruby Linin. After John's service in World War II, he worked in construction and the oil shale industry. John and Lola had two children: George and Betty Jo "BJ" McQuiston. Both children were raised on Parachute Creek and graduated from Grand Valley High School.

When Albert and Gladys moved into town, John and Lola took over their home and farm on Parachute Creek. Their son, George, was killed in a truck-train accident in 1958 while he was working for the Union Carbide Company in Rifle. Daughter BJ became a nurse and worked for many years at the Veterans Hospital in Grand Junction (see McQuiston Family). John Allen was killed in a ditch cave-in in 1973 while working for the Bureau of Mines at Anvil Points. His wife Lola died in 2005 and both are buried in the Russey-Hurlburt Cemetery.

Lola (Linin) Allen, wife of John Allen, ca. 2000s.

Albert and Gladys's third child, Mildred (Tabscott), was born in Grand Valley in 1920. She graduated from Grand Valley High School in 1938 and a short time later married and moved to Alaska and

---

[118] *US federal census, 1910-1920.*

remained there where she and her husband owned a business.

Gladys and Albert also had a foster child, Elsie Richardson Obermeyer, who lived with them while she finished high school. She traveled to California where she continued her profession as a telephone operator working for various companies. In 2012, she was living with her daughter, Lynn McEachern, in Denver. Elsie passed away April 25, 2013, in the Denver area.

It was not uncommon for Albert and Gladys to have others staying with them over the years, such as the Nair brothers, Paul and Chuck, who stayed and worked with the Allens for several years.

Albert and Gladys operated a dairy and sold milk, cream, and eggs to local markets. For years Albert raised hay and farmed a ranch near what was called the "Yellow Barn" just one-half mile up Parachute Creek. Albert and Gladys lived on their farm until 1947 when they moved to a cabin along Parachute Creek adjacent to Grand Valley. A few years later, they moved into the town of Grand Valley. Albert died in 1983 at the age of ninety-seven and Gladys in November 1990 at the age of ninety-five. They are both buried in the Russey-Hurlburt Cemetery.

JOHN B. HURLBURT – THE FAMILY PATRIARCH | #2

John Breeden Hurlburt, known as JB, was born October 4, 1839, in Scott County, Iowa, the third of seven children of his parents, Isaiah and Rebecca (Breeden) Hurlburt. His father, born in Canada, became a US citizen. His mother was a native of Kentucky, who died in 1846. In his youth, Isaiah was the captain of a steamboat on the Great Lakes.

During 1854, JB, at the age of fifteen, made the long and lonesome overland trip with a team of oxen to California from Scott County, Iowa. The finding of gold in California had been the big attraction. His first work was mining in Placer County, California. In 1859, he moved to Oregon where he worked splitting rails for a short time, but then returned to Butte, California, where he farmed for the next ten years.

In 1870, JB Hurlburt married Martha A. "Mattie" Rock of Shasta City, California, and they moved to Lawson County, California. Here, JB continued farming for another thirteen years before leaving for Colorado in 1882.[119] He left Northern California June 1, 1882, with a partner, Martin Billiter, trailing a combined herd of 2,000 sheep. East of the Sierra Nevada Mountains, they met two other sheep men (Benner and Lee), each with 1,000 head of sheep, and the four men joined their herds.

Included with this large herd of sheep were the owners, some herdsmen, and wagons, all headed east to Colorado. JB had left his wife and five children in California. They reached the Green River in eastern Utah to find that the bridge had been washed out. After waiting several days until the bridge could be repaired, they arrived in Meeker on October 1, 1882, four months after leaving California.

He was advised in Meeker by an Indian scout, LS Kelly, to go over to the Grand River where the grass was higher than the sagebrush and the winters were milder and not so long. Chief Colorow, a Ute Indian, agreed with this advice, noting that the snow in the Meeker country often got "two Ute Indians deep" in the winter.[120]

After leaving a team and wagon in Meeker, JB and Martin Billiter traveled over the Government Road from Meeker to the Colorado River valley and downriver some sixteen miles. There, the men found an ideal site near a stream where JB might graze his sheep and bring his family.

JB Hurlburt arrived at the confluence of Parachute Creek and the Colorado River the day he turned

---

[119] Bowen, *Progressive Men of Western Colorado*. 1905.

[120] Murray. *Lest We Forget*. 1973.

**The extended Hurlburt family gathers for Thanksgiving in 1907 (age in parentheses).
L to R, back row: Martha "Mae" (Hurlburt) Burnside (23), Jessie (Hurlburt) Baughman (15), Mark Hurlburt (30), Lottie (Hurlburt) Shehorn (21), Fred Hurlburt (18), Minnie (Hurlburt) Clarke (28) holding Minnie Clarke (2), Winnie (Hurlburt) Christensen (11), Luther Hurlburt (32), Olive (Curry) Trimmer (15), Frances (Hurlburt) Trimmer (35) holding son Joseph Trimmer (1), Rebecca Lou Wayne (25) holding Mae Wayne (1); middle row: Learner Clark (5), Jim Trimmer (13), Frances Trimmer (9), Daisy Hurlburt (8), Fern Wayne (4), and Elsie Clarke (7); front row: Jim Clarke (3), John Breeden Hurlburt (68), and Martha "Mattie" (Rock) Hurlburt (55).**

forty-three years old. Here, he found a lone individual, Hungry Mike, who was interested in selling his place. JB bought the cabin and land for $100. Hungry Mike moved on and was never heard from again.

JB and Martin Billiter spent the winter of 1882 in Hungry Mike's cabin. He had done a good job in building the cabin with peeled cottonwood logs. The roof was covered with deerskin topped by a layer of soil.

In the spring, David Evans, commonly known as Doby, walked into the valley and was hired by Hurlburt. The three men cleared about an acre of land and planted a garden using all the seeds they had available. They also made a ditch to Parachute Creek so they would have irrigation water.

JB went back to California to get his family. He returned with his wife and their children: Frances (Trimmer), Luther, Mark, Minnie (Clarke), and Rebecca (Wayne). They traveled by train to Rawlins, Wyoming, and located the team that he had left earlier. After three days, they gathered everything they owned and headed for the Grand River valley. They brought with them a strong box containing all their money, important papers, and the Bible. On the back of the wagon was a wire coop containing twelve hens and one rooster and a box holding such essential tools as an axe, planes, a saw, and a level needed for sighting ditches and other leveling activities.

The family arrived after dark and spent their first night on Parachute Creek in Hungry Mike's cabin. They woke in the morning to find that Doby had built a snug dugout, twenty-six feet square, and it was to this structure that the family moved. In this new home, the family set up their stove, tables, and other necessary living furniture and used the area as a kitchen and general family room. The cabin became the sleeping quarters. The dugout that Doby had built provided adequate shelter for the family, and the garden provided a generous supply of vegetables. With abundant deer nearby, the family had plenty to eat to survive. As the rest of the family settled in, Billiter, Doby, and JB spent a good part of the summer cutting and hewing logs to build a larger home.

Hurlburt had purchased four sections of choice land along Parachute Creek when he bought the cabin from Hungry Mike. He sold off portions of this land over the years and continued to build up his real estate activities, but never ranched again. Hurlburt's work paid off. He helped establish the town of Parachute in 1885 and turned the old Hurlburt cabin into the first school in 1889. He gave the land for the First Christian Church, built in 1898, which is still in operation today. He was instrumental in promoting orchards in the valley and adjacent mesas; he served two years as president of the Farmer's Club and served as secretary of the local school board, adding a view that influenced the management of the educational system of the valley for years. Though his influences on the community were everlasting, JB Hurlburt died April 14, 1923, and is buried in the Russey-Hurlburt Cemetery. His wife Martha died in 1940 and is also buried there.

Martin Billiter, who accompanied JB Hurlburt from California to Parachute, was born in Ohio in 1842. Only a minimal amount of information about him was found. He came to the Parachute Creek valley in September of 1882 with JB Hurlburt, bringing his sheep from California. He was a big help to the Hurlburt family in establishing the town and community of Parachute. He was a member of the Christian Church, Myron Reed Post, and the Grand Army of the Republic (GAR). Martin made his home in Parachute for twenty years until he passed away October 11, 1901.

JB HURLBURT'S CHILDREN | #2

Twelve children were born to John Breeden "JB" and Martha Ann "Mattie" (Rock) Hurlburt; many of them stayed in Grand Valley all their lives. Details of the family follow.

FRANCES ELLEN (HURLBURT) TRIMMER | #2

Frances Ellen was the first child born in Pittsville, Shasta County, California, on September 4, 1872. When she was eleven years old in 1883, she, along with five siblings, moved with the family by train and wagon to the Parachute area. She married Joseph Trimmer June 3, 1889, in Parachute, and together they had six children. After living in Parachute for some time along the lower reaches of Parachute Creek, the family eventually moved to Washington State. Frances died January 7, 1938, and is buried in Everett, Washington. Additional information on Joseph could not be found.

LUTHER LEE HURLBURT | #2

Luther Lee was the first son born to JB and Mattie Hurlburt. He was born April 24, 1875, in Pittsville, California, and came with his family to Colorado when he was eight years old. He was a bachelor for most of his life, until he married Mary Emma Hedrick when he was fifty-three years old. They had no children. Luther was a sheep rancher and owned land along with his brother Mark. They ran their sheep on the high plateaus of the Parachute Creek area. Furthermore, he raised hay on the Hurlburt ranch along Parachute Creek, and remained in Parachute for most of his life. In his later years, Luther served as a consultant on the movie *Yellowstone Kelly*. His journey came to an end on December 10, 1969, at the age of ninety-four years. Luther is buried in the Battlement Mesa Cemetery in Parachute.

MARK PITT HURLBURT | #2

Mark Pitt, the second son, was born March 30, 1877, in Pittsville, California. He was six years old when the family travelled to Parachute. He never married but did help raise his orphaned niece and nephew, Daisy (Looney) and Oscar Shehorn. He was a rancher and landowner and was one of the first to own a John Deere two-cylinder tractor. He often had well-grown alfalfa hay and was seen mowing it with this (putt-putt) tractor on numerous occasions. Mark died April 5, 1970, and is buried in the Russey-Hurlburt Cemetery.

MINNIE HESTER (HURLBURT) CLARKE | #2

Minnie Hester made the trip to western Colorado with the rest of her family when she was three years old. She was born March 30, 1879, in Pittsville, California, and married Joseph S. Clarke on January 1, 1895. They had seven children, with four reaching adulthood. Joe Clarke disappeared in Wyoming in 1909, and was never heard from again. Minnie returned to Parachute with her children and homesteaded property outside of the town of Parachute. She operated the local telephone company office for a number of years. She eventually moved into a new home in Parachute. Minnie died in Rifle, January 8, 1961, and is buried in Russey-Hurlburt Cemetery.

REBECCA (HURLBURT) WAYNE | #2

The youngest of the Hurlburt family to leave California and move towards western Colorado was Rebecca Lucinda "Lou," born February 16, 1882, in Pittsville, California. She was a small girl when her father came back to California to bring the family to Colorado. Lou married Herbert Claude Wayne May 30, 1902, and they had ten children. Herbert was a farmer, but the family spent only a short time in Colorado before moving to Idaho. Their first child was born in Colorado. Lou died February 21, 1962, in Hillsboro, Oregon.

MARTHA MAE (HURLBURT) BURNSIDE | #2

Martha Mae was born in Parachute May 25, 1884. It is thought that her mother may have been pregnant with Mae when the family moved from California to western Colorado. Mae married Fredrick Burnside November 22, 1910, and they had five children, all born in the town of Parachute. Fred was a farmer but was also involved with the lumber industry. Mae died on December 12, 1978, and is buried in the Russey-Hurlburt Cemetery.

LOTTIE BELLE (HURLBURT) SHEHORN | #2

Lottie Belle was the seventh child born to JB and Mattie. She was born May 15, 1886, in Parachute and for a time taught at one of the schools on Parachute Creek. She married Joseph Shehorn September 12, 1913, and they had three children. Joe was a laborer on the railroad. Both Lottie and Joseph died on the same day, February 20, 1920, from the Spanish flu. Three days later, Anna Belle, their youngest daughter, died. Tragically, the three had survived the worst years of the disease which devastated entire families worldwide in 1918-19, only to succumb as the pandemic finally came to an end. They all are buried in the Russey-Hurlburt Cemetery. Their two remaining children, Daisy, age five, and Oscar, age three, went to live with their grandparents, JB and Mattie Hurlburt. Lottie's brothers, Mark and Luther, also helped a great deal in raising these two children.

Eight members of the J. B. and Martha Hurlburt family, ca. 1939. L to R, Minnie Clark, Mae Burnside, Martha Rock Hurlburt (mother), Jessie Baughman, Rebecca Lou Lucinda (Hurlburt) Wayne, Daisy Green, Winifred Christensen, and Luther Hurlburt. Photo taken Oct. 4 at Mae Burnside's home in Meeker, Colorado.

FRED FISHER HURLBURT | #2

Fred Fisher was the third son and eighth child of the Hurlburt family. He was born January 1, 1889, in Parachute. Fred and Alice Pearl Baughman, sister of Jessie (Hurlburt) Baughman's husband, "Yone" Baughman, married on August 27, 1912, and they had four children. In 1918, Fred went to work for the Denver & Rio Grande Western Railroad in Grand Junction and moved in 1927 to work for the Union Pacific Railroad in Utah as a car-man. Fred was very active in the Masonic Lodge. He died in Ogden, Utah, on March 31, 1968, and is buried in the Ogden City Cemetery.

MARGARITE ANN HURLBURT | #2

Margarite was born March 15, 1890, but lived only nine months. She died in December of 1890 and is buried in the Russey-Hurlburt Cemetery.

JESSIE EVELYN (HURLBURT) BAUGHMAN FAMILY | #2

Jessie Evelyn, a long-time resident of Parachute Creek, was born in Parachute July 24, 1892. Their home was about one and a half miles west of the town of Parachute and on the south side of Parachute Creek. She married Jonathan Curtis "Yone" Baughman May 13, 1912. (A detailed description of Yone and Jessie's family may be found earlier in this report). Yone Baughman died of a stroke in 1929, leaving a pregnant wife and six children. Jessie's brothers, Mark and Luther, who were already helping with Lottie and Joseph's son and daughter, also helped put food on the table for their sister Jessie and her children. Jessie died January 7, 1977, and is buried in the Russey-Hurlburt Cemetery.

WINIFRED WINNIE (HURLBURT) CHRISTENSEN | #2

Winifred "Silvery Winnie" was born September 1, 1896, in Parachute. She married Henry J. Christensen June 1, 1917, and they had no children. He died in 1932 and Winnie lived her remaining forty-four years in Parachute. She died September 21, 1976, and is buried in the Russey-Hurlburt Cemetery.

DAISY JUNE (HURLBURT) GREEN FAMILY | #2

Daisy June was the youngest of the JB and Martha Hurlburt children. She was born June 1, 1899, and lived most of her ninety-five years in Parachute. Daisy married Robert Ernest "Bob" Green October 6, 1917, in Glenwood Springs. He was born 1891 and spent thirty years as a US mail carrier in the Parachute area. Daisy was an active correspondent for the *Grand Valley News* for years and participated in most of the local events. She was a charter member of a ladies aid organization called "The Willing Workers," formed in 1921. She contributed much to the community of Parachute for some fifty years, was a friend to everyone, and was held in high esteem in the community.

Daisy and Bob had two children: Evelyn (Green) Lewis and Robert Eugene "Bobby" Green. Evelyn was born in 1918 and spent most of her life in the state of Washington. Bobby was born in 1933.

Their son "Bobby" Green was a graduate of Grand Valley High School. He attended Colorado School of Mines, graduated, and became a certified engineer. He worked as a heavy metal mining engineer in Peru and other foreign countries during his career, spending much of his time in copper mining. He married his high school sweetheart, Gloria Samples, and together they traveled the world. He and Gloria retired after thirty years and live in Tucson, Arizona.

Daisy died on December 20, 1994, of cancer in Sequim, Washington, where she had gone to live with her daughter Evelyn, who took care of Daisy in her last year. Bob and Daisy were both buried in the Russey-Hurlburt Cemetery.

VAN HORN FAMILY | #3, 1

Lyman E. Van Horn was born September 1, 1899, in Parachute. His father Martin T. Van Horn was from New York and his mother, Kate Van Horn, also came from New York. Lyman worked for the D&RG Railroad, retiring as foreman for the Grand Valley section of the railroad. He married Gladys Butts when she was eighteen years old in 1920. They spent most of their life in Grand Valley.

Lyman and Gladys had three children as follows: Nola M., born in 1921; Ruth, born in 1923; and Lyman C. Jr., born in 1926. Lyman E. Van Horn had a brother, Wes, who played the violin (fiddle) and was frequently called on to play for the many dances in the Grand Valley community. Wes worked for Mr. Wheatley at the *Grand Valley News* for a number of years and he took over the *Grand Valley News* when Mr. Wheatley died in 1937.

The Van Horn Ranch was a deeded fifty-five-acre island property owned by Lyman C. Van Horn. It was located at the mouth of Parachute Creek and was surrounded by the Colorado River at one time. The Hurlburt Ranch was north and just across the creek on the east side, forming the northeast boundary to the Van Horn ranch. The channel surrounding the ranch on the north was slowly drying up in the 1940s. There were several hundred acres of meander land (floodplain land owned by the government) that surrounded the island. The farmland had received irrigation water from an elaborate flume that had been built to carry the water across the incoming northwest river channel. This channel was cut off shortly after the flume was built. To continue to obtain irrigation water for fields beyond the channel, a ditch was built from Parachute Creek across the channel to carry water to a hay field of some twenty-five acres on the south end of the property.

This Island Ranch had a lot of large cottonwood trees and brush along the waterways that provided good winter shelter and feed for livestock and wildlife. Paul Lindauer leased this property for his cattle winter range. When Lyman Jr. and Betty Sue (Stone) inherited the property and decided to move to California, Paul bought the property in the late 1940s.

At some time during the 1950s, the government decided to place the government owned land surrounding private property in the floodplain (called meander land) on the adjacent landowners' tax rolls. This transferred ownership of the meander land surrounding the Island Ranch from the government to Paul and Bessie Lindauer. That land was used for many years as the wintering and calving range for 100-plus head of cows. The property was sold to a New Jersey firm by the partnership of Ivo and Sydney Lindauer who had purchased the family ranch in the late 1970s from their parents and operated it for a number of years. The partnership was dissolved later and the New Jersey firm sold the island ranch a few years later to the Barrett Gas Development Company. A greenbelt was established by the Lindauers between the river and the Island Ranch prior to selling the property that they had owned for over thirty years.

NOLTE AND RUPP FAMILY

The Englebert Rupp family, who emigrated from Germany in 1887, lived on the lower end of Parachute Creek. They farmed immediately south of Parachute Creek about one mile downriver and south of the town of Grand Valley. A granddaughter of the Rupp family, Anna Rupp, married Paul Nolte in the 1930s in Grand Junction. They farmed the Rupp property, and Paul did custom work with his new International Harvester H tractor. He often plowed fields for neighbors and others of the valley. He obtained his irrigation water from the Diamond Ditch that was a diversion from Parachute Creek. This ditch irrigated their farm along with several others on its way down, ending at the Nolte farm.

Anna spent much of her life as the clerk for the Grand Valley Lumber & Supply Store. Harry Koch of Aspen built the store in response to the potential needs of the Hallett Ditch Company, which was building the Havemeyer Ditch. Following a 1913 fire that destroyed his and many other buildings on First Street in Parachute, Koch built a new large brick building and restocked it with lumber, harnesses, machinery, and a variety of other hardware supplies. HT Sukeforth managed this store for over forty years, adding groceries, dry goods, gasoline, and many other items commonly used in a rural community. Their business thrived and the store was very successful for many years.

When HT Sukeforth retired, Anna and Paul took over management of the store. Paul managed the store and Anna looked after the books and inventory. After Anna died in 1963, Ed Koch sold the store to Marvin and Roberta "Bobbi" (Benson) Wambolt who ran the store for some five years before closing the doors during a time of economic slowdown.[121] Bobbi, age eighty-four in 2015, spent most of her life on Parachute Creek and was a great help in identifying and confirming many individuals and dates found in this report. Anna (Rupp) Nolte died in Grand Junction at the age of sixty-five and Paul died on November 16, 1967. Their burial site is not known.

OTHER STOCKMEN ON THE PARACHUTE CREEK DRAINAGE

The Michael O'Toole family came to the Parachute area in 1887 and homesteaded on Battlement Mesa. The family settled on a large ranch adjacent to the road leading up from the Colorado River to Morrisania Mesa.

---

[121] Murray. *Lest We Forget.* 1973.

The O'Toole brothers, Edward, Charles, Joseph, John, and Hugh, were frequently seen on Parachute Creek and on the summer range of the Book Cliffs. John, Charlie, and Hugh all worked on the ranch while Ed O'Toole was in the horse business. Joe, the third oldest of the O'Toole brothers, was a ranch foreman for the Morrisania Land and Cattle Company. They also ranged their cattle on the Book Cliffs. Their brands were Z/H and Bar D Seven.

Joseph Clemency "Joe" O'Toole was a quiet man and good friends with the East Fork cowmen, always working with them to take care of his cattle. Joe was born in Parachute in 1889 and lived well into the early 1970s. He moved to California in his later years.

The O'Tooles ran about 700 head of cattle and raised some twenty stacks of hay. They also bought hay from the Clark and Jenny Ranch. In mild winters, they would winter their cattle on oil cake on the Colorado River and into the cutoff country towards Roan Creek. Many local cattlemen did this in the early days. They also borrowed money from the Federal Reserve Banks as security in connection with their ranch operation, should the prices of cattle drop. One of the O'Toole boys drowned in the Colorado River when he got caught in an undercurrent.

Other stockmen in this country were Phillip Waterman, Billy Aymer, Watson Dickerson, Bill Hughes, and several others whose information was not found. These folks all ranged on the Book Cliffs up Parachute Creek. Phillip Waterman wintered his cattle for some years on the Otis Murray Ranch on Wallace Creek where they received excellent care. Sam Wasson was one of the popular livestock men on Parachute Creek. Many in the valley considered Sam to be a grand person. When he was the local postmaster in the 1920s, he would open the post office day or night to give people their mail.

There were other ranchers and farmers who lived on Parachute Creek during the period covered in this incomplete history. However, only those whose information was found in the four-year search for families have been included. Hopefully, over the years, as more information comes to light, it may be added to this story.

CHAPTER 8

Life along the Creek

RECOLLECTIONS OF EARLY PIONEERS OF PARACHUTE CREEK AND GRAND VALLEY

In the early days, Bus Pasquire and Philip Waterman operated a barbershop in Grand Valley, followed by Ben Anderson.

Two of the old-timers that are gone were Phil Moore and Saro Pickett who won the bronco riding at the Grand Valley Day show. Doc Wilson won the roping contest.

Grand Valley had one of the top baseball teams in Western Colorado. Some of the major players were Ross Conner, Harry Wasson, Beech Zediker, Cuny Milner, Paul Baum, Clarence Ulrey, Ben Anderson, and Cottonington.

Zel Herman and his brothers, who operated a large hay ranch on Wallace Creek, came to Parachute Creek to hunt, fish, and have picnics.

Charlie Sawyer had a ranch on Wallace Creek and baled his hay for transfer across the Colorado River. They floated the hay across by boat and cable, then loaded the hay on freight cars at Una to be shipped elsewhere.

The Dutton family of Wallace Creek were frequent visitors at Grand Valley and Parachute Creek. Mrs. Dutton's sisters homesteaded on Wallace Creek in the early days where they raised hay and grain.

In 1913, Harve Sprague was the first to file on land above the ledges of West Fork on Parachute Creek. He had a record of shooting wolves for a period of some thirty years and was noted for raising large work mules.

In the lower Willow Creek, Margie Segar Von Rosenberg Sipprelle homesteaded in 1920. She sold out to the oil shale company.

Lydia and Doctor Jacobson had a homestead on the fork of Willow Creek and Bear's Run. At the head of Willow Creek was Esther Homequist Hackett. She had filed on land and was a talented artist. She also sold to the oil companies.

Henry Wilda, Anna McCosh, Dan Webster, and Bob Latham homesteaded in the Circle Dot area. The Wilda Trail built by Mr. Wilda was a five-year project, which, for a distance of about five miles, led from the foot of Parachute Creek into Circle Dot mountain ranch.

The Carpenters, from Iowa, lived next to Fern and Glen Eastman, who homesteaded on Circle Dot. Frances Smerchek was at the head of Circle Dot. On the hill south, where one would find the Rondels and Roy Hungerford along with the John Cox family, and the Crawford family's homestead. Some of these folks farmed up there and packed their machinery on horses and mules to their homestead. They packed off milk and cream on packsaddles and took it to the railhead for shipment to creameries. Fred Barrith had a thrashing machine up on his homestead. Barrith lived up there and operated a dairy on Mt. Callahan using the Riley Gulch trail. He also packed cream on horses off the mountain.

These homesteads were on the West Mountains south of Parachute Creek while others, identified below, were on the Old Mountain, east and south of the East Fork of Parachute Creek.

Cade Benson homesteaded in Rulison Gulch on top of the Book Cliffs by way of the Granlee Trail and he operated a dairy at his homestead. In later years Fay Stanton and Irish Sherwood operated dairies and packed their cream off on horses. Buck Bailey, Tom Cline, and the Pritchard family homesteaded there, also. They ran some cattle and sold their holdings to the oil shale people. John Boleran, an ironworker from Pueblo, homesteaded at the head of Bear's Run.

– As told by Paul Lindauer & Harry Hansen; recorded in 1972

EARLY LIFE OF A COWBOY IN THE PARACHUTE CREEK AREA

The cowboys always looked forward to roundup time for it was like going to a fair or rodeo. Lots of mornings we put on a rodeo when some of them cold-back horses were saddled, sometimes before daylight.

I remember one time in Parachute, when the round-up crews gathered the whole bunch. All of these cattle were at the head of Ben Good Ridge where Yellow Jacket takes off for North-water on the East Fork cattlemen's range. This was in the fall of 1918. Frank Squires of the Rifle boys was range boss; Walter Oldland was the boss of the Piceance, and Sam Wasson of the Grand Valley crew.

The main herd there consisted of 1,400 cattle in one bunch and we managed to get them all worked before dark according to brands and owner's marks. Following that, we had to move them to holding pastures and later trailed them to railroad stockyards where they were shipped to markets.

The town of Grand Valley has always boomed. In those days, during shipping time, there were three hotels, two saloons, a couple of livery barns, and a blacksmith shop that did considerable business in shoeing horses.

First, we would go up on the mountains around September 20. Two or three men would take their bedrolls and an average of seven saddle horses for each person. They then would head over to the Figure Four Springs, a tributary to Piceance Creek, and come around with the Piceance Creek wagon to the East Fork cattle range.

It took about two weeks to gather the cattle there and we would pick up strays belonging to the Grand Valley stockmen. In those days we had no drift fences and about 150 cattle would stray off the range to the Piceance Creek area. After this was done, we would ride our own range, which was all public domain in those days, and hold them in the Wasson pasture, located on the Book Cliffs in upper East Fork of Parachute Creek, until time to ship.

We would then trail to the railroad stockyards that was about twenty-four miles and load an average of twenty cars of cattle with thirty cattle in each car. Some of the big fat four-year old steers would need to turn their heads sideways to enter the door of the cars. These cattle were sold to the packers and slaughtered, then placed on the market as eatable beef.

In those days there were lots of coyotes, bobcats, and all sorts of predatory animals. No gophers or moles were visible. In later years when the predatory animals were destroyed, the gophers and moles took over and chewed up the parks and bottomlands, eating the roots and crowns of the grass and storing tremendous amounts of this vegetation in large mounds. This was their winter feed supply.

The grass in early days was three feet high all over the country, and then the gophers and moles returned. About 1929, during the panic, they returned as the predatory animals had been killed off. Now we have more rodents that are a food source for coyotes, bobcats, and eagles; however, in 1974, the grass is returning as a result of management by the Bureau of Land Management.

In the early days, we used three cow camps for the cowboys. The Wasson Cabin on East Fork of upper Parachute Creek was built in 1913 by the Wassons, O'Tooles, Watermans, and Hallie Parkhurst. Another cabin, built in 1914 by Everett Tracy on North water, could be used if needed. Bill Clough of Rifle owned the cabin in later years. In 1926, my brothers and I built a cabin on the north slope of Long Ridge next to Yellow Jacket. This cabin has served to meet the needs of cowboys needing a place to stay overnight or stop for lunch in the more recent times.

– Recorded, Paul Lindauer in 1972. [122]

Note: In 2015, the Lindauer Cow Camp remains present and is used by cowmen as needed, but rarely for tourist people or recreation. It now has a padlock to secure the items inside.

TRAGEDIES OF THE AREA

Harve Creek's father was killed in a gun duel on top of Mount Callahan off of the Parachute Creek valley. A horse fell on Lee Johns and Ross Latham on Mt. Callahan and both suffered broken legs. Ross Latham, Sim Stowell, and Eli Etchison were doing assessment work on oil shale claims when a rockslide caved in on the assessment hole they were digging, killing Etchison. A mule killed a Hispano sheepherder on Mt. Callahan.

There were a few other tragedies like a shooting match in a Grand Valley dance hall in the early days where no one was killed but a powder mark was left on one fellow's head. A tragedy occurred on July 30, 1921, when an oil shale tramway located in Wheeler Gulch some four miles up Parachute Creek collapsed. A cable on the upper end of the tramway gave way as men were leaving work and were on their way down. As the cable came loose from the upper end of the tramway, it came twisting and writhing down the hillside, scattering men and machinery all the way down. Men were thrown from the small car in which they were riding and others were killed or injured as the car struck the bottom of the tramway. One individual refused to ride down because he considered it too dangerous and was walking along the tramway. His body was cut in half by the twisting cable as he traveled down. Seven men were killed and three were injured in this accident.[123]

While most everyone was concerned with the tramway, the Grand Valley Bank was robbed at the same time with the loss of some $5,000 in cash and $15,000 in securities. This occurred during a major thunderstorm, so locals did not recognize the dynamiting of the safe. The robbers also used blankets covering the safe to muffle the sound. The robbery occurred on Monday, Colorado Day, August 1, and the bank had been closed for two days. Although detectives were on the case immediately, no arrests were ever made.

In the late 1940s, another tramway was built, this time by the Union Oil Company of California. Due to the steepness of the hillside and the dangers associated with its operation, it was abandoned after a loss of one life and a road was built in its place. A new location was identified where the shale

---

[122] Lindauer, "Early Life of a Cowboy," 1972.

[123] Murray. *Lest We Forget*. 1973.

could be pushed over the cliff and slid or rolled down the hill to a collection point.

There were serious accidents on the East Fork Range in early days. Watson Dickerson had a knife kicked into his thigh by a calf, inflicting a terrible gash. A tourniquet was applied to his leg and then hot poultices and he was ready to go home in four days to recuperate.

Julius Lindauer was bucked off of a horse while carrying an ax that resulted in severing an artery on the side of his head. Several cowboys tried to stop the bleeding with no success. Ivo Lindauer, the author, made the wild ride for help from Bull Gulch camp to the upper Lindauer Ranch to telephone for a doctor. He made this twelve-mile trip in less than one hour and was met on the road by Dr. Dean Moore from Rifle after the local physician, Dr. Miller, refused to come to the end of the road. Julius nearly bled to death; however he recovered after two or three weeks. It was a close call with the loss of so much blood.

Fred Werhonig's brother Rudolph drowned in the Colorado River near the Van Horn Island when he was thrown from an overturned boat. One of the O'Toole boys drowned in the river one mile above the bridge at Grand Valley. He was swimming with some other boys and was caught in a current. Two high school boys, Melvin Martin and John Bruckner, drowned at the Colorado River Bridge at Grand Valley in 1954. An effort by Sid Lindauer and Tom Spangler to rescue them was not successful. That ended the swimming in the Colorado River for a period of years.

One of the early homesteaders on or near the head of West Fork was the Sumner family, consisting of three girls and two boys. A bucking horse in one of the Oldlands' corrals killed Tim Sumner. Tige Sumner was the other boy who lost his life. He would go down the mountains on snowshoes part way once every six weeks to the Lindauer Ranch to pick up his mail, a distance of about sixteen miles. In the spring of the year, the snow was crusted in the mornings so he could walk the first six miles on snowshoes and walk the rest of the way without them, pick up his mail, and start back to where he left his snowshoes.

This particular day, Paul Lindauer loaned him a horse to ride the first eight miles. He then turned the horse loose, which came back to the ranch. A warm Chinook wind had come up on this March 20 day and the snow had melted. Tige broke through about four feet of snow and wore himself out trying to get back to his snowshoes. His mother found him the next morning frozen to death. The word of this tragedy reached Piceance Creek. Ray Finier and Art Ebler recovered the body by using four horses and traveling ten miles with a sled, and then skiing in on snowshoes with a toboggan, before bringing the body out by way of Piceance Creek. The Sumner family lived there for three years, and then lost their homestead.

LAST TRAIN ROBBERY

A lonely spot on the banks of the Colorado River known as Streit's Flat, just three miles west from the town of Parachute, was the scene of one of the last train robberies in the West.

Harvey Logan, a member of Butch Cassidy's notorious "Hole in the Wall" gang known as Kid Curry, was looking for gold when the westbound Denver & Rio Grande train stopped at Parachute in the middle of the night. It was June 7, 1904. Kid Curry and his cohorts had made ample preparations.[124]

A man clambered onto the train and, pointing a gun, ordered the engineer to continue to Streit's Flat. Once there, he was joined by two more men. The three outlaws forced the baggage master to open the baggage car. Then, using dynamite, they blew up the safe and a good part of the baggage car.

---

[124] Gulliford, "They Robbed the Wrong Train," 1983.

Top left: The first robber climbed onto the coal tender and confronted the engineer as the train left the station.

Top right: The robbers fled across the river in a boat they had stashed on the river bank.

Lower right: The train robbers escaped from the river on horseback.

What they saw—or didn't see—must have been a big disappointment. The gold they expected to find had apparently been sent on an earlier train.

The thwarted threesome jumped off the train and ran to the Colorado River, where they had hidden a boat. They rowed across the river, then mounted horses they had tethered there earlier. They rode east toward Battlement Mesa, stopping to steal fresh horses whenever their mounts slowed.

Meanwhile, a posse was formed including lawmen from Grand Junction and Parachute as well as several local ranchers. The outlaws and their pursuers crossed Battlement Mesa, and exchanged gunfire on Mamm Creek, several miles to the east. Somehow, the desperadoes got away, and fled farther east.

The posse caught up with them at East Divide Creek. The would-be train robbers hid behind rocks, calling out to their pursuers to "go back or get hurt." No luck. The posse opened fire. As the gun battle raged, one of the robbers was hit. Posse members heard him vow to "finish the job" himself, then a single gunshot. All was quiet as they crept up to the rock. Behind it lay a dead man, shot in the chest and head.

The remaining two outlaws fled on foot, leaving behind their horses which also lay dead. The men were never apprehended or identified.

The Pinkerton Detective Agency later confirmed identification of the dead train robber as Kid Curry, Harvey Logan. His body was taken to Glenwood Springs, where it was buried near Doc Holliday's grave.

The events of the train robbery have been painted by Jack Roberts, a well know painter of western art who had a studio in Redstone, Colorado. Three of his paintings are on display in the Parachute Administrative Office/Court Room in the town of Parachute. After he completed these paintings, he prepared three drawings depicting the events and gave them to his son, Gary Miller, (owner and manager of Miller's Dry Goods in Rifle). [125]

LOCAL NEWSPAPERS

The first newspaper in Parachute was called *The Parachute Index* first published on October 15, 1895, by JB Hurlburt & Company. It became the official newspaper with a new name, *Grand Valley News*, in 1904. This occurred as the town changed its name to Grand Valley as reported by both Erlene Murray, author of *Lest We Forget*, and Floyd McDaniels, the last editor of *The Grand Valley News*. When Elmer Wheatley moved his family to the recently renamed town of Grand Valley in 1913, he purchased the *Grand Valley News*. A dedicated Democrat, he continued editing and publishing this newspaper until his death July 23, 1937, at the age of sixty-three years. Elmer and his wife ran the old printing press with a gasoline engine

Wes Van Horn worked for Wheatley for a number of years before taking over the newspaper. He regularly published the *Grand Valley News* weekly until leasing it to Floyd McDaniels. While Floyd was in high school, he worked with Wes and learned typesetting and the operation of the *Grand Valley News*. After graduating from high school in 1948, Floyd left Parachute and attended college for one year and then leased the paper in 1949. He continued working with the paper until 1951 when he discontinued his lease and entered the military.

Following Floyd's service time, he returned to college and finished his degree in secondary education. After a short stay in Virginia and some teaching, Floyd returned to Grand Valley in 1956 and bought the *Grand Valley News* from Kenneth Becktell. He published the newspaper for almost fifteen years and then sold the building to the State of Colorado for the new Interstate Highway (I-70), which would be coming through his property. The *Grand Valley News* was the major newspaper for information on Parachute Creek for nearly 100 years.

EARLY DAY BLACKSMITHS

Blacksmiths were a critical part of the Parachute Creek community in the early days of wagons, buggies, and horses. There was a strong need for someone to sharpen plowshares, shoe horses, and construct other farm items from steel as needed. It was the artistic blacksmiths who were able to meet this task. Not only did they fix buggy and wagon wheels, but they often had a livery stable nearby where weary travelers could overnight their horse or where one could rent a team, a wagon, or a saddle horse as needed to travel around the area.

Some of the early homesteaders who came to Parachute Creek brought their blacksmith skills with them, and some families such as the Wheelers set up shop in town as the demand for blacksmiths was great. Charlie Davis was one of the first blacksmiths; later John Helm, Walter Wheeler, Fred Werhonig,

---

[125] Munsell, *Colorado Artist Jack Roberts, Painting the West*. 2015.

and Sam Seder left their record as good blacksmiths. Harry Hoag was the last local blacksmith and was known for the power hammer that he used to make plowshares. This hammer was sold to Paul Lindauer who used it for years. It was sold to the Silt Historical Society in Silt, Colorado, where Bill Smith, the blacksmith and caretaker of the Silt Historical Society, is now in possession of it. Harry Morrow and Delbert Cox operated a garage in Parachute in the early days, followed by John Wheeler and Chet Spitler.

WOLVES ON PARACHUTE CREEK

Wolves have been around for a long period of time, much before man arrived. Yet, the fear that wolves created remains today. Much of this fear has resulted from the nature of the animal, considering that wolves are equally as fearful of humans. The two rarely encountered each other. While the popularity of the "Little Red Riding Hood" story and "the big bad wolf" has caused many to fear the wolf, the real dangers were much worse.

When livestock were brought to the New World, they were another food source for wolves, and lone wolves took advantage of free-ranging livestock. When colonists began losing stock, they lashed out at wolves with folklore and physical violence, creating a long-lasting fear that has been passed from generation to generation. "Little Red Riding Hood" was just one example of the extensive propaganda. Wolf bounty programs mushroomed throughout the West resulting in a near extinction of wolves. In 1906, the US Biological Survey (BBS) was established to examine the impact of wolves on livestock, but as the result of extensive lobbying by livestock owners, the Bureau became a wolf-extermination unit. Even a famous biologist and artist, John James Audubon, promoted the destruction of wolves that nearly eliminated the gray wolf by 1950. The Bureau of Biological Survey continued to promote wolf destruction through their propaganda. Wolves were major problems for ranchers at the head of Parachute Creek in the early 1900s. Since there was little big game to prey on, wolves would chase yearling calves and chew up the hams on the ones they caught. Until the first of July, local ranchers would have as many as twenty-five yearlings in for doctoring with carbolic acid and tar until they healed up. Ranchers used every method that they could think of in an attempt to eliminate the wolves.

In 1929, Arthur Carhart, a *Denver Post* writer and conservationist and Stanley Young, coauthor of the Bureau of Biological Survey (BBS), published *Last Stand of the Pack*.[126] This was to be an account of the extermination of the last wolves in Colorado. Young headed a federal program designed to kill every last wolf in Colorado. About that time, Bill Caywood of Piceance Creek, known as a government trapper, came on the scene and started trapping these wolves.

Bill Caywood was born in 1871 and lived on his ranch along Piceance Creek in Rio Blanco County near Meeker with his wife, Laura, and six children. He was a farmer and an independent trapper before joining the BBS in 1915. He was hired by the local stockmen to reduce the number of wolves that were damaging and eating their young livestock and decimating the deer herds. During 1912 and 1913, "Big" Bill Caywood, as he was called, killed 140 wolves for which the local stockmen paid him $50 per head. In his book, Carhart described Caywood:

> [He was] big shouldered, slightly stooped, not quite bowlegged but evidently a rider of cow land trails. Caywood represented the type that put much of the work into the winning of the western wildernesses.

---

[126] Carhart, *Last Stand of the Pack*, 1929.

A rancher asked Caywood what he was going to do when all the wolves were gone, and Caywood said that he was unsure, but he couldn't live in the city.

> I've just got a lot of love and respect for the gray wolf. He's a real fellow, the big gray is. Lots of brains, I feel sorry for him. It's his way of livin'. He don't know better. And I feel sorry every time I see one of those big fellows thrashing around in a trap bellowing bloody murder . . . Guess I'm too much a part of the outdoors to hold any grudge against animals . . . it's part the way that wolves go after poor defenseless steers, murder does and fawns and drag down bucks that helps me go out and bring them in.

Ambivalence stalks Caywood in another death scene:

> "You poor old devil," cried Bill huskily as he stooped to the dying wolf. "You poor, lonely, old, murdering devil."

In a period of fifteen years, he had practically wiped out all of the wolves except for one called "Old Rags." It took Caywood a year and a half to catch him and he did so by turning his traps upside down, for the old wolf would dig under the trap that was set straight up and snap it with his foot. That contributed to ending the career of one of the best trappers in the country, causing him to retire and eventually move to Delta, Colorado, where he lived for many years before passing away, as reported by some (Parachute) "old-timers."

Caywood wrote Carhart in 1930 to say how much he liked his book *Last Stand of the Pack* that made him famous. However, he added, "The demise of the wolf also had consequences for the wolfer."

In 1935, Arthur Carhart and Stanley Young alerted Caywood to rumors of a pack of old buffalo lobos running over toward the Big Salt Wash and the Cathedral Bluffs area (Rio Blanco County). Carhart recalled, "I told him then if they were genuine lobos and you were going to be sent; I want to go along if it was OK with you."

By that time, Young was rising to the top of the BBS back in Washington, DC, but the BBS had other ideas. They forced Caywood to retire. "No one will hire a crippled old man," Caywood told Carhart.[127] Young stood firm, but both Caywood and Carhart changed their minds over time about the wolf. Carhart told Mary Austin, "my sympathy, too, was with the old renegades and I think the hunters feel somewhat the same way. Personally, I feel that we are floundering dangerously and ridiculously with our wildlife. A lot of so-called 'conservation' is bunk."

It was not until the late 1960s that attitudes began to change with a greater understanding of the wolf in the environment and its role in the ecosystem. By the early 1970s, the eradication of wolves slowed with the passage of the Endangered Species Act. Since then, wolf populations have increased. However, the number of wolves in Colorado has not returned, and only rarely is one sighted.

Today, there is a major effort underway by a variety of conservation agencies to bring the gray wolf back to the lower Rocky Mountains. The Sierra Club and the Defenders of Wildlife have been leaders in trying to save the wolf.

---

[127] Ibid.

CHAPTER 9

Parachute Creek Ranching and Farming Community Becomes an Industrial Site

In 1910 there were thirty-four families living on Parachute Creek. By 1950, the number had increased to fifty-eight families, and the author knew most of them. In 1974, however, there were approximately eight families left, with four owning their own property.

In 2012, only one of the original families still owned their ranch and farmed their property. Oil and gas companies have purchased all of the other properties on Parachute Creek. Some have been leased back to tenant farmers and ranchers.

The Parachute Creek Valley now contains many natural gas wells. (See maps in Appendix I.)

PARACHUTE MINING DISTRICT (PMD)

Although the District was formed in the spring of 1890, there appears to be no record of the early meetings. On July 9, 1918, at a meeting in Elmer Wheatley's office of the *Grand Valley News*, the Parachute Mining District held its meeting. From then until April 8, 1935, minutes were kept of the organization. Joseph Bellis was elected secretary of PMD in 1918 and maintained the records of this group that met occasionally to discuss oil shale development in the valley.

JB Hurlburt, president of the PMD, called the July 9, 1918, meeting to order and noted that all five officers were present, including TE Bailey as vice president, Sadie Streit as secretary, and two others, Morton Rowley and HM Streit. President Hurlburt noted anyone "owning or having an interest in a mining claim or other property" was eligible for membership in the organization.

Several people were elected to membership including Joseph Bellis, James Doyle, Mary Duplice, JL Herwick, Oren H. Herwick, Guy Herwick, William Ulrey, EE Wheatley, and Judd Sipprelle.

Over the next seventeen years, various meetings were held but due to the unsuccessful development of an oil shale industry, the president and TE Bailey asked secretary Bellis to write up the minutes and file them with the Garfield County Clerk after all had signed them. This brought to a close the planned development of oil shale by the Parachute Mining District organization.[128]

OIL SHALE MINING ON PARACHUTE CREEK

Oil shale in Colorado, found in the Eocene Green River Formation in the northwestern part of the state, developed from fluctuating water levels of Lake Uinta, a fresh water lake that underwent long periods of desiccation in climates ranging from dry-subtropical to moist subtropical. This change occurred some forty-eight to fifty-two million years ago in the geological Eocene Period. Karl Newman, in his report to the Rocky Mountain Association of Geologists (1980), describes the Green River Formation as follows:

> The Green River formation was originally named and described as the Green River shale in southwestern Wyoming by Hayden (1869). In his report he stated a little east of Rock Springs station a new group commences composed of thinly laminated chalky shale, that I have called the Green River shale, because they are best displayed along Green River. They

---
[128] Murray, *Lest We Forget*, 1973, p.144.

are evidently of purely fresh-water origin and of middle Tertiary age. The layers are nearly horizontal and, as shown in the valley of Green River, present a peculiarly banded appearance. One of the marked features of this group is the great amount of combustible or petroleum shale, some portion of which burn with great readiness and has been used for fuel in stoves.

Colorado's oil shale is found in the Eocene Green River formation in the northwestern part of the state. The Green River formation underlies much of the Roan Plateau, Battlement Mesa, Piceance Creek basin, and some of the Grand Mesa. The Piceance Creek basin has the greatest oil-shale resources of the region. It is estimated that where oil-shale beds are at least ten feet thick, the shale resource yields at least thirty gallons per ton, which contains about 118 billion barrels of recoverable oil. Less oil-rich beds, yielding from fifteen to thirty gallons per ton contain an additional 602 billion barrels of recoverable oil. The Green River formation in the Piceance Creek basin is subdivided into four members, that vary in thickness and lithology. These are the Douglas Creek, Garden Gulch, Parachute Creek and Anvil Points members.[129]

In Newman's 1980 report, he notes that in 1931, Bradley discussed two members, the Garden Gulch Member and the Parachute Creek Member that are directly related to the Parachute Creek region as follows:

> The member (Garden Gulch) was named by Bradley (1931), for exposures at Garden Gulch, a tributary to Parachute Creek north of Grand Valley in Garfield County. The unit, about 700 feet (213 m) thick, consists mostly of light gray, thinly laminated, slope-forming, paper shale lying above the Douglas Creek member. Some of the shale is low-grade oil shale; rarely is it rich oil shale. Mud cracks are relatively abundant and fossils, though rather rare, include ostracodes, gar scales, fish and leaves. Bradley (1931) named the beds above the Garden Gulch member, along Parachute Creek, the Parachute Creek member. This member is a cliff-forming unit, about 1,000 feet (305 m) thick, dominated by rich oil shale. Some mudstone and tuff bed areas are also present. Notable fossils such as fly larvae and gar scales, ostracodes and leaves occasionally are found. Bradley also identified other fossils found in the Green River formation of the Piceance Creek basin that included algae, pelecypods, gastropods, fish scales, fish, insect larvae, insects, turtles, crocodiles, pollen and spores. He noted that no mammal remains have been reported from the Green River formation.[130]

In the 1880s and early 1900s, hard rock miners began to move west with their families as the mining industry was declining and the government was opening lands for settlements. When the miners moved into the Parachute Creek Valley some 130 years ago, they became ranchers and farmers with aspirations of raising their families in their new surroundings and being able to provide food and shelter for them. Those that arrived first got the pick of the land and were able to establish profitable ranching operations. However, it wasn't long before too many had moved into the valley and no more land was available for settlement. Consequently, many of the late arrivals ended up with smaller acreages and then had to locate on the poorest soil sites of the valley.

As World War I spread across Europe, the United States became concerned about their naval oil re-

---

[129] Newman, *Geology of Oil Shale in Piceance Creek Basin, Colorado*, 1980, pp. 199-203.

[130] University of Colorado at Boulder. "What Every Westerner Should Know About Oil Shale."

sources and had begun to obtain oil from coal. They thought that oil shale might also be a reliable source. Consequently, in 1913 the US Geological Survey began exploring several sites, including the Western Slope of Colorado, where they knew oil shale existed. In 1916, President Woodrow Wilson withdrew 45,444 acres from the public domain occurring in the Piceance Creek Basin where the East Fork Cattlemen today graze their herds. This withdrawal was originally identified in 1924 as the Naval Oil Shale Reserve (NOSR). Later, it was changed and more acreage was added and titled NOSR 1 with 37,550 acres and NOSR 3 of 18,040 acres. Claims were filed in this area and men were hired to dig assessment holes in an effort to show sufficient work to patent the claim.[131]

The attempt to obtain and process the petroleum product from the extensive amounts of oil shale in the ledges of Parachute Creek was an ongoing task during the 20th century and continues today. Many individuals have given their lives in an effort to get the oil out of the shale. The petroleum material in oil shale is known as "kerogen." It is a tar-like substance classed as a valuable complex carbohydrate that when refined can be processed into a fuel for use in airplanes, autos, pharmaceuticals, and over one hundred different items including plastic products.

High-grade shale that is found in the cliffs of Parachute Creek in the Green River Formation above the valley, often contains over thirty gallons of oil per ton of shale rock. Here, some of it occurs in a dark mahogany vein and is often sought out for research projects. Further west in the Piceance Basin, oil shale is found at lower elevations, and on plateaus where mining from the top down was possible and did occur in the late 1980s.

In the early 1940s during WWII, Paul Lindauer was contacted by the US Navy to collect samples of oil shale from a site they had selected on the east edge of the Naval Oil Shale Reserve. This site was to be the Rifle Oil Shale Project as determined by the Synthetic Fuels Act in 1944 and was located at Anvil Points, an undeveloped area high on the cliffs of the Roan Plateau. A camp was established one mile east of Rulison on the Colorado River flood plain. The necessary men, equipment, and horses needed to access the site were obtained and kept there. A trail was developed from the Colorado River valley floor to the base of the cliffs where the mahogany vein could be reached. The mining was basically by hand with a pick, hammer, shovel, drill bits, and dynamite. The shale gathered from the cliff was placed in gunny sacks and packed on horseback down to the campsite. From this point it was transferred by rail to a US Naval Research Station in Maryland.

A year later in the spring of 1945, the US Bureau of Mines began the base development of an oil shale plant in a new community called Anvil Points. Over the next two years, a community with seventy-four homes was built, and a mine was opened to supply shale to a retorting plant at the base. This research project operated until 1956 when the Synthetic Fuels Act of 1944 expired and the plant was closed down. Since that date, the plant has operated on a small scale producing oil from shale for various clients, including an extended Australian project carried out in the Paraho research facility that was located east of the Anvil Point Facility. They have continued this work to date and recently announced a new venture and name for a web site named Shale-Tech.com.[132]

The Anvil Points project was decommissioned and cleanup was completed between 1984 and 1986. The property was placed under the management of the Bureau of Land Management in 1987. A small operation has continued processing oil from shale at the Anvil Points location. The shale is shipped in from various locations including Europe and Australia for analysis and some processing.

---

[131] Fouch et al, "Oil and Gas Resources of US Naval Oil Shale Reserves 1 and 3, Colorado, and Reserve 2, Utah," 1994.

[132] Shale Tech International Services LLC website, accessed 2014.

The Union Oil Company of California began buying properties in the 1920s and by the later part of 1940 had developed an extraction process called a "rock pump." In this process, the crushed rock is placed in the bottom of a heated retort and is moved up as the hot gases moved down, thus, retorting the crude oil from the shale. They tested the process from 1954 until 1958 in a pilot program using the Unocal A process at the plant site on the purchased Peter Lindauer and Sons Ranch. During this time period they were able to process over 1,200 tons of raw shale per day and once reported that they had produced 1,500 barrels of crude oil in one day. Production quantity ranged from ten to ninety-five gallons per ton of oil shale, but averages were closer to thirty-five gallons/ton. When the shale is processed by heat in a reservoir, the waste product expands some 20 to 25 percent and it is very sticky, like toffee, and causes many problems in removal. At temperatures below 98 degrees Fahrenheit the petroleum product extracted, "kerogen," changes to a solid. The shale must be heated to near 975 degrees Fahrenheit to extract this product from the shale.

As prices for oil declined worldwide, the 1950s plant closed in 1961, but the quest for production of oil from shale continued. A consortium of oil and gas companies including Total Oil Shale Company (Tosco), Standard Oil of Ohio, and Cleveland Cliffs Iron Company created the Colony Oil Shale Project that proposed a commercial oil shale retort in 1963. This plant was to be located a few miles north of the Union Oil Company's 1950s plant using Unocal B process that was a reverse of the A process. Atlantic Richfield joined the project in 1969 and they attempted to retort oils from shale using the Tosco II retorting technology. The project was suspended in 1974. Ashland Oil and Shell Oil Company joined the project, but in the late '70s, most was sold to Atlantic Richfield, leaving Tosco with 40 percent and Atlantic Richfield with 60 percent. Atlantic Richfield sold their share to Exxon who planned a $5 billion oil shale commercial plant project. This massive project lasted for approximately two years; however, on May 2, 1982 ,"Black Sunday," they closed the project and sent 2,000 workers home, thus devastating the local community. Andrew Gulliford, in his text *Boomtown Blues, Colorado Oil Shale, 1885-1985*[133] described in detail the problems that occurred when Exxon shut down its operation, and he also describes the development of oil shale and its impact on local populations. Much of the other oil shale data was found via the Internet.

Fred Hartley attempted a second effort to extract oil from shale through the development of the Unocal Oil Shale Company while using newer technology. A processing/upgrade plant was built on Parachute Creek three miles up from the town of Parachute. It was connected through heated pipelines to a retort located about twelve miles up Parachute Creek and two miles north of the 1950s plant. From 1985 until 1991 the production facility was able to produce 4.6 million barrels of synthetic crude during five years of operation at a cost of nearly $6.5 million.[134] When this company was not able to show a profit, the shareholders terminated its operation and sold the company to Chevron Oil. The plant was taken over by another company and later sold to American Soda, who extracted baking soda from deposits of nahcolite found in association with oil shale. This ended the extraction of oil from shale in Parachute Creek until newer technology came along. Fred Hartley, the executive officer and president of the Union Oil Company of California (Unocal), had spent over thirty years attempting to develop an oil shale industry and make a dent in the billions of barrels of oil that are locked up in the shale rock. He died in California in 1990 at the age of seventy-three.

---

[133] Gulliford, *Boomtown Blues, Colorado Oil Shale, 1885-1985*, 1989.

[134] Wikipedia, "Colony Shale Oil Project," January 19, 2015.

SODA ASH AND SODIUM BICARBONATE PRODUCTION

From the 1930s until the 1980s, the Union Oil Company of California, known by locals as Unocal, purchased a number of ranches up and down Parachute Creek. In the early 1980s, they decided to build an upgrade/processing refinery on some of their properties located about three miles up Parachute Creek and west of the town of Parachute. This facility was needed to support their oil shale retort operation. The history of changes at this location is complex; thus, a historical review of the last thirty plus years at this site is significant to understanding the changes that have occurred on Parachute Creek following the demise of the oil shale plants and upgrade refining facility.

In the 1950s and '60s, Irv Neilson had worked as a geologist with Union Oil Company of California in their mining and retorting of oil shale at the Parachute Creek plant located on the Peter and Sons Lindauer Ranch (see details of oil shale production under the oil shale title). Neilson also worked with Marathon Oil Company doing exploration in the Piceance Creek area for nahcolite ($NaHCO_3$). He was instrumental in starting a small solution mining industry under the title of American Alkali and spent many years obtaining the necessary permits to extract sodium bicarbonate. This chemical substance occurred in deposits of nahcolite and was found in a prehistoric lakebed in oil shale formations in the Piceance Creek Basin north of Parachute Creek. The Piceance Creek facility converted sodium bicarbonate solution to a more stable soda ash. This soda ash was eventually piped down from the high plateau on Davis Point, located between Middle Fork and West Fork, to the Parachute Creek Basin. This material was piped further down Parachute Creek beginning in the year 2000 to the former Unocal Upgrade Refinery west of the town of Parachute and sold as sodium bicarbonate and soda ash.

Unocal had developed plans for an upgraded refinery that was in production from 1985 until 1991 when it was shut down. For the next eight to nine years, Celina Akin, an environmental specialist for the company, and her team worked to close out the ponds in the Piceance Creek Basin, dismantling building structures at the mine bench and wetter bench and reclaiming 9.6 million tons of retorted shale taluses that were in East Fork. The Unocal Upgrade Refinery and Administration office building sat idle from 1991 until 1999 when American Soda purchased the site and facilities. As the administration office building was being remodeled, Kurt Neilson (Irv Neilson's son), the general manager of the project, hired a contractor to replace many of the office walls with glass since soda ash is used in the production of glass. This brought many positive comments from soda ash customers and in addition the workers felt more like a team not separated by walls.

In 2000, American Soda started a commercial production of soda ash and sodium bicarbonate from the Piceance Creek Basin. They were successful for several years, raising their production of soda ash from 294,000 tons in 2001 to 521,000 tons in 2003. During this same period, their production of sodium bicarbonate went from 55,000 tons in 2001 to 77,000 tons in 2003.

When natural gas prices continued to rise and the price of soda ash and sodium bicarbonate went down, Williams Production RMT Co., a 60 percent partner in the American Soda Parachute venture, suffered losses from their investment in "Enron," the large company that went bankrupt. Williams divested themselves of everything that was not core business for their company to raise funds; thus, American Soda went up for sale.

In 2004, as prices dropped for American Soda products, Solvay Chemicals purchased the operation, for they were very interested in becoming a major player in the sodium bicarbonate business in North America. They sought to be recognized similar to that of Armand Hammer and his baking soda success. However, after five years of operation they decided to mothball their plant and it sat idle for several years. It is rumored in the valley that Solvay paid some $30 million for a plant that cost nearly $450 million to build, including the 44-mile dual pipeline.

Solvay Chemicals took over the property with the intention to continue the production of sodium bicarbonate and a variety of other products. The solution mining facility and well field in the Piceance Creek Basin was shut down and there has been no more solution mining at this site by Solvay. They sold the 44-mile pipeline to Enterprise shortly after they acquired it. This pipeline that was originally used to move soda ash in solution was now moving natural gas and water from the Piceance Creek Basin to the Parachute Creek Basin.

A railroad siding had been constructed from the main Denver & Rio Grande line in Parachute to the plant site, but was removed when American Soda decided to discontinue their operation; however, it was replaced when Solvay took over the operation. Solvay Chemicals, Inc. is the owner of the Parachute American Soda operation whose name was on all the permits and leased property. They continued to operate for several years with all land owned, leased, and other assets under the American Soda name. Although they have considered changing it to Solvay, in the fall of 2014 they decided not to make the change at this time.

Solvay currently has thirty-three employees and a few resident contractors. During earlier operations, American Soda had 176 employees at their two sites. Solvay Chemicals has been good to the local community by contributing to the Grand Valley Schools, to the Kiwanis, and regularly donating to the Wildlife Rehabilitation Center in Silt. They have leased twenty-six of their acres at no cost to the Grand Valley Park Association for a new Event Center and Rodeo Grounds. Solvay Chemicals ship their product, sodium bicarbonate, by train carloads and trucks all over the nation while their raw product of soda ash comes via rail car from the Green River Trona Basin. They have five grades of sodium bicarbonate which are used in food manufacturing, industrial chemical applications such as chemical balance in swimming pools, flue gas desulfurization, as sanding media, and pharmaceuticals. They have placed their products into three categories: food, industrial, and animal.

NATURAL GAS INDUSTRY ON PARACHUTE CREEK

In the search for energy sources in the oil shale reserves of the Williams Fork Formation and the Mesa Verde Formation in Northwest Colorado, specifically in the Piceance Creek Basin, natural gas was found in a number of exploratory wells. It had been known for some time that these Cretaceous Formations contained oil shale, coal, and natural gas.

However, the permeability of the sandstone reservoirs and the lack of easy access did not make the development of a natural gas industry economical.

The Atomic Energy Commission (AEC) in December of 1967, as an effort to find a peaceful use of atomic energy, partnered with the US Bureau of Mines to develop a project that they hoped would improve the extraction of natural gas from low-grade deposits. In this project, called Operation Plowshare or "Gasbuggy," a 29-kiloton nuclear device, nearly twice as large as the 15 kilotons used at Hiroshima, was detonated in a sandstone layer at a depth of 4,227 feet below the surface. This occurred above the Mesa Verde Formation in Leandro Canyon, New Mexico. The location was a site approximately twenty-seven miles southwest of Dulce, New Mexico, in the Carson National Forest. The blast created a rubble chimney eighty feet wide and 335 feet high above the blast center. A minimal amount of gas was obtained, but was considered too radioactive for commercial use. The project did suggest a larger nuclear device might do a better job. There was no apparent external damage.

In the fall of 1969, the Austral Oil Company of Houston, Texas and the US Atomic Energy Commission sponsored a second project. In this test, a nuclear device equal to 40,000 tons of TNT was detonated at a depth of 8,430 feet underground in the upper Cretaceous portion of the Mesa Verde Formation. The nuclear device was forty times as large as the Hiroshima device. The purpose of this project was to determine the economics of developing the Rulison natural gas field east of Parachute, Colorado, and recovery of gas. The AEC was also interested in the ground motion effects or damage that might affect future exploration of natural gas. Large quantities of natural gas were liberated but less than anticipated. The gas was radioactive and unsuitable for home applications. The gas could not be sold economically, since a fear of radiation expected from fracking with nuclear energy was a concern of the local residents in the community and throughout Parachute Creek. The nuclear blast did little external damage other than stopping some springs and creating others. A few chimneys were cracked but no major structural damage occurred. The blast did, however, fracture the rock base and created a reservoir of radioactive gas. Natural gas from the Rulison Project well was considered unusable and the well was closed.

A third natural gas experiment was held near Rio Blanco, Colorado, in 1973 under Fawn Creek, thirty miles southwest of Meeker. This project was sponsored by the AEC, CER Geonuclear, and the Equity Oil Company and was in a rural area with no homes. Three 33- kiloton bombs were simultaneously detonated in a shaft at different levels 1,779, 1,900, and 2,039 feet below ground level. Gas did collect in the cavity and the explosion produced fissures, but it was also radioactive. Efforts were made to reduce the radioactive tritium levels to near one percent, which was nearly harmless to the public; however, the public continued to resist any radioactivity. The experiment did accomplish some goals and the project was declared a success, but the results reported from this test were minimal. The gas collected was contaminated with tritium radiation, making it unacceptable for use.[135]

These three natural gas projects created much interest in the oil and gas industry. Many of the major players who were property owners in the area were actively developing a plan for the development of gas wells and pipelines in western Colorado during the 1970s. The natural gas field of Parachute Creek developed rapidly through the 1980s. Barrett Resources was one of the first to begin a drilling program on properties and leases that they held on Parachute Creek in 1984. The Department of Energy, Northwest, FINA, and Exxon also had drilled a few wells during this time. Barrett Resources was the only operator that stayed and kept an active drilling program moving forward. In 1996, Barrett Resources built an administration building one mile west of the town of Parachute and placed their operation at this site. In 2001 Barrett Resources sold their operation to Williams, who expanded the facility in 2007 to some 53,000 square feet. In January 2012, the exploration and production business/operation was transferred to WPX Energy Rocky Mountains, LLC (WPX Energy); an energy company based in Tulsa, Oklahoma, operates this facility at the present time. Barrett Resources continues to hold leases in the Parachute Creek region. Williams retained their pipeline facilities and other assets. Peak productions were obtained between the years of 2005 and 2009. WPX took over all drilling operations at the beginning of 2014 and had about 250 individuals working in the Parachute Creek area at that time.

In 2013, WPX Energy opened a new well in Riley Gulch that was called "The Beast." They found gas in this well, in the Niobrara Formation some 10,000 feet below the surface, which was in abun-

---

[135] Wikipedia. "Project Rio Blanco," accessed June 24, 2015.

dance with high pressure. This well produced 1 billion cubic feet (BCF) of gas in the first 100 days of production as compared to a typical well in the Williams Fork Formation that produces 1-2 BCF during its lifetime of twenty-five to thirty-five years. The "Beast" is still going strong in 2015 and has a favorable outlook for the future.

Barrett Resources and Williams had built 800 pads by 2011 and drilled 4,500 wells by 2012. WPX had drilled another 950 wells in 2012 with peak production of 950 MMCF within the Parachute Creek area. The Bureau of Land Management reported in the summer of 2014 that they had a record of 5,433 wells on Parachute Creek, 4,471 being on private land. Nine hundred and sixty-two (962) were on federal surfaces. The location of these wells may be seen in Appendix I. This satellite image over-layered with the well sites illustrates the intensity of drilling that has occurred on Parachute Creek. It also illustrates the use of the land, and one can see that there is little land left for agriculture or ranching. Most of the drainage is now covered with well pads. In addition, one must consider the space required for roads, wells, pipelines, and other facilities needed to service the producing wells.[136]

The depression of natural gas prices in 2010 impacted the industry for several years, forcing companies to cut back their operations and in some cases move to other productive basins, such as that found in northeastern Colorado. Technological advances in the development of new methods for drilling wells, using hydraulic fracturing and drilling horizontally have made gas well drilling very profitable. More than twenty wells can be drilled from one pad at this time.

WPX continued to drill wells along Parachute Creek in 2015. The investment in facilities and production equipment including extensive pipelines and roads suggests that the natural gas energy companies will remain in the Parachute Creek drainage for years to come. Barrett Oil and Gas, Williams, WPX Energy, and Encana Energy have a long history of working productively with landowners including locating well pads in a place convenient to the landowner, installing fencing, cattle guards, or digging stock watering ponds. According to WPX Energy, the future of the natural gas industry looks promising and is expected to survive for well over the next thirty years.

ENCANA ENERGY ENTERS THE GAS INDUSTRY ON PARACHUTE CREEK

Encana Energy is a leading North America energy producing company. In 2011, they produced 446 million cubic feet (MCF) per day from 141 net wells in the Piceance Creek Basin, which includes Parachute Creek drainage. In 2012, Encana purchased, from the Union Oil Company of California, the North Parachute Creek Ranch and adjacent properties consisting of some 45,000 acres. The base operation is located on the old Peter Lindauer and Sons Ranch and extends up the three forks (West, Middle, and East forks) of Parachute Creek and on to some of the nearby high mountains adjoining these drainages. They have over 650 producing wells with an estimated combined production of 200 MCF per day. One of their well pads houses fifty-one individual wells that were drilled at that site.

Encana Energy built a 56,000 square foot regional headquarters in the town of Parachute that was opened in the fall of 2012. They have some 200 employees working in and out of this three-story building. They report that their workers live in the Grand Valley area that extends west of Grand Junction to east of Rifle. The new building and site is one of Encana's largest field offices. In the town of Parachute, Encana opened a new compressed natural gas (CNG) station as an effort to continue to expand their North American infrastructure of CNG and liquefied natural gas (LNG) fueling. They

---

[136] Pittman, "Oil/Gas Wells on Parachute Creek—2014." Interview by author. October, 2014.

continue to influence their drilling rig fleet and other fleet vehicles to run on natural gas. This service facility is available to the public and they now own and operate five public stations in Colorado, Wyoming, Louisiana, and Alberta, Canada.

In 2004, Encana became involved in natural gas production in the Parachute Creek region although they were active east and south of Rifle for many years prior to this date. Encana owns or leases some 800,000 acres in the Parachute Creek area including the adjacent mountain ranges bordering the drainage. They have drilled some 3,000 wells in the area since 1990, primarily in the Williams Fork Formation and have obtained both gas and oil from these wells that averaged about 450 million cubic feet of production per day. Most of their wells are drilled to a depth of 6,000 to 7,000 feet below the surface.

In 2012, Doug Hock, spokesman for Encana Oil and Gas, reported that drilling for natural gas in the Parachute Creek area would continue to be profitable based on the increased value of natural gas liquids (NGL), an area where they will tend to concentrate their efforts in the future. In 2013, Encana sold much of their natural gas holdings in Canada and invested in properties in Texas and other lower forty-eight states. In Colorado, Encana USA employs and contracts some 1,000 workers with net production in 2012 of 1.6 billion cubic feet per day and 11.6 thousand barrels per day of oil and natural gas liquids.

In November 2013, the *Daily Camera* newspaper of Boulder, Colorado, reported that Encana planned to cut 20 percent of their work force in the Parachute office and Piceance Basin. They plan to focus on the development of resources in the Denver-Julesburg Basin. In 2014, Encana had no active drilling operations on Parachute Creek. However, they continue to support a bright future for natural gas development in the Piceance Basin that includes Parachute Creek.

Encana has contributed significantly to the local communities. According to their public relations office, they awarded 711 grants in the Piceance Basin equal to $9,273,803 and their employees have made donations that were matched by Encana. In addition they have provided millions of dollars in revenue to the state, county, and local governments including contributions to countless charitable organizations, schools, and Little League teams in the Grand Valley.[137]

---

[137] Kent, "Encana Public Relations—Contributions to Local Community," E-mail interview by author. 2014.

CHAPTER 10

Changes in the Parachute Creek Valley in the Last Eighty-plus Years

In the 1930s following the Great Depression, ranches were purchased by a variety of major oil and gas industries for future exploration and development of an oil shale industry or a natural gas industry. Some of the oil and gas companies purchasing property were: Union Oil and Gas Company of California, Sinclair Oil and Gas, Phillips, Atlantic Richfield, Cleveland Cliffs, Chevron, Mobile, Tosco, and Exxon. The decade following the depression of the 1930s up to WWII, was a time that the ranches and farms began to rebuild their herds and stabilize their operations.

As the Second World War began and the United States became involved, there was a great demand for new soldiers. Parachute Creek and the community of Grand Valley supplied many more than their share of individuals between the age of eighteen and thirty-five for the war. Older family members took over the responsibilities of the men who went to war while some left the valley to work in shipyards, aircraft facilities, and other places as needed. Prices for farm and ranch products increased during the war years, and when soldiers were able to return home in the mid-1940s, they found their properties in good shape and their livestock herds increased.

As the Korean War started in the 1950s, a draft call again went out for men needed in the military service. Many of the valley's younger men volunteered while others were drafted, leaving their families with the responsibilities of taking care of the home place. Parachute Creek properties continued to be sold to the oil and gas companies. While the Union Oil Co. of California (Unocal) built and opened an experimental oil shale plant, the plant remained in production for nearly ten years but closed in 1961. However, the quest for oil that could be extracted from shale continued as described in more detail earlier in this manuscript.

Although it has been said that the government promoted the oil shale booms that busted over the years, the future hope of an imminent oil shale industry crippled the livestock industry. Ranches were sold to oil and gas companies, which restricted access and in some cases completely prohibited it. In order to reduce the property taxes being paid, some buildings were burned or removed. Travel to the upper regions of Parachute Creek was cut off and tourism was eliminated from this area.

THE EXODUS OF PIONEERS AND THEIR FAMILIES FROM PARACHUTE CREEK

There are many reasons why the original fifty-eight-plus families and most of the other families identified in this manuscript left Parachute Creek. One could say that economics was a major problem, and most would be right. To make a living on a small farm was difficult when their product prices remained low and all their needs and living expenses continued to rise. In this cold desert environment, one must irrigate crops to keep them living and reaching harvest time. These ranchers and farmers were in competition with most regions in the United States where adequate rain takes care of their crops. Irrigating crops takes time and is expensive, especially if one needs to hire an irrigator. The fields must be prepared beyond planting the crop to include corrugates needed to distribute the water evenly if not using the old standard method of damming the ditches and flooding the fields. If money is available, some ranchers buy gated pipes or use other methods to provide equal distribution of their water. In addition, the soils on Parachute Creek are not very fertile and, in many cases, are alkaline with much clay. Consequently, this requires annually fertilizing each field, and this cost rose dramatically in the last half of the 20th century.

As early residents of Parachute Creek became aware of higher living standards and job security outside the valley, they questioned why they were saddled with low-paying and sporadic jobs here. Consequently, they sold their property and moved on, hopefully to a better life. Those individuals that wanted to continue ranching sold their property to waiting energy companies and bought elsewhere or retired from ranching.

A number of the sons and daughters of ranch families entered military service upon graduating from high school, and a few made this their life career. Others moved on knowing they did not want the hard work that they had seen their mothers and fathers endure to keep food on the table for their family. They sought a more reliable source of income and envied the conveniences of urban living and the entertainment the media had shown them. A few went to college and entered a professional career that took them from the valley. It was difficult for family members to follow in the steps of their parents when families were often large, and there wasn't room for more than one family to survive on the meager returns from their small ranch or farm.

Job availability was another problem in the valley since energy companies were taking over the properties of Parachute Creek and often brought in their own employees from many locations throughout the nation. There was an increase in employees at times, but few local or permanent jobs were offered. Employment became more difficult to find and the education requirements continued to go up. During boom stages in the valley, energy companies provided many more jobs but most lasted only for a few months and only a small number were semi-permanent.

However, when the bust came, and it always did, the employees left en masse and owners of businesses and property were left with the cleanup and unpaid bills. The local residents soon became leery of any new developments or proposal for energy development.

IMPACT OF CLOSING PUBLIC ACCESS TO WEST, MIDDLE, AND EAST FORKS OF PARACHUTE CREEK

A secondary impact to the local community resulting from the industrialization of Parachute Creek has been prohibiting public access to the three main drainages that create Parachute Creek. A gate approximately ten miles up from the town of Parachute now blocks public access to the drainages of West Fork, Middle Fork, and East Fork. The upper reaches of these drainages contain one of the more diverse wildlife habitats in the region. There are many deer, elk, and a fairly large population of bears in these three drainages. The author of this manuscript observed five different bears on one trip up East Fork as he rode to check on facilities and conditions of the East Fork cattle range. At another time, he observed a group of at least fifty elk wintering in the valley. There are also many birds and small mammals in the area.

At the end of the East Fork Canyon, one finds a spectacular waterfall of several hundred feet. In the 1980s, the Union Oil Company of California reported that closure restrictions were necessary for public safety, as they were forcing shale rock off the ledges to the valley below. The county commissioners agreed to the closure of this livestock road on October 12, 1982; however, there have not been any rocks pushed over the ledges for many years.

Encana Energy has drilled many wells in the East Fork valley since purchasing the Union Oil Company property. Ranchers who have grazing permits on the East Fork cattle range retained access to the drainage and the three-mile public road that is now considered a private road.

When the East Fork valley was open to the public, many families would hike up to the end of the road and have a picnic, then hike on up to see the East Fork Falls and maybe do some trout fishing in the upper

East Fork drainage looking west.

East Fork Falls is no longer accessible for the general public.

reaches. It stands today as another obstacle restricting the local population from enjoying their natural environment in a peaceful and enjoyable manner.

Thus, today, ranching on Parachute Creek is in trouble and almost absent. As long as there are livestock grazing permits on the mountain ranges and cattle and sheep have a high value as a protein source, livestock ranchers will find ways to utilize the thousands of acres of vegetation for their animals and make the protein of these animals available as a human food. Economics and, in particular, prices for beef and lamb will determine the final availability and usage of this protein source.

The Parachute Creek valley of the 1800s and 1900s supported many small, single-family ranches, farms, and homes. It is now giving its mineral resources to the public in the forms of non-renewable fuels, baking soda, and energy fuel for heating and transportation. The beautiful green valley is now an industrial site with many wells, pipelines, roads, and support facilities needed to extract these substances and for the workers needed to maintain these facilities. It has been a trade-off with a few benefiting much more than others.

What will the valley look like fifty or 100 years from now? Will it continue to be an industrial site for oil shale after most of the natural gas has been extracted? Will sodium bicarbonate continue to be produced in the valley?

Will it ever return to a ranching valley?

APPENDIX I

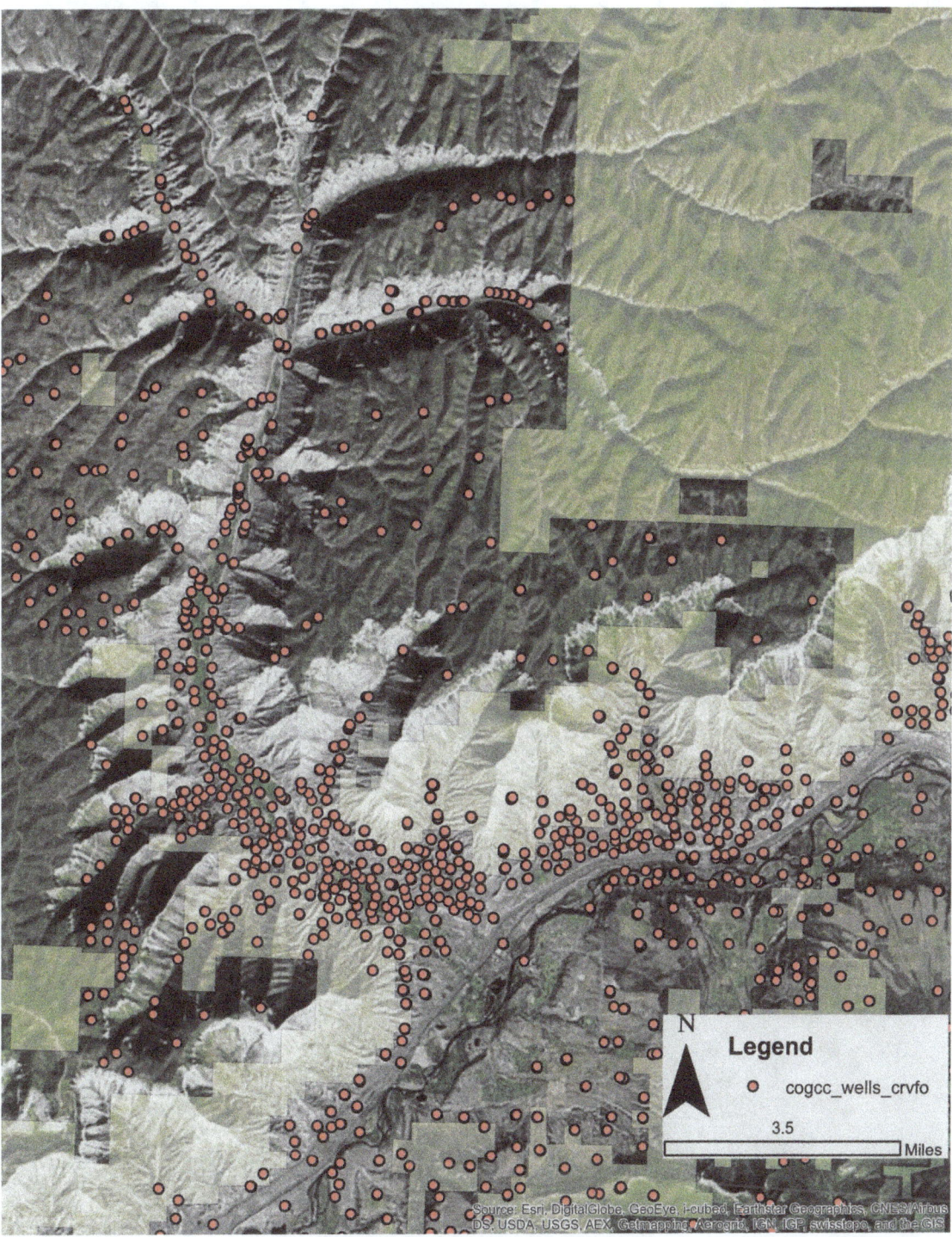

Satellite image of natural gas drilling pads on Parachute Creek and adjacent drainages. Image provided by Isaac Pittman and David Boyd with the Colorado River Valley Field Office of the Bureau of Land Management, Department of the Interior, 2014.

WPX Energy Inc. "Gas/Oil Pads on the Parachute Creek Drainage - 2014."
Traci Houpt (landman) interviewed by author. October, 2014.

APPENDIX II

WATER FLOW AND FLOODING OF PARACHUTE CREEK

Early reports of the Parachute Creek stream flow in the late 1890s indicated that it often dried up in its lower reaches. The shale in the upper portion of the creek is very porous, and water drifts downward with ease. Ranchers and farmers in need of water to irrigate their crops built dams and ditches to divert water to newly cleared fields. Following the unsuccessful building of a storage dam on West Fork, irrigation was promoted on the upper reaches of Parachute Creek. As the fields were irrigated, much of the water ended up back in the stream channel. This activity resulted in more water being available in the lower regions of the creek. For most years, the farmers and ranchers had sufficient water on the lower section of Parachute Creek to irrigate their crops. Rarely was it necessary for the water commissioner to limit water only to those with the first recorded right.

An attempt was made to determine the years of major flooding of Parachute Creek from local residents and state records. However, limited as it may be, the data does reveal the variations of the stream flow throughout a year. Hydrologic data for the Parachute Creek drainage has been gathered since 1922 and retained in the US Geological Survey, Denver Library, in the Colorado Water Science Center. Data has been obtained at several points along the drainage. The following two graphs illustrate the discharge where Parachute Creek enters the Colorado River. The first graph illustrates the extreme variations over a period of seven years from 1922 until 1928. Emily Wild of the US Geological Survey at the Denver Federal Center provided this data.[138]

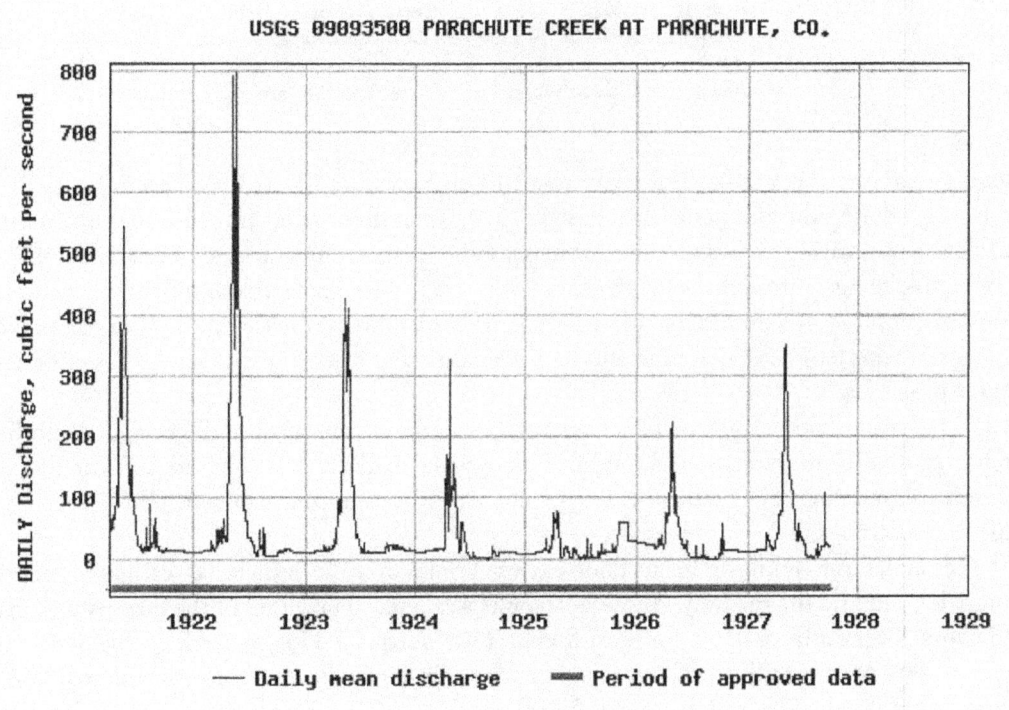

---

[138] *U S. Geological Survey Flood Chart of Parachute Creek, Colorado. 1928-1929.*

The variations in the following graph show the result from high spring runoffs to summer flooding, drought conditions, and possibly the lack of data gathered. This last graph illustrates in detail variations that occurred from April 21 through September 1921 in the daily mean discharge.

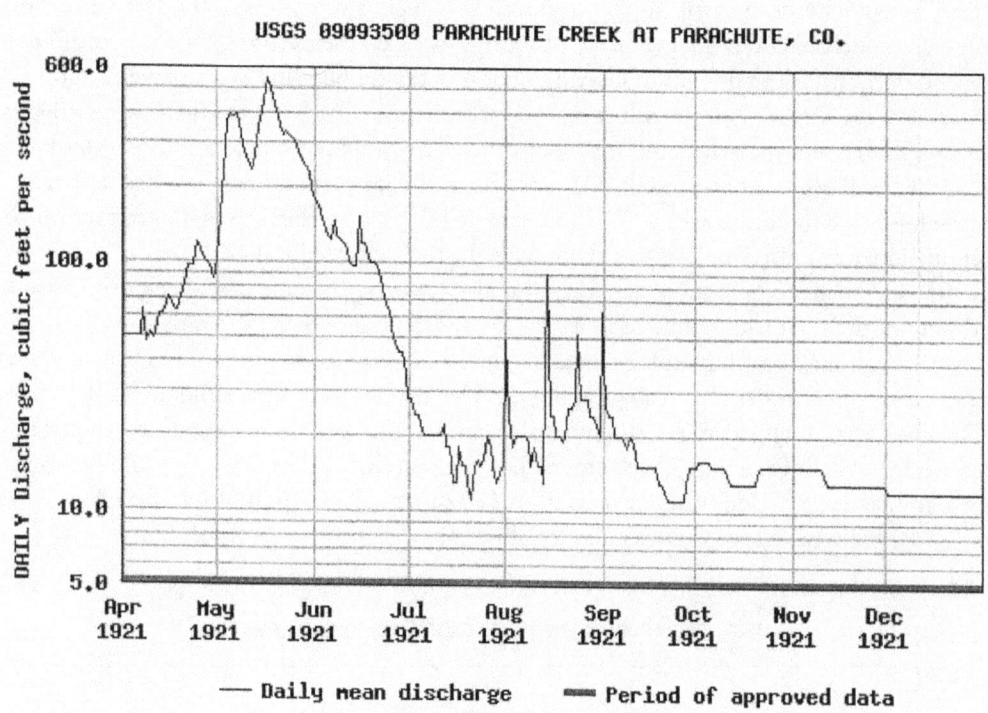

Flooding has been a continuous threat to residents on Parachute Creek. Mrs. Lavern Bailey had a narrow escape during the afternoon of August 5, 1929, when floodwaters from a cloudburst overtook her while she was driving to Grand Valley from her father's ranch on Parachute Creek. She was fortunate to be able to jump from the vehicle before it was swept through a fence and finally came to rest in a field about 300 yards from the road. Although it didn't tip over, the car was torn to pieces. The *Rifle Telegram* reported that much mud and rock were carried down onto the Charles Patterson and CE Tracy properties.

In 1935, a major flood came down Parachute Creek and took out most of the bridges. Ruth Benson reported that the muskrats were scrambling all over the roadway near the bridge in Grand Valley, which was still standing. They went there to see the big floodwater coming down. This flood washed out the lower part of the Russey-Hurlburt Cemetery.

Wheeler Gulch is well known for its floods. Several times over the years it has washed rock and debris on fields and into the roadway. A special channel was built to take care of the excess water that would come down during a flood; for most floods, it was adequate. However, with some floods, the water continues to go over the banks and washes debris on the fields. Martel Sherwood, Red Walters, and Francis Stanton had major impacts on their fields from this flooding.

BIBLIOGRAPHY

Alexander, Thomas G. date unknown. "The Walker War." Utah History to Go
http://historytogo.utah.gov/utah_chapters/american_indians/thewalkerwar.html

Boulton, Alice. *Silt, Colorado, Homesteads, 1880-1940*. Silt, Colorado: Silt Historical Park, 2009.

Bowen, A.W. *Progressive Men of Western Colorado*, Illustrated. Chicago: A.W. Bowen & Co, 1905.

Carhart, Arthur Hawthorne, and Stanley Paul Young. *The Last Stand of the Pack*. New York: The US Bureau of Biological Survey (BBS), 1929.

City of Parachute Administrative Office. Parachute, Colorado.

Conetah, Fred A. *A History of the Northern Ute People*, Edited by Kathryn L. Mackay and Floyd A. O'Neil. Salt Lake City, Utah: Published by the Uintah-Ouray Ute Tribe, printed by the University of Utah Printing Service, 1982.

Crow Canyon Archaeological Center. "Peoples of the Mesa Verde Regions," http://www.crowcanyon.org/EducationProducts

Davis, Robin. "Ute Indians." September 20, 2010. http://uteindians.blogspot.com.

FitzPatrick, V. S. *The Arbuckle Cafe: Classic Cowboy Stories*. Yellow Cat Flats, Utah: Yellow Cat Pub, 1999.

Fouch, Thomas, Craig Wandrey, David Taylor, William Butler, John Miller, Steven Prensky, Lynn Boone, James Schmoker, and Robert Crovelli. "Oil and Gas Resources of US Naval Oil Shale Reserves 1 and 3, Colorado, and Reserve 2, Utah." 1994. http://pubs.usgs.gov/of/1994/0427/report.pdf

Fritz, Percy Stanley. *Colorado, the Centennial State*. New York: Prentice-Hall, Inc., 1941.

Garfield County Clerk & Recorder's Office, 109 8 Street, Suite 200, Glenwood Springs, CO. 81601.

Genealogy, Family Trees & Family History Records, Ancestry.com. http://ancestry.com

Grand Valley News, "Obituaries." February 16, 1962.

Grand Valley News, "Parachute, a Misnomer According to Government Employee—Is a Ute Word." June 30, 1910.

Gulliford, Andrew. *Boomtown Blues, Colorado Oil Shale, 1885-1985*. Boulder, Colorado: University Press of Colorado, 1989.

Gulliford, Andrew, ed. "They Robbed the Wrong Train," *The First Hundred Years 1883-1983*. Glenwood Springs, Colorado: Gran Farnum Printing, 1983.

Hayden, F. V. et. al: *Eighth Annual Report of the United States Geological and Geographical Survey of the Territories: Embracing Colorado and Parts of Adjacent Territories: Being a Report of Progress of Exploration for the Year 1874*. Washington, [D.C.]: G.P.O., 1876.

Hayden, F. V., A. D. Wilson, Henry Gannett, George B. Chittenden, Gustavus R. Bechler, William H. Jackson, Walter J. Hoffman, Leo A. Packard, F. D. Owen, and H. H. Nichols. *Ninth Annual Report of the United States Geological and Geographical Survey of the Territories: Embracing Colorado and Parts of Adjacent Territories: Being a Report of Progress of the Exploration for the Year 1875*. Washington [D.C.]: G.P.O., 1877.

Hayden, F. V., Charles A. White, F. M. Enlich, A. C. Peale, William H. Holmes, and A. D. Wilson. *Tenth Annual Report of the United States Geological and Geographical Survey of the Territories: Embracing Colorado and Parts of Adjacent Territories: Being a Report of Progress of the Exploration for the Year 1876*. Washington [D.C.]: G.P.O., 1878.

Hughes, J. Donald. *American Indians in Colorado*. Boulder, Colorado: Pruett Publishing Co., 1977.

Hughes, J. Donald, Calvin H. Jennings (PI), and Carl W. Ritchie & Richard P. Taylor (Field Assistants). *A Cultural Resource Inventory of the Union Oil Company Property in Parachute Creek, Garfield County, Colorado*. Fort Collins, Colorado: Laboratory of Public Archaeology, Dept. of Anthropology, Colorado State University, 1975.

Kent, Sandy. "Encana Public Relations - Contributions to Local Community." E-mail interview by author. October 1, 2014.

Kerr, Andy and Mark Salvo. "Livestock Grazing on the National Park and Wilderness Preservation System." *Wild Earth*. Vol. 10, No. 2. Summer, 2000.

Lindauer, Paul. "Early Life of a Cowboy." Interview by Betty JoAnn Lindauer. 1972.

_____. *A Little Cabin Away From Town*, 1940s.

McManus, Carol. *Bess: A Woman's Life in the Early 1900s*. Ouray, Colorado: Western Reflections, 2004.

_____. *Ida: Her Labor of Love*. Ouray, Colorado: Western Reflections, 1999.

Michael, Daniel T., descendant of Tom Glover, 2008 (written communication)

Munsell, F. Darrell. *Colorado Artist Jack Roberts, Painting the West*. Charleston, SC: The History Press, 2015.

Murray, Erlene D. *Lest We Forget*. Grand Junction, Colorado: Quahada, Inc., 1973.

Newman, Karl R. "Geology of Oil Shale in Piceance Creek Basin, Colorado." Rocky Mountain Association of Geologists Symposium, 1980.

Ogden, Roberta. "A Wilderness Sojourn: A Summer of Railroading," Grand Junction, Colorado *The Daily Sentinel*, October 29, 1972.

Patrick, Val. *The Arbuckle Café*. Yellow Cat Flats, Utah: Yellow Cat Publishing, (Classic Cowboy Stories), 1998.

Petrakian, Gracie Wynn. *Land of Tall Grass*. Publishing with Gracie, LLC, 2010.

Pittman, Isaac and David Boyd. "Oil/Gas Wells on Parachute Creek - 2014." Colorado River Valley Field Office of the Bureau of Land Management. Interview by author. October, 2014.

Reading Club of Rifle, Colorado. *Rifle Shots; The Story of Rifle, Colorado*. Rifle: Rifle Reading Club of Rifle, Colorado, 1973.

Shale Tech International Services LLC. "Shale Tech International Services LLC." http://shaletech.com

Silbernagel, Robert. *Troubled Trails: The Meeker Affair and the Expulsion of the Utes from Colorado*. Salt Lake City: University of Utah Press, 2011.

Smith, P. David. *Ouray, Chief of the Utes*. Ouray, Colorado: Wayfinder Press, 1986.

Starbuck, La Verne. *Children Came: Some from Log Camps Others from Ranches. The Valley West Dispatch*, September 27, 1989.

The Parachute Centennial, "*Grand Valley Proud*." Grand Valley Historical Society. 2008.

US federal census, 1870-1940: various volumes: Provo, UT, accessed online.

University of Colorado at Boulder. "What Every Westerner Should Know About Oil Shale." http://www.centerwest.org/publications/oilshale/2history/0history.php

Van Pelt, Bill. "Report on 60th Anniversary of the Chosin Reservoir Battle, Korea, November-December of 1950 as Reported by Ronald Reagan." Interview by author. 2012.

Wheeler, Mrs. Donald. *History of Ransom S. Wheeler and Harriett Ferris Wheeler*. Edited by Mrs. Gary

_____. Parachute, Colorado: Family Published, 1994.

Wikipedia. "Colony Shale Oil Project." January 19, 2015.

Wikipedia. "Project Rio Blanco." https://en.wikipedia.org/wiki/Project_Rio_Blanco

Williams, (Gardner) Ann, and Wayne Payton. *No Market for 'Em*. [United States]: Ann Williams, 2012. Self-published.

Witt, Anita McCune. *I Remember One Horse: The Last of the Cowboys in the Roaring Fork Valley and Beyond*. Aspen, Colorado: W-H Pub, 2002.

Wolfe, Tom. *Arthur Carhart: Wilderness Prophet*. Boulder, Colorado: University Press of Colorado, 2008.

WPX Energy Inc. "Gas/Oil Pads on the Parachute Creek Drainage - 2014." Traci Houpt (landman) interviewed by author. October, 2014.

Young, Richard K. *The Ute Indians of Colorado in the Twentieth Century*. Norman, Oklahoma: The University of Oklahoma Press, 1997.

INDEX

A

Akin, Celina 141
Alber, Anna Mae 69, 109, *110*
Alber, Carl 07, 108-109, *109*, 110
Alber, Carl Jr. "Bud" 108, 109, 110, *110*
Alber, Edna Mae (Goble) 108-109, *109*
Alber, Fred xv, 109
Alber, Hulda (Frick) 108
Alber, John "Henry" 108
Alber, Tom 109
Allen, Albert 43, 112, 118-120
Allen, Betty "BJ" (m. McQuiston) xv, 119
Allen, George 119
Allen, Gladys (Patterson) 43, 97, 106, 112, 118-120
Allen, John 119
Allen, Lola (Linin) 119, *119*
Allen, Mildred 119-120
American Soda 140, 141-142
Anderson, Ben 97, 129
Anvil Points 60, 94, 102, 104, 118, 119, 138, 139

B

Bailey, Bertha (m. Lindstrom) 98
Bailey, Betty (m. Arnold) 98
Bailey, Bivian 95, *95*, 97
Bailey, Buck 130
Bailey, Daniel Burdette 98
Bailey, Earl *95*, 97-98, *97*
Bailey, Emma 97
Bailey, Frances (Zediker) 98, *98*, 102, 154
Bailey, George *95*, 97
Bailey, George Wilbur 98
Bailey, Iva (m. Wetzel) *95*, 98
Bailey, Joy (m. Stone) 98, 99, 102
Bailey, LaVern 95, 98, *98*, 102
Bailey, Martha "Alice" (Jessup) 95, *95*
Bailey, Maud (m. Cline) 41, *95*, *96*, 96-97, 100-101
Bailey, Olive (m. Shoults) *95*, 97
Bailey, Pearl *95*
Bailey, Ruth Marie (m. Cutter-Roberts) 98
Bailey, Thad 79, 108
Bailey, Thelma (Anderson) *97*, 97-98
Bailey, Thomas 76, *95*, 95-96, 137
Barrett Gas Development Co. 126, 144
Barrett Resources 143, 144
Barrith, Fred 129

Baughman, Alfred Orville 111
Baughman, Alice Pearl (m. Hurlburt) 111, 124
Baughman, George Woodman 111
Baughman, Jessie (Hurlburt) 37, 110-111, *121*, 124, *124*
Baughman, John Curtis 111
Baughman, Johnathan "Yone" 110, 111, 124
Baughman, Juanita "Neta" (M. Rector) 111
Baughman, Luther David 111
Baughman, Norman Mark 111
Baum, Paul 109, 129
Becktell, Kenneth 134
Bellis, Joe 39-40, 42, 62, 104, 137
Benedetti, Estella "Faye" (Armstrong) 105
Benedetti, George 37, 48, 105-106
Benedetti, Georgie (m. Williams) 105
Benedetti, Vera (m. Quinn) 105
Benedetti, Vesta (m. Crawford) 105
Benson, Arcadious "Cade" 42, 43, 44, 46, 148
Benson, Cade Lyle 45, 129
Benson, Charles 41, 42, *43*, *44*, 43-46, 94
Benson, Charline (m. Gibbons, Allen) 41, 44, 45, *45*, 87
Benson, Clara Bertha (Gardner) 38, *38*, 39, 42, 53
Benson, Elvis 42, 43
Benson, Gregory Charles 45
Benson, Helen Ruth (m. Arnett) 44, *45*, 46, 154
Benson, Leta Ruth (Funk) 41, 43-44, *44*
Benson, Marjorie Merle (m. Lange) xv, 41, 44, *45*
Benson, Pamela Rose (m. Brock) 44-45, *45*
Benson, Roberta "Bobbi" Jean (m. Wambolt) xv, 41, 44, *45*, 46, 126
Benson, Sadie Winifred (m. Letson) 42
Benton, George 30, 58, 61
Benton, Nettie (Fogel) 58
Benton place 30, 58, 61, 77, 80, 83, 101
Billiter, Martin 12, 14, 17, 24, 25, *25*, 120, 121, 122
Black Sunday 140
Blue/Lindauer ranch 81, 114
Boleran, John 130
Book Cliff School viii, 30, 32, 40, 51, *55*, *67*, 67-69, 79, 87, *96*, 105
Brown, Carl 14, 24
Brown, Colene 114
Brown, Johnny 114

159

Bruckner, Arle 58, 81
Bruckner, Betsy Marlene (Clarke) 80
Bruckner, Edsel *55*, 69, *79*, 80, *80*,
Bruckner, Eyer xv, *79*, *80*, 80-81
Bruckner, Janke 81
Bruckner, John *79*, 81, 132
Bruckner, Maude (Bumgardner) 80, 81
Bruckner, Rose (Benton) 58, 59, 61, 81
Bruckner, Samuel "Floyd" *79*, 79-80, 81,
Bruckner, Samuel Fredrick *79*, 79-80
Brunot Treaty 7
Bumgardner, Calvin 54, *80*
Bumgardner, Clarence 54, *80*, 103
Bumgardner, Clark Ella "Cora" (Wheeler) 53, *53*, 54, *54*, 55, *62*, *67*, 69, 73, *73*, *74*, 74-75
Bumgardner, Eileen "Boots" (Clarke) xv, 56, 57, *57*, 68
Bumgardner, Gene 54, *55*, 56-57, *57*, 69, 74, *80*
Bumgardner, James 54, *54*
Bumgardner, James "Jim" Robert 54, *74*, *80*
Bumgardner, Jeanne May 56, 57
Bumgardner, Joseph 54, *54*
Bumgardner, Maude 54, *54*, 69, *79*, 80, *81*
Bumgardner, Mike 56, 57
Bumgardner, Paul 54, 55-56
Bumgardner, Philip Gene 54, *69*
Bumgardner, Robert *53*, *54*, *55*, 53-55, 75
Bumgardner, Rock 56, 57
Burnside, Fredrick 123

C

Callahan, Mike 26
Carhart, Arthur 135-136
Cattle and sheep wars 13-14
Caywood, Bill 135-136
Chevron 140, 147
Clarke, Elsie *121*
Clarke, Jim *121*
Clarke, Joseph S. 123
Clarke, Learner *121*
Clarke, Minnie (Hurlburt) *121*
Clayton, William 47
Cline, Coda 86, 99, 101
Cline, Cody *67*
Cline, Donald Dean 97
Cline, Edna 101
Cline, Erward *96*, 97
Cline, Gladys 101

Cline, John *67*, 73, 74, 99-100
Cline, John Wesley 99-100
Cline, Larry Leon 97
Cline, Olive (m. Stanton) 89, *96*, 96-97
Cline, Robert 101
Cline, Sarah (unknown) 73, 74, 100
Cline, Teresa "Terry" 96
Cline, Thomas Edison 99, 100-101
Cline, Tom 49, *67*, *96*, 96-97, *100*, 130
Cline, Vera 96
Cline, Verna 97
Cline, Wayne 96
Cline. Willie (m. Haley) *67*, 99, 100
Clough, Bill 131
Colony Oil Shale project 140
Cox, Alice "Ma" (Dykes) 48
Cox, Clifford 48
Cox, Delbert 48, 135
Cox, Frank 48, 50
Cox, Fred 48
Cox, Jacqueline "Jaq" (unknown) 48
Cox, Johanna 48
Cox, John 48, 49, 129
Cox, Maude 48
Cox, Nellie 48
Cox, Sig 48, 62
Crawford, David xv, 48, 49, 51, 52, 69
Crawford, Doris (Sutherland) 41, 49, 50, 51, *51*, 68 see also Kerlee
Crawford, Eva Lou (m. Smith, Harris) 51, 52, 69
Crawford, Gabriel Purdy "Purd" 41, 49-50, *50*, 51, 68
Crawford, "Jack" 51, 52, 69,105
Crawford, John *50*, 50-51, *62*, 105, 129
Crawford, Lena (Gordon) 50, *50*
Crawford, Oren 50, *67*
Crawford, Titus 50
Crawford, Vesta (Benedetti) 52, 105
Creek, Harve 131

D

Davenport, John 24, 25, 26, 27, 29, 38
Davidson, Andy 76-77
Davidson, Bob 76, 77
Davidson, Nettie 77
Davidson, Olive Alice (Dutton) 77
Davidson, Velma (m. power) 77, 117-118, *118*
Davidson, Winnie 77

Davis, Charlie 134
Davis, Sharon 77
Davis, Sherrill (m. Powell/LaDonne) 77
Dawson, Bob *62*
Dere, Anna (Stoffer) 21, *21*
Dere, Beverly 23, *23*
Dere, Catherine *21*, 22-23, *28*
Dere, Charlie 23
Dere, Chris *21*, 22, 62, 80
Dere, Frank *21*, 22, 23, *28*
Dere, Frederick *21*, 23
Dere, Joseph *21*, 22
Dere, Margaretha 21-22, 27, *27*, *28*, 29, 36
Dere, Philip 21, *21*, 25, 111
Dere, Philip Jr. *21*, 22
Dere, Stanford "Bud" xv, 23, *23*
DeWitt, Bill 70
DeWitt, Birdie (Wheeler) 67, 69, *70*, 73
DeWitt, Dean 70
DeWitt, Dee 70
DeWitt, Elmore 69
DeWitt, Elvin 69-70, *70*
DeWitt, Frank 85, 86
DeWitt, James 70, 75
DeWitt, Mabel 70
DeWitt, Martin *69*, 70
DeWitt, Virginia 70
Dickerson, Watson 132
Doyle, James 137
Duplice, Mary 137
Dutton family 77, 29

E

Eastman, Fern and Glen 129
Ebler, Art 132
Encana Energy 144-145, 148
Etchison, Ei 131
Exxon 140, 143, 147

F

Finier, Ray 132
Freeland, Flora Edna (Perham) *40*, 41, 56, 68, 71-72
Freeland, Marcus Dee 41, 53, 57, 60, 62, 67, 68, 70, *71*, 71-72, *82*, 83
Freeland, Marcus Dee Jr. 68, 69, 71

G

Gardner, Albert 99, 105
Gardner, Charles A. *38*
Gardner, Clara Bertha 38, *38*, 39, 42, 53
Gardner, Frank 38
Gardner, George 37-38, *38*
Gardner, Harry C. 38, *38*
Gardner, Harvey *38*
Gardner, James "Jim" 116, *117*, 118
Gardner, Laura (Osborn) 116, *117*
Gardner, Mary Elizabeth "Liz" (Wayne) 37-38, *38*
Gardner, Mary "Mate" (m. Riley, Smith) *38*, 39, 53, 54
Gardner, Mona (Kemper) 69, 99, 105
Gardner, Vern 46, 47, 56, 89, 117
Gardner, Walter *38*
Geology 1-2, 137-139
Gibbons, Florence 69, 87
Gibbons, Gertrude Caroline "Carrie" (Hansen) 85, 87
Gibbons, Harry Arthur "Sonny" 44, *55*, 87
Gibbons, Theodore "Theo" 80, 85, 87
Gibbons, Walter Ernest 87
Glover, Alice (Gates) 57, *58*, 59-61, 68
Glover Cabin 57, *58*, *59*, 60, 78, 79
Glover, Lucinda "Lou" 59, 60, 61, *67*, 71
Glover, Queenie (m. Shaw, Steuck) 57, 59, 60, *60*, 67, *67*
Glover, Tom 41, 50, 57-61, *58*, 71
Gordon, Paul 50
Grand Valley Bank *64*, 131
Grand Valley News 3, 61, 116, 125, 134, 137
Granlee, Beulah 41, 42
Granlee, Clara (Clayton) 41, 42, 47
Granlee, Milton C. 40, 41-42, 61
Granlee, Milton Dean 41, 42
Granlee, Ruth 41, 42
Granlee School *40*, 40-41, 43, 44, 46, 71, 113
Green, Robert "Bobby" xv, 125
Green, Evelyn 125
Green, Robert E. "Bob" 125
Gulliford, Andrew xi-xii, xiv, 140

H

Hackett, Esther Homequist 129
Haley, Alice 100
Haley, Charles 100
Haley, Ida 100

Hansen, Robert "Harry" xiii, 29, 44, 68, 80, 83, 85-86, *85*, 88, 93, 94, 113, 130
Hansen, Marlene (m. Trent) 86
Hansen, Mary 85
Hansen, Peter 85, 87
Hansen, Thelma (Zediker) 56, 68, 85, 86, 93
Hartley, Fred 140
Hayden, F.V. 3, 137
Hayward, Christy (m. Koeneke) xv
Hayward, Judith xv
Helm, John 134
Herman, Zel 129
Herwick, Guy 137
Herwick, JL 137
Herwick, Oren H. 137
Hilliker, Adelbert "Bert" *67*, 69, 87
Hilliker, Edwin 63, 68, 87
Hilliker, Gertrude 41, *67*, 87
Hoag, Harry 135
Hock, Doug 145
Hoffman, David 94, 102
Hoffman, Sarah (unknown) 94
Huber, Iris (Wasson) 107-108, *108*
Huber, Ray 107-108, *108*
Hughes, Bill 113, 127
Hungerford, Roy 129
Hungry Mike 4, 121, 122
Hurlburt, Alice Pearl (Baughman) 124
Hurlburt, Blanche (m. Sandstrom) 76, *76*
Hurlburt, Daisy (m. Green) 121, *124*, 125
Hurlburt, Frances (m. Trimmer) 25, 121, *121*, 122
Hurlburt, Fred 111, *121*, 124
Hurlburt, John Breeden "JB" 13, 14, 17, 24, 37, 40, 53, 54, 56, 72, 111, 120-125, *121*, 122, 134, 137
Hurlburt, Jessie see Baughman
Hurlburt, Lottie (m. Shehorn) 25, *121*, 123-124
Hurlburt, Rebecca "Lou" (m. Wayne) 25, 121, *121*, 123, *124*
Hurlburt, Luther 25, 121, *121*, 122, 124, *124*
Hurlburt, Mark xiv, 25, 55, 121, *121*, 123, 124
Hurlburt, Martha "Mattie" (Rock) 25, 120, *121*, 121-122, *124*
Hurlburt, Martha Mae (m. Burnside) *121*, 123, *124*
Hurlburt, Mary Emma (Hedrick) 122
Hurlburt, Minnie (m. Clarke) 121, *121*, 123, *124*
Hurlburt, Winnie (m. Christenson) *121*, *124*, 124-125

J
Jacobson, Lydia and Doctor 129
Jasinowski, Gloria (Kramer) xv, 33
Jensen, Betty (m. Carr) 69, 75
Jensen, Roy 75-76
Jensen, Charles "Sharky" 23, 75, *78*
Johns, Lee 131
Johnson, Chas. *76*

K
Kerlee, Buck 39
Kerlee, Dean 39
Kerlee, Doris (Sutherland, m. Crawford) 49, *51*, 51-52
Kerlee, George 48-49, *49*, 51-52, 80
Kerlee, Harrison 48-49
Kerlee, May (White) 49
Kerlee, Ollie (Hollenbeck) 49
Killian, Dollie 47
Killian, James 47-48, 49
Kramer, Clifford 33
Kramer, Curtis 33

L
LaDonne, Sherrill (Davidson) xv
Latham, Bob 129
Latham, Ross 131
Lenhart, Emma (unknown) 115
Lenhart, Forrest Drake 115
Lenhart, Freeman FJ 99, 112, 115-116
Lenhart, Katie 115
Letson, Otto 42
Lewis, Albert Wayne 78, *78*
Lewis, Alice (Johnson) 58, 60, 68, 77-78
Lewis, Anna May 78, *78*
Lewis, Charles 58, 60, 77-79
Lewis, Charles Jr. xv, 78, *78, 79*
Lewis, Ella (m. Hedrick) xv, 69, *78, 79*
Lewis, Ethel Jane (m. Gardner) *78,* 79
Lewis, Glen Andrew 78, *78*
Lewis, Laura 69
Lewis, Willard 58, 77
Lindauer, Alice (Quinn) 63-64
Lindauer, Bessie (Shults) xii, xiv, 24, 30-31, *30*, 69, 113-114, 126
Lindauer, Betty (Baughman, m. Mead) 37, *37*
Lindauer, Betty JoAnn "BJ" (Barstow) xiii, xv, 114-115, *119*, 167

Lindauer, Carl vi, 29, 35
Lindauer, Diane xv, 37
Lindauer, Dylan Ivo xv, 114, 167
Lindauer, Edith (Evans) 31-32, *32*
Lindauer, Edna Maude "Midge" (Wurts) 35, *36*
Lindauer, Felix Richard 27, *28*, 29, 31-32, *31*, *32*, *34*, 55, 63, 64
Lindauer, Felix Orland 32, *34*, 55, 63-64, *64*
Lindauer, Ferdinand 26-27
Lindauer, Gary 35
Lindauer, Gerald xv, 64
Lindauer, Iva (Taylor) 34
Lindauer, Ivo xi, 114-116, 126, 132
Lindauer, Janelle (m. Carlson) 114
Lindauer, Judy 37
Lindauer, Julia 114
Lindauer, Julius 29, 33, 36-37, *37*, 105, 132
Lindauer Karl vi, 27, *28*, 34, *34*, 36
Lindauer, Larry 35
Lindauer, Leland 37
Lindauer, Leslie 35
Lindauer, Lorraine (m. Brown, Weston) 114
Lindauer, Louis vi, 27, *35*, 35-36, *36*
Lindauer, Mary (m. Satterfield) 64
Lindauer, Mary Margaret, 63, *64*
Lindauer, Michael 114
Lindauer, Mindy 115
Lindauer, Norman xv, 37
Lindauer, Paul iv, v, xiii, xiv, 24, 27, *28*, *29*, *30*, 29-31, 74, 86, 99, 113-115, 126, 130, 131, 132, 135, 139
Lindauer, Peter 21-22, 24, 25, 26-29, *27*, *28*
Lindauer, Robin 115
Lindauer, Rose 27, *32*, 32-33, *33*
Lindauer, Ruth (Bennett) 115
Lindauer, Sandy 115
Lindauer, Sydney 115, 132
Lindauer, Virginia (Marchi) 114
Lindauer, Zelmo 114
Logan, Harvey "Kid Carry" 132-134

M

Mabee, Al 112-113
Mabee, Mildren (Radtke) 112-113
MacLennan, Lynda (Lindauer) 115
MacLennan, Kenneth 115
MacLennan, Kevin 115
Madden, Vera (Stanton) 89, 90

Marks, Victor *69*
Marling, Georgia "Jody" 32, 64
Martin, Melvin 132
Maxfield, Abram 13
McCosh, Anna 129
McDaniels, Floyd 134
McKay, David 112
McKay, Evalee xv, 111
McKay, Evelyn (Wasson) 111-112
McKay, Michael 112
McKay, Stanley 88, 111-112
McManus, Carol (Herwick, m. Crawford) xiv, 52
McQuiston, Jody 88
McQuiston, Louise 88
McQuiston, Nita (Cummings) 88
McQuiston, Richard 88
McQuiston, Shirley 88
McQuiston, Ted xv, 87-88
McQuiston, William "Ted" Jr. 88
Meeker Massacre 4, 7-8, 63
Methodist Church 401, 42, 52, 60, 80
Miller, Gary xv, 134
Mills, Grant V. 68, 85, 86, 101
Mills, Katherine 86
Mills, Lawrence 86
Mills, Mary e. 86
Milner, Cuny 129
Moore, Dean 132
Moore, Phil 129
Morrow, Harry 135

N

Neilson, Irv 141
Neilson, Kurt 141
Nelson, Anna Leona (Reynolds) 91
Nelson, Dena G. (m. Thompson) xv, 92
Nelson, Leila (Ogden) 92
Nelson, Mabel 74
Nelson, Mary Gertrude (m. Plowman) 91
Nelson, Reuben "Windy" *82*, *83*, *84*, 91-92, *92*
Nelson, Robert 74, 80, 91
Nelson, Ruby F. (m. Wolfe) 92
Nelson, Sarah Kathleen (m. Ridgway) 91

O

Obermeyer, Elsie 120
Ogden, Bill 46-47, 69
Ogden, Bill Jr. xv, 47

Ogden, Charlie 92
Ogden, Mary Ann 47
Ogden, Perry 47
Ogden, Roberta (Funk) 41, 43, 46-47
Oldland, Walter 130
Orona, Cordero 114, 167
Orona, Delcia 114, 167
Orona, Howard "Howie" 114, 115
Orona, Sarah (Lindauer) 114, 115, 167
O'Toole brothers 127, 132

P

Pasquire, Bus 129
Parachute Index 4, 134
Parachute Mining District xi, 26, 96, 137
Parachute, name 3-4
Parkhurst, Hallie 24, *24*, 33, 131
Parkhurst, Irving 24, *24*, 25
Parkhurst, Madeline (Kramer) 24
Patterson, Charles 106, 172
Patterson, Charlton "Chella" 106
Patterson, Ellen Gertrude (Wilson) 106
Patterson, Helen 69
Payton, Alberta (Gardner) *104*, 104-105
Payton, Chester "Art" 102-103, *103*
Payton, Clarence Wayne *104*, 104-105
Payton, Dale Arthur 103
Payton, Dorothy 103
Payton, Lily Marie 103
Payton, Mabel (Rasmussen, m. Peak) 102-103, *103*
Payton, Norman 32, 88, 104, 105
Payton, Viola (Christian) 103
Payton, Warren "Binks" 105
Pickett, Saro 129
Power, Adeline "Addie" (Osborn) *116*, 116-117, *117*
Power, Ed *116*, 116-117, *117*
Power, Edward Granville 116, *117*
Power, Leslie *117*
Power, Lexie Ruth 117
Power, Lloyd 117-118, *118*
Power, Lloyd Alfred (son of Ed) 116, *117*
Power, Lloyd Alfred Jr. (son of Lloyd) 118
Power, Lois Lorene (m. Hurla) xv, 118
Power, Mary Alice (m. Miracle) 118
Power, Ralph 117
Power, Robert Joe 118
Power, Shirley Lavonne (m. Brackett) 118
Power, Velma 117

Power, Velma (Davidson) 117-118, *118*
Power, W. Glen 116, 117, *117*
Pritchard family 130

Q

Quinn, Charles "Chuck" 105

R

Riley, Bill 47
Riley, Frances 39
Riley, Hugh 39
Riley, Leslie *117*
Roberts, Jack 132, 133
Rowley, Morton 26, 27, 29, 137
Rupp/Nolte Ranch 126

S

Sandstrom, Ernest 76, *76*
Sawyer, Charlie 129
Seamens, Darrell 107, 109
Seamens, Julia (Alcock) 106-107
Seamens, Kenneth 107
Seamens, Myrtle (Sill) 107
Seamens, William 106-107
Seder, Sam 135
Semsack, Charlene (Kramer) xv, 33
Shaw, Alice 59
Shaw, Joseph 123-124
Shaw, Oscar 123, 124
Shaw, Tom 59, 61
Shehorn, Daisy 123, 124
Shehorn, Joseph 123, 124
Shehorn, Oscar 123, 124
Sherwood, Arch *82*, 82-83, 90, 93
Sherwood, Lester "Irish" 82, 84-85, 93, 101, 130
Sherwood, Mae (Phillips) *83*, 83-84
Sherwood, Martel 45, 58, 61, *82*, *83*, 83-84, *84*, 93, 101
Sherwood, Viola (m. Walters) 82, 90, 92, 93-94, 101
Sherwood, Zula "Madge" (Zediker) 82, 93
Shults, Claude 69
Shults, Walter 60, 61
Shults, Winfred *33*
Sinclair Oil & Gas Co. xi, 32, 63, 147
Sipprelle, Judd 23, 41, 137
Sipprelle, Margie Segar Von Rosenberg 129
Smerchek, Frances 129
Smith, Bill 135

Smith, Roslyn 39, 53, 54, 69
Solvay Chemicals 141-142
Spangler, Tom 132
Spitler, Chet 135
Sprague, Harve 129
Squires, Frank 130
Stanton, Amy S. (m. Severson) 88
Stanton, Bessie Ellen (m. Grainger) 88
Stanton, Billy 85, 90
Stanton, Clifford Marlon 89
Stanton, Clyde 89
Stanton, Daniel 83, 89-90
Stanton, Emma (Sherwood) 82, 85, 90, *90*, 93, 101
Stanton, Fay "Buck" 90-91, 130
Stanton, Francis 85, 90, *90*
Stanton, Guy 89, *89*
Stanton, Henry 88-89
Stanton, Henry Clements 88
Stanton, Olive (Cline) 89-90
Stanton, Ortha (Robertson) 89
Stanton, Terry (m. Barnhill) 90
Stanton, Vera (m. Madden) 88, 89, 90
Stanton, Verna (m. Reed) 90
Stanton, Viola (Bunker) 88
Stanton, Viola (m. Gardner, Larson) 89
Stanton, Wayne 89, 90
Stone, Audrey (m. Moore) 99
Stone, Betty Sue (m. Van horn) 99, 126
Stone, Earl 98-99
Stone, Jack 98, 99
Stone, Rose (Wilhite) 98-99
Stone, Thelma (m. Thompson) 99
Stone, Theo 99
Stowell, Sim 131
Streit, HM 137
Streit, Sadie 137
Streit's Flat viii, 9, 132
Sumner, Tige 132
Sumner, Tim 132

T
Tanney, Bill 28, 95
Tracy, Everett 131
Train robbery 132-134
Trimmer, Jim *121*
Trimmer, Joe 25, *25*, 26, 27, 29, 122
Trimmer, Joseph Jr. *121*
Trimmer, Olive (Curry) 121

U
Ulrey, Clarence 129
Ulrey, William 137
Union Oil Co. of California xi, 23, 24, 32, 34, 37, 39, 41, 45, 52, 58, 74, 78, 92, 104, 110, 112, 131, 140, 141, 144, 147, 148
Ute Indians 3, 5-11, 26, 50, 72
Chief Colorow 72, 120
Chief Ouray 7, 8, 9
Chief Walkara (Walker) 6

V
Vail, Carl 119, *119*
Vail, Helen (Allen) 119, *119*
Van Horn, Gladys (Betts) 125-126
Van Horn, Lyman 115, 125-126, 150
Van Horn, Lyman Jr. 99, 125, 126,
Van Horn, Nola 125
Van Horn, Wes 125, 134
Vivian, Gov. John C. *78*

W
Waterman, Philip 108, 127, 129, 131
Walters, Bruce "Red" 44, 78, 86, *93*, 93-94, 98, 154
Walters, Pauline (m. Threlkeld) xv, 84, 90, 94
Walters, Mary (m. Stanton) 89
Wasson, Eva F. (Hunter) 112
Wasson, Harry 129, 131
Wasson, Sam B. 30, 112, 127, 130, 131
Wayne, Fern *121*
Wayne, Herbert Claude 123
Wayne, Mae *121*
Webster, Dan 129
Werhonig, Fred 132, 134
Werhonig, Rudolph 132, 134
Wheatley, Elmer 116, 125, 134, 137
Wheatley, Lois 116
Wheatley, Lucia 114, 116
Wheeler, Elmer 74
Wheeler, Harriet (Ferris) 72
Wheeler, Isaac *67*
Wheeler, James Ferris 53, 54, 69, *72*, 72-74, *73*, 100
Wheeler, John Albert *62*, *67*, *72*, 73, 75, 80, 135
Wheeler, Lemuel Adolf 68, 73
Wheeler, Lula "Bobbie" *62*, 74
Wheeler, Lulu May (De Witt) 73, 75

Wheeler, Mabel (Nelson) 74
Wheeler, Mary Louise (Weber) 54, 69, 72-74, *73*
Wheeler, Ransom 72
Wheeler, Robert "Bob" 24, *74*
Wheeler, Walter Kern 51, 69, 74, 134
Wilda, Henry 129
Williams, Charley 105
Williams Gas and Oil 58, 59, 112
Williams, Harold 105
Williams, Marsh 46, 70
Williams Production RMt Co. 141
Williams, Sam 116
Wilson, Alyce Jane (Ritter) 62
Wilson, Beryl (m. Miner) 61, 62
Wilson (Gillium), Beulah (m. Margolius), 61, 62
Wilson, Charles W. "Billy" 61
Wilson, De Etta (Arner, m. Gillium) 61
Wilson, Doc 17-18, *17*, 32, 40, 50, 60, 61-63, 87, 129
Wilson, Frank 18
Wilson, Howard xv, 62
Wilson, Marshall xv, 62
WPX 143, 144

Y
Yeoman, Blanche (m. Johnson) *62*, 67, *67*, 69, *76*
Yeoman, Clifford *62*, *67*
Yeoman, Ellen (Shimel) 62
Yeoman, Elmo *62*, 67
Yeoman, Enos 60, 61, 62-63
Yeoman, Grace 62
Yeoman, Jesse *62*, *67*
Yeoman, SB 41
Yeoman, Steven 67
Young, Stanley 135

Z
Zediker, Allen "Lloyd" 46, 102
Zediker, Beech 98, 102, 129
Zediker, Lucretia (Alexander) 86
Zediker, Thomas Jefferson "TJ" 86

ABOUT THE AUTHOR

Ivo Lindauer grew up along Parachute Creek, the third generation to live and ranch in the canyons and on surrounding mesa tops.

His grandfather, Peter Lindauer, purchased a homestead at the head of Parachute Creek in 1902, and his father Paul established a ranch on the East Fork branch. One of five children, Ivo Lindauer grew up on the ranch eleven miles from Grand Valley (now known as Parachute), and spent his boyhood years moving cattle and machinery up and down the drainage. His neighbors were cowboys, and life followed the rhythms of the seasons as they moved their livestock up to the high country for summer grazing and back to the canyons before snow fell. They hunted and fished, and looked out for one another.

In the course of Lindauer's lifetime, he has watched a dramatic transformation of the landscape that helped shape him. Once dotted with cattle ranches and fruit orchards, Parachute Creek is now dominated by energy development and natural resource extraction. Lindauer and his family are the only remaining ranching landowners along the entire creek.

After graduating from Grand Valley High School in 1949, he attended the University of Colorado and Colorado State University, where he earned a BS degree in science. His first job surveying spruce beetle infestations for the US Bureau of Entomology was interrupted by service in the Marine Corps, including a year in Korea. Following his discharge, he married transplanted Ohioan Betty Jo Ann Barstow and the couple settled near the family ranch. In addition to ranching, Lindauer worked as a coach and science teacher at Silt, Colorado.

He returned to the University of Northern Colorado (UNC) to pursue teaching certification, along with his wife. He eventually earned an MA in biological sciences and later a PhD in botany and plant ecology from Colorado State University (CSU). He joined the faculty at UNC. During his career there, he took leave to serve as a visiting scholar at two universities in Australia.

As a field and floodplain ecologist, Lindauer led numerous field trips for teachers and students as well as organizing and leading sixteen week-long float trips down the Colorado River in the Grand Canyon studying the unique ecology and geology of the area. He also spent two years in Washington, DC, with the National Science Foundation as a program officer assisting in awarding grants to universities and schools for training teachers and producing teacher training materials.

In the course of his career, Lindauer founded and was president of the Colorado Biology Teachers Association, and was president of the National Biology Teachers Association, president of the Colorado Nature Conservancy, and director of several NSF grants and teaching projects. He was grand marshal of the Grand Valley Rodeo and Parade in 2003 and served on the board of the Grand Valley Educational Foundation in all offices including president from 2000 to 2009.

After retiring in 1996, he and his wife returned to his childhood home. The couple have traveled extensively since their retirement, including three around-the-world trips and six weeks in Scotland. Ivo and Betty Jo have two daughters, Julia Lindauer and Sarah Orona, and three grandchildren, Dylan Lindauer (24), Cordero (19) and Delcia Orona (18), and one cat, Spook (10).